To Keep the Land for My Children's Children

Documents of Salish, Pend d'Oreille, and Kootenai Indian History, 1890-1899

To Keep the Land for My Children's Children

Documents of Salish,
Pend d'Oreille, and
Kootenai Indian History,
1890-1899

edited by
Robert Bigart
and
Joseph McDonald

published by
Salish Kootenai College Press
Pablo, Montana

distributed by
University of Nebraska Press
Lincoln, Nebraska

Publication of this book was made possible through the generosity of the Oleta "Pete" Smith Endowment Fund of the Montana Community Foundation.

Cover design: Corky Clairmont, artist/graphic designer, Pablo, Montana.
Cover illustration:

Library of Congress Cataloging-in-Publication Data:
Names: Bigart, Robert, editor. | McDonald, Joseph, 1933- editor.
Title: To keep the land for my children's children : documents of Salish, Pend
    d'Oreille, and Kootenai Indian history, 1890-1899 / edited by Robert
    Bigart and Joseph McDonald.
Description: Pablo, Montana : Salish Kootenai College Press, [2020] |
    Includes biographical references and index.
Identifiers: LCCN 2020006203 | ISBN 9781934594278 (paperback)
Subjects: LCSH: Salish Indians--Montana--History--19th century--Sources.
    | Kootenai Indians--Montana--History--19th century--Sources. | Kalispel
    Indians--Montana--History--19th century--Sources.
Classification: LCC E99.S2 T6 2020 | DDC 978.6004/979435--dc23
LC record available at https://lccn.loc.gov/2020006203

Published by Salish Kootenai College Press, PO Box 70, Pablo, MT 59855.

Distributed by University of Nebraska Press, 1111 Lincoln Mall, Lincoln, NE 68588-0630, order 1-800-755-1105, www.nebraskapress.unl.edu.

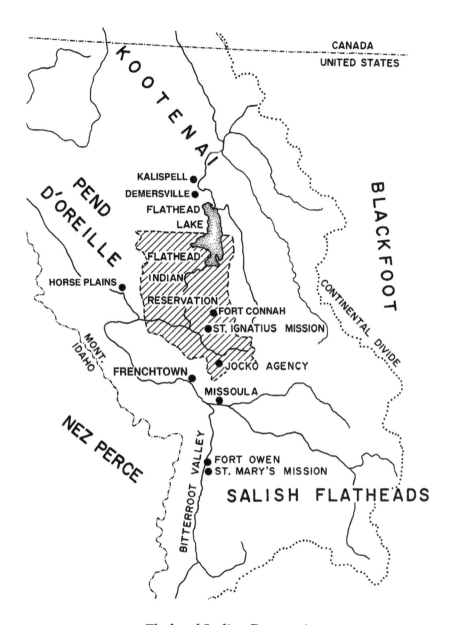

CANADA
UNITED STATES

KOOTENAI

PEND D'OREILLE

BLACKFOOT

KALISPELL
DEMERSVILLE
FLATHEAD
LAKE

FLATHEAD
INDIAN
RESERVATION

HORSE PLAINS

CONTINENTAL DIVIDE

FORT CONNAH
ST. IGNATIUS MISSION

MONT.
IDAHO

JOCKO AGENCY

FRENCHTOWN

MISSOULA

NEZ PERCE

BITTERROOT VALLEY

FORT OWEN
ST. MARY'S MISSION

SALISH FLATHEADS

**Flathead Indian Reservation
Showing Tribal Territories
and Surrounding Towns**

Table of Contents

Detailed Table of Contents

Introduction

The decade of the 1890s on the Flathead Indian Reservation in Montana saw the culmination and intensification of some of the survival challenges that confronted tribal leaders through the nineteenth century. The 1890s also witnessed the heartbreaking climax of the struggle of Chief Charlo and the Salish Indians to develop an independent and self-supporting Salish community in the Bitterroot Valley. The period introduced the doleful impact of a biased white-controlled justice system and predatory economic interests in western Montana.

Four Indians were hung for murder in Missoula in 1890, but whites who murdered Indians escaped punishment. In the 1890s, tribal leaders labored to hold the agency controlled Indian police and Indian court accountable. Serious crimes were tried in off reservation courts with varying degrees of justice. Bootlegged alcohol fueled violence and death on the reservation.

At the same time white neighbors threatened tribal resources. In the early part of the decade, Agent Peter Ronan and Kootenai leaders tried and failed to protect Kootenai farmers just north of the reservation boundary. A predacious Missoula County government developed new and novel legal theories to justify collecting county taxes from reservation mixed bloods. The federal government pressured the tribes to sell the northern part of the reserve and accept allotment.

The historical sources provide glimpses of economic development and daily life on the reservation. Duncan McDonald and Charles Allard, Sr., developed a hotel at Ravalli and a stage line across the reserve, among other business enterprises. Historical records have also survived describing church celebrations at St. Ignatius Mission and fleeting glances of everyday tribal life.

Written sources provide insight on reservation affairs in the 1890s, but they give only a partial picture of the period. The sources do, however, describe leaders and a community that actively looked out for their interests and fought to protect tribal independence and assets.

Cautions, Biases, and Selection Strategies

The documents of Flathead Reservation history in this collection were selected because they offered valuable information about the tribes. However, because they were written records, they also reflect the biases and bigotry of the white men and women who wrote the records. The readers need to look beyond the bigotry to see the specific incidents being described.

The editors have given preference to statements by individual Indians or chiefs or descriptions of specific activities. The documents chosen needed to be readable and make sense on their own. Normally historians rely on many small, short references in diaries or newspaper articles which do not tell a full story.

The documents have not been edited to remove bigoted words or references. However, an offensive term describing Indian women has been rendered as "s...." The editors have only rarely used "sic" to indicate mistakes in the original. We feared that inserting sic into the text after every error would make the sources hard to read.

The most important authority for tribal history is the oral traditions of the elders. The written sources contribute towards telling history, but they do not give the history. Hopefully, the documents reproduced here will supplement the oral tribal histories currently being collected and written by the Salish-Pend d'Oreille Culture Committee in St. Ignatius and the Kootenai Culture Committee in Elmo, Montana.

Complementary Sources

Readers of Salish, Pend d'Oreille, and Kootenai Indian history between 1890 and 1899 will want to also look at some other books of historical sources published by Salish Kootenai College Press. Of particular interest would be the second volume of Agent Peter Ronan's letters that were published in 2014: Peter Ronan, Justice To Be Accorded To the Indians: Agent Peter Ronan Reports on the Flathead Indian Reservation, Montana, 1888-1893. Selected Ronan letters describing the views and actions of tribal members have been reprinted in this volume of documents, but the full Ronan collection included much information about other reservation events not covered in this book. Robert J. Bigart, editor, Zealous in All Virtues: Documents of Worship and Culture Change, St. Ignatius Mission, Montana, 1890-1894 (2007) included more detailed descriptions of life in the early 1890s at St. Ignatius Mission than have been reproduced in this book. Hopefully, the present volume can serve as an introduction to the broader world of written evidence about tribal history between 1890 and 1899. The citations for the source of each document in this volume will allow readers to do follow up research and learn more about the context of the events described.

Uneven Justice in Nineteenth Century Montana

Many of the surviving historical sources from the 1890s relate to crime and law and order on the reservation. Indian courts and Indian police were controlled by the government agent. The most serious crimes were tried off the reservation in federal courts with all-white juries. Two Kootenai and two Pend d'Oreille Indians were convicted in 1890 of murdering white men and hung in Missoula. The documents reproduced in Chapter 1 describe the arrests, trials, and hanging of the four Indians. Agent Peter Ronan argued that the trials were fair because the men were represented by competent lawyers and much of the testimony came from Indian witnesses (Doc. 12). Ronan did, however, sign a petition calling for the commutation of the death sentences to life imprisonment (Doc. 13). In contrast, the murderers of Kootenai Chief Eneas' son in Kalispell and Pend d'Oreille Chief Michelle's relatives in Chouteau County were never arrested or punished.

The four men had been captured by the Indian police or surrendered to prominent Indians, but in 1895, when it came time to collect the reward, members of the white posse asked for the money (Doc. 17). In 1892 when a white man, Robert Philips, was accused of murdering Felix Burns, an Indian, Agent Ronan and leading tribal members struggled to get Philips punished (Doc. 16). No record was found indicating how the Philips case finally turned out.

Many other documents relate to Indians accused of crimes, but they only convey glimpses of isolated events and rarely give the Indian perspective. In February 1892, fifteen Indian police visited Missoula to arrest Indians who had fled the reservation to avoid arrest for crimes committed on the reserve. (Doc. 35) Three months later, Adolph Barnaby was convicted of assaulting Alex Ashley while drinking at a dance on the reservation. (Doc. 36)

Most of the surviving accounts give the police version of events. For example, years later Harry Stanford, a white policeman, told of arresting a Kootenai Indian named Lame Louis for being drunk in Kalispell in 1892. (Doc. 41)

A strange case occurred in 1893, when Angus P. McDonald, a mixed blood adopted into the tribes, was drinking with two white men off the reservation. McDonald passed out and woke up later with his arm around the corpse of one of the white men, Curley Stevens. McDonald was found innocent by an all-white jury. (Doc. 44) In 1894, Daniel Larose, a mixed blood, was acquitted of the murder of William King, another mixed blood, at a reservation dance. (Doc. 48)

One of the more spectacular and convoluted cases was an 1895 incident that presumably arose out of a mistaken translation of Louison's comments at a pre-Lenten dance. Agent Joseph Carter had Louison arrested for encouraging the Indian dance after Carter had sent orders for it to end. Then three Indians were arrested and jailed in Missoula for trying to free Louison. According to Duncan McDonald, Louison had actually tried to stop the dance, but his statement was mistranslated by the Indian policeman. McDonald hired a lawyer to get the three Indian prisoners released from the Missoula jail on a writ of habeas corpus. The three Indians were then rearrested by the United States Marshal and taken to the federal court in Helena. But the United States Attorney could not find any laws they had broken, and they were released. (Docs. 56 and 68)

A few months later in 1895, Charlie Kickinghorse was jailed as a witness after being robbed by two white men in Missoula. While in the Missoula jail, Kickinghorse was assaulted by white inmates because he refused to pay them protection money. (Doc. 59)

An Indian woman was murdered in Kalispell in February 1896 in one of a series of cases of whites shooting Indians in the city. (Doc. 69) No record was found of anyone being arrested and punished for this murder.

In 1896 Missoula authorities threatened to arrest Indians who failed to observe state game laws while hunting off the reservation. (Doc. 72) Conflict over hunting rights was to continue until well into the twentieth century.

A curious case in tribal court in 1897 attracted newspaper attention. The three sons of Louis Clairmont were sleeping with the same young lady on the reservation. When she became pregnant, the Indian judges did not know who was the father. The judges threw all three in jail. Louis Clairmont hired a white lawyer from Missoula to intervene, but the court refused to let the lawyer participate in the case. (Doc. 77)

Bitterroot Removal

The 1891 removal of the Bitterroot Salish Indians to the Jocko Valley was one of the most painful events in tribal history. Retired Army General Henry B. Carrington had negotiated with Charlo in 1889. The Salish had struggled to develop their farms and were making progress, but their dreams of making a self-supporting community in the Bitterroot Valley were dashed by drought. The Salish crop had failed in 1889. They understood they were to move in the spring of 1890, but bureaucratic delays pushed the move to the fall of 1891. After the 1889 agreement, they did not plant crops in 1890 and 1891 and had to sell off their equipment and belongings to survive the two-year hiatus. Until the Salish-Pend d'Oreille Culture Committee publishes the oral history of the tribe, we have only Carrington's one-sided eyewitness account. His description of the removal emphasized his personal role and was insensitive to the trauma, pain, and disappointment surrounding the removal (Doc. 18).

Newspaper accounts of the removal were cryptic and failed to catch the human drama involved (Docs. 20-23). One very telling note recorded whites vandalizing the vacant Salish farms. While the Salish had respected the property of their white neighbors, a few Bitterroot whites lost no time in plundering the newly vacated farms left by the Indians (Doc. 24). The historical sources provide some detail about the removal, but they leave us with almost as many questions as answers.

Glimpses Into the Lives of Tribal Members

The historical sources provide important information about the lives of prominent tribal members in the 1890s, especially Duncan McDonald and Charles Allard, Sr. These two men operated businesses that served white travelers going through the reserve.

McDonald was well known among white travelers who patronized his hotel at Ravalli. Two examples included in this collection are the spring 1891 account of a Helena Independent correspondent (Doc. 30), and an 1895 letter from H. M. Kingsbury published in a Thompson Falls newspaper. (Doc. 58) However, McDonald was also active in tribal politics in opposition to the Flathead agent. In February 1894, Duncan organized a protest meeting at St. Ignatius which endorsed a petition complaining about incorrect surveys on the northern and southwestern boundaries of the reservation. (Doc. 49) When Agent Joseph Carter arrested three Indians for insurrection and jailed them in Missoula, McDonald hired an attorney and got the prisoners released on a petition of habeas corpus. (Doc. 56) In August 1896, Carter was alarmed when he heard that McDonald might be appointed U.S. Commissioner to screen reservation cases for the federal court. According to Carter, "Imbued as he [McDonald] is with Indian prejudices, justice could not be expected of him." (Doc. 60) In 1896, McDonald leveled a series of complaints against Carter's administration of reservation affairs. (Doc. 68) McDonald took part in a buffalo roundup on the reservation in 1891. (Doc. 32) In 1894, McDonald was interviewed by a Spokane, Washington, newspaperman and lamented the passing of the traditional Indian way of life. (Doc. 52)

Charles Allard, Sr., was well known both for his stage line between Ravalli and the foot of Flathead Lake and his buffalo herd. Fortunately, Allard recounted his life story to a newspaper reporter in 1895. (Doc. 55) In 1890 and 1891,

Allard's stage carried many passengers traveling to the Upper Flathead Valley. (Doc. 26) Allard organized a roundup of his buffalo herd in the fall of 1891. (Doc. 32) For a short time in 1893, Allard exhibited the buffalo as part of a wild west show that toured Montana and the Midwest. The show went bust later in the year. (Doc. 46)

The historical sources also provided information on the lives and descriptions of the homes of tribal members in the 1890s. A number of newspapermen met Michel Revais, the blind agency interpreter. In 1892, a Helena newspaper interviewed Revais about his life. (Doc. 37) During the summer of 1890, Palmer Henderson attended a religious service led by Revais at the Jocko Agency church. (Doc. 28) Revais was interviewed by a Missoula reporter in September 1890. (Doc. 29) He also assisted Henry Carrington during Carrington's negotiations with Chief Charlo in the Bitterroot Valley in 1891 (Doc. 18).

Chief Charlo appeared frequently in the 1890s sources. In 1891, Charlo was the central figure in the removal of the Salish from the Bitterroot Valley (Doc. 18). Later in the decade, Charlo led tribal efforts to prevent the sale of reservation land. (Doc. 74) In October 1893, a Missoula newspaperman described a visit to Charlo at his home in the Jocko Valley. (Doc. 47) A few years later in 1897, a group of Jesuit scholastics visited Charlo at his home and were given Indian names. (Doc. 83) Especially valuable was the account related by Victor Vanderburg about Charlo's life in the Jocko Valley after 1891. (Doc. 42) The information about Charlo should be used with caution because some of the writers were competing with Charlo over land and other government policies.

Another tribal leader who appeared frequently in the 1890s sources was Baptist Kakashee, the church chief and tribal policeman at St. Ignatius Mission. In 1896, Kakashee led the Indian delegation greeting Bishop John Brondell when he arrived at Ravalli for the St. Ignatius Day celebration. (Doc. 71) In 1897, a Jesuit scholastic recorded Kakashee's role in law and order at the mission (Doc. 83), and another Jesuit described him at the 1897 Christmas eve celebration at the mission. (Doc. 81)

The sources also related visits to the homes of Antoine Moiese and Francois Saxa in 1890 (Doc. 28), and Alex Matt in 1893. (Doc. 47) In the twentieth century, the life of Clara Ducharme Cramer, a mixed blood tribal member, was recorded in a biographical collection. She was born in Frenchtown and moved to the reservation with her white husband in about 1892. (Doc. 43) The written sources only give glimpses of their lives, but they can complement family and tribal oral history.

St. Ignatius Mission

Many of the historical sources included descriptions of St. Ignatius Mission in the 1890s and church celebrations. In 1890, Palmer Henderson visited St. Ignatius and also reprinted the program for the celebration presented for Easter 1890. (Doc. 28) A letter by J. F. Nugent described the festive greeting tribal members gave Bishop John Brondell for the 1896 St. Ignatius Day festivities. (Doc. 71) A Jesuit visitor wrote a detailed description of the St. Ignatius Christmas Eve service in 1897. (Doc. 81) That same year, Thomas McKeogh, a Jesuit scholastic, provided an account of the mission, school, and services. (Doc. 83) Katie Ronan, a daughter of Agent Peter Ronan, in 1897 wrote a description of the St. Ignatius Good Friday service. (Doc. 89) Descriptions of the church and school at the Jocko Agency were available from 1890 (Doc. 28) and 1893. (Doc. 47) The 1890s were the height of the growth of the St. Ignatius Mission. The mission declined in the twentieth century as government support dried up.

Kootenai Indian Allotments

Agent Peter Ronan's effort to protect Kootenai Indian farmers just north of the reservation boundary was a long story of disappointment. Even more remarkable was the ability of Kootenai Chief Eneas to persuade tribal members to trust the government and refrain from violence to assert their claims to their farms and allotments off the reservation.

The Kootenai Indians had long used a meadow north of their village at Elmo for grazing and hay for their stock. They understood that this land was on the reservation, but the official survey ran the boundary line south of where the Kootenai expected. The official survey turned out to be in error in the tribes' twentieth century U.S. Court of Claims case, but in 1891 the Kootenai meadow land was considered public domain. Agent Peter Ronan made off-reservation allotments to Kootenai farmers north of the reservation and the Kootenai proceeded to improve their allotments. (Doc. 33)

Agent Peter Ronan spent considerable time in the last three years of his life trying to get the United States Government to protect the rights of the Kootenai Indian allottees north of the Flathead Reservation boundary. At one point he was able to get the United States Marshal to remove whites who had trespassed on the allotments, but unfortunately the white men just returned after the marshal left. (Docs. 34 and 38)

After Ronan's death in 1893, the Flathead Indian agents paid little attention to the rights of the Kootenai allottees and the government left the white trespassers in possession of the lands until the early twentieth century when the trespassers were allowed to pay small sums to the Kootenai to relinquish their rights. For more information see the numerous Ronan letters to the Commissioner of Indian Affairs about the trespassers in Peter Ronan, *Justice To Be Accorded To the Indians: Agent Peter Ronan Reports on the Flathead Indian Reservation, Montana, 1888-1893*, ed. Robert J. Bigart (Pablo, Mont.: Salish Kootenai College Press, 2014), pages 225 through 367.

The Flathead Reservation Economy

The documents provide a partial look at the reservation economy in the 1890s. The buffalo were gone, other game populations had crashed, and many sites for gathering wild plants had been fenced by white farmers. Tribal members needed to find new ways to support themselves and their families. One income source was working for the Flathead Agency. In 1892, a number of tribal members were employed to dig an irrigation ditch in the Jocko Valley to serve the farms being developed by the newly removed Bitterroot Salish. An Anaconda Standard reporter described how tribal members contracted the excavation work by the yard and shared the labor within families. (Doc. 40)

According to Agent Joseph Carter, in the 1890s many tribal members engaged in seasonal work for off reservation farmers and the more prosperous Indian farmers and ranchers on the reservation. (Doc. 53) Livestock were becoming an ever more important part of the reservation economy. In 1895, a newspaper reporter described a roundup of horses on the reservation open range. Cattle owners were anxious to reduce the number of horses so more grass would be available for cattle. (Doc. 62) By the end of the 1890s, sales of cattle were the foundation of the reservation economy.

One facet of the new economic order was employment in rodeos and wild west shows off the reservation. A series of June 1897 performances in Anaconda were covered in detail by the local newspaper. (Doc. 75)

Tribal leaders realized that protecting reservation land was critical in preserving the economic independence of the tribes. In the 1890s, predatory white interests were plotting new ways to steal Indian assets. In 1895, W. H. Smead, a future Flathead Agent, pushed a memorial through the Montana Legislature asking for the allotment of the Flathead Reservation. Of course, the allotment policy also provided for the forced sale of "surplus" land to white settlers at less than market value. (Doc. 54)

In 1895 a Missoulian reporter learned that in 1892 the late Agent Peter Ronan had advised against allotment or land sales on the reservation because of fierce opposition from the Indians. The reporter was offended that allotment was not pursued "simply because a few Indians had prejudices in the matter." (Doc. 57) Ronan's action postponed allotment on the Flathead Reservation for twelve years, until Senator Joseph Dixon imposed the policy on the tribes in 1904 over vigorous objections from tribal leaders.

In the late 1890s, the government sent the Crow, Flathead, Etc., Commission to negotiate for the sale of the northern part of the reservation. Chief Charlo and other tribal leaders resolutely refused to consider any land sales. Despite the rejection, the commissioners were determined to pressure the tribes into a land sale. (Doc. 74) The commission returned to the Flathead Reservation in September 1898, but tribal members again said no. Chief Charlo spoke for the tribes. He wanted the government to carry out earlier agreements before the tribes considered any new promises. No transcript of the meeting has survived, but, according to a newspaper report, Charlo declared: "You think this land is good. So do I. You want it. I propose to keep it for my people, their children and their children's children." (Doc. 86)

As the federal government was trying to get reservation land, the Missoula County government levied taxes on reservation mixed bloods. As early as 1895, a Missoula County sheriff came on the reservation and seized the property of a tribal member to settle a contested debt. (Doc. 61)

In the fall of 1897, Missoula County began a major effort to collect taxes from reservation mixed bloods. The Commissioner of Indian Affairs responded that mixed bloods living on the reservation were exempt from county taxes. (Doc. 78) In the summer of 1898, Chief Aeneas Paul of Ronan complained about both the federal attempt to buy part of the reservation and the Missoula County efforts to tax tribal members. (Doc. 85) County officials collecting the taxes were ordered off the reservation by the chiefs. In 1898, the Deputy County Treasurer was confronted by Chief Aeneas Paul. The deputy responded: "What I want to tell that old Indian is that he may go to h— . . . . Tell him that this is not his country, but that it belongs to the government at Washington." (Doc. 85) Despite the efforts of the Flathead Agents and the decisions of the Commissioner of Indian Affairs, Missoula County was determined to collect taxes. In 1899, the county argued that mixed bloods whose Indian blood was from non-Flathead Reservation tribes were taxable. (Doc. 88) The United States District Court decided several cases in the early twentieth century, but the county officials continued their predatory assault on the reservation well past 1899.

Other Aspects of Reservation Life

The historical sources recorded little about daily life on the reservation, but a few glimpses have survived in the record. In the summer of 1891 white tourists on Flathead Lake had a friendly interaction and competition with some young Kootenai Indians. (Doc. 31) A newspaper report in 1895 described the medicine tree in the Bitterroot Valley. (Doc. 63) In 1896, baseball teams were organized at St. Ignatius and the Jocko Agency. (Doc. 70) One of the Morrigeaus came to the aid of a distressed white woman traveling across the reservation in 1897. In this case, a dispute arose over clothes the Morrigeaus loaned the woman. (Doc. 80) In 1897 author Hamlin Garland visited the reservation and recorded his observations of the St. Ignatius town and a mixed blood fiddle dance. (Doc. 82)

When he was interviewed in 1976, tribal elder Blind Mose described the earliest powwows in the late 1890s. (Doc. 87) Finally, Montana State University professor Morton Elrod began scientific research on the reservation in 1899. He left a series of amusing vignettes of reservation life at the turn of the twentieth century. (Doc. 92)

The written documents are not the "the history" of the tribes, but they do contribute some useful information to complement the oral history now being compiled by the Salish-Pend d'Oreille Culture Committee. In the meantime, the editors hope the reader enjoys this journey through the Flathead Reservation in the 1890s.

Robert Bigart
Joseph McDonald

Chapter 1

Uneven Justice in Montana Courts

1890-1892

Document 1

Trial of Larry Finley for Murder

March 1890

Source: "Finlay the Murderer," *Missoula Daily Gazette*, March 14, 1890, page 4, col. 2; "For His Life," *Missoula Daily Gazette*, March 18, 1890, page 4, col. 3; "He Gets Ten Years," *Missoula Daily Gazette*, March 19, 1890, page 4, col. 2; "Finlay Talks," *Missoula Daily Gazette*, March 20, 1890, page 4, col. 1.

Editors' note: Larry or Laurence Finley had a long record of trouble with the law. The pursuit and arrest of Larry Finley, accused Indian murderer, emphasized law and order problems on the reservation in the late 1880s. He was captured by Al Sloan, a mixed blood Chippewa Indian who had married into the Flathead Reservation tribes, in May 1889 on the Sun River. In May 1889, Finley made a statement accusing Pierre Paul and Lalasee of murdering two white men on Jocko River in the summer of 1888. For a biographical sketch of Lawrence Finley's career see Peter Ronan, *"A Great Many of Us Have Good Farms": Agent Peter Ronan Reports on the Flathead Indian Reservation, Montana, 1877-1887*, ed. Robert J. Bigart (Pablo, Mont.: Salish Kootenai College Press, 2014), pages 400-401.

Finlay the Murderer.
An Interview with the Slayer of Jocco, the Indian.

A *Gazette* reporter interviewed Larry Finlay, the man to be tried on Monday for the murder of the Indian, Jocco, at Demersville, last April, at the county jail this morning. Finlay is in apparent good spirits and anxious to have his trial begin, believing that he will be acquitted. To the reporter he told the following story of the murder: He thinks it was on the first day of last April that he went from Demersville to Ashly, where he had been drinking to some extent, and met his cousin, who induced him to return to Demersville with him. Arriving at Demersville the two went to their camp, when Jocco, the Indian, came up to their tent drunk and wanted to fight, and run the entire camp out. Finlay and his cousin became afraid of the Indian. They did not want to run away from him, but went into one of the tepees. Jocco followed them in and began fighting with the cousin. Finlay interfered and told the Indian to let his cousin alone as he was not able to grapple with him, being his inferior in strength by large odds, when Jocco replied, "If you don't let me fight with him I'll fight with you. I am down on you people any way," at the same time striking him twice in the face." Finlay says that he then pushed the Indian away from him, but he came at him again, and when he came up the third time he picked up a stick about three feet long and two inches in diameter and struck him over the head with it, felling him to the ground in front of the tent.

He then sat down and told his cousin to let him lay there, that if he came up again he would fix him. Finlay says that he did not think he had killed the Indian, and walked up town and began drinking at the various saloons. Soon after one of the Indians came to him and told him that Jocco was dead. He asked this Indian how he thought the other Indians would feel about it, and the messenger told him that he thought the Indians would rather see Jocco dead than alive, as he was a "bad Indian" and of a very quarrelsome nature, but advised Finlay to leave the country for a time until the excitement had died out. Finlay then left the reservation and went to Sun River, where he was arrested. He says that he had intended coming back in the fall, and did not think the officers wanted him for killing "that feller," as he expressed it, or he should have come back of his own accord and delivered himself up to the authorities.

Finlay is a half-breed, 24 years old. He was raised on the Jocco reservation where he has a mother and two sisters living.

* * * * * * * *

For His Life.
Larry Finlay on Trial for the Murder of Jocko, the Indian.

Larry Finlay was brought into district court this morning to answer to the charge of murder. The prisoner took a seat beside his counsel, Messrs. Reeves & Stiff, and seemed entirely unconcerned. At different times when testimony was being given he grinned and smiled, having from his actions and appearance, undoubtedly, explicit faith in his being acquitted.

It did not take long to get a jury and after three quarters of an hour's time the following gentlemen were sworn and the trial began: T. J. Farland, B. N. Harris, Geo. White, W. H. Patrick, W. H. Ellis, G. R. Woodard, A. J. Gibson, P. Thomander, T. J. McClurg, Isaac Patty, C. E. Johnson and G. B. Woods. Michael Rivaes was sworn as interpreter in the Flathead Indian language and Dave Finlay in the Kootenai language.

The first witness put on the stand on the part of the state was Baptiste Finlay, who testified as follows: I live at Dayton creek, alongside of Flathead lake. Larry Finlay is my cousin. I knew Jocko; he was Kootenai Indian. I saw Larry and Jocko together close to Demersville on the day of the murder. Paul,

Tom and Sophie were with him. Paul, Tom and Larry were camped about half a mile from Demersville. In the evening Larry and Jocko came into camp; they had a bottle of whisky each, when they came into the tepee. They sat down and Jocko wanted to say something to Tom, and Larry, wanted to say something to Tom. Jocko slapped Larry on the face, not very hard. I said to Jocky [sic] I don't want any quarrel or any fight here. I was sitting down; Jocko was behind me. When I said this he got up before I could get up and he grabbed me by the coat collar and dragged me along. We both grappled and fell. I fell on top of Jocko, and held him on the ground.

I held Jocco down because he was a mean man, especially when he drank, and I did not want him to fight in our camp. While I was holding him Larry jumped outside the tepee and the first thing I knew was that Larry struck Jocco over the head with a stick. I hollered to Larry "Stop! Stop, he's dead already!" and Larry then struck him twice again. He struck him three times. Jocco laid there dead. I saw wounds on Jocco's forehead. His forehead was all broken in. There was no other trouble between Jocco and Larry except that each one wanted to talk to Tom first. This is the only trouble I know of they had. I was at the tepee all the time during the trouble. After I found that Jocco was dead I went home, and from there went towards the agency. There were in the tepee Jocko, Larry, Paul, Tom, Sophie and myself. Paul has gone across the mountains. Tom is up at the Blackfoot agency now.

Cross-examination: I knew Jocko a long time. Jocko was a big Indian. When he was sober I never knew him to fight, but when he drank whisky he would fight. He was drinking on this occasion. He was regarded by the people as a fighting man, and when drinking whisky he was known to fight men, women and children, and make them run from him. He was a dangerous man when drinking. He had a club in his tepee all the time.

Sophie Finlay was the next witness. In taking her testimony it required two interpreters, Michel to Dave Finlay and Dave to Sophie. Sophie took the stand, and like all other women showed a degree of bashfulness. She testified in substance: I knew Jocko in his lifetime and know Larry. I did not see the trouble between Larry and Jocko. I was camped with Baptiest [sic] and Paul and Tom and their wives last spring. Jocko and Larry came to the camp together. They had whisky. Larry had the whisky. When they came in Tom was not in the lodge. Soon after Tom came in. Jocko wanted to talk to Tom first. When Larry struck Jocko the first blow he had the stick in both hands. The witness substantiated the testimony given by Baptiste in all other respects.

Court re-convened at 2 o'clock and the cross examination of Sophie began, which lasted fully an hour. The witness testified on cross examination that when Jocko slapped Larry they all got alarmed and became afraid. That Finlay was just like Jocko when under the influence of liquor, quarrelsome and of a fighting and brutal disposition. The witness contradicted herself somewhat in regard to the position in which Jocko laid and where Finlay stood, but with this exception the cross examination of the witness did not differ materially from her direct testimony.

W. H. Gregg testified: I live at Demersville. Demersville is about twenty miles from the Indian reservation.

This closed the testimony on behalf of the state, and the defense put Mr. Gregg on the stand as its first witness. He is testifying as we go to press.

* * * * * * * *

He Gets Ten Years.

Arguments in the Finlay murder trial began this morning at 10:30. Mr. Webster on behalf of the state occupied fifteen minutes in his opening address. He was followed by Messrs. Reeves & Stiff on behalf of the defense, who occupied the rest of the morning. Mr. Webster closed this afternoon and Judge Marshall instructed the jury at half-past two o'clock.

The jury, after being out an hour and a quarter, returned a verdict of guilty of manslaughter, and fixed the sentence at ten years imprisonment in the state penitentiary.

* * * * * * * *

Finlay Talks.

A *Gazette* reporter this morning had a talk with Larry Finlay, who was yesterday convicted of manslaughter and sentenced to ten years' imprisonment in the penitentiary. Finlay says that the expected to be acquitted, that the sentence was pretty rough, and that Baptiste, his cousin, swore falsely; that he had been prejudiced against him. Had he been set free he would have aided the officers in getting Pierre Paul and La-La See, the Indian desperadoes, and should he had been a thousand miles away he would have come to testify against them as he was an eye witness to their depredations. Finlay will be taken to Deer Lodge by Sheriff Houston in a day or two.

Document 2

Antoine Finley Accused Pascal of Murder

July 1890

Source: "A Shooting Affray," *The Inter Lake* (Demersville, Mont.), July 11, 1890, page 3, col. 3; "Killed for Money," *Missoula Gazette* (daily), July 15, 1890, page 1, col. 5.

Editors' note: These articles gave one side of the violent death of a white man, J. M. Dunn, a white prospector, allegedly killed by Pascal, a Kootenai Indian. Pascal was captured by the white justice authorities, tried, and hung in Missoula in December 1890.

A Shooting Affray.

Another human being has entered the great beyond. On July 4th, while Antoine Finley was holding down a drunken Indian named Goosta, while he was being secured so as to be moved where he could do no harm, Wm. Finley approached and tried to take him off so as to liberate Goosta. As they arose Antoine pulled out his revolver (which Finl[e]y seized by the muzzle) and placed it close to Finley's abdomen and fired, the ball intering [sic] about two inches above and to left of umbilicus. He lived until Saturday afternoon. Immediately after death a coroner's inquest was held over his remains. Drs. Sanders and Coe when placed upon the stand both testified that it would be impossible to determine the exact cause of death with out a post mortem examination, upon which the inquest was postponed until Sunday at 1. P. M. when a post mortem was held and the testimony of the witnesses taken by the Cornor's jury. They rendered a verdict that one William Finley came to his death from a pistol shot fired by one Antoine Finley, a half-breed, and said shot was fired intentionally. He is now in jail here [Demersville] pending his trial which is set for next Monday.

* * * * * * * *

Killed for Money.
A White Man the Victim of an Indian's Cupidity.
Antoine Finley Tells of a Horrible Murder Committed by Pascale.

A brief account was published yesterday about the finding of a white man's bones in the Flathead country, the man having been murdered by an Indian. The Inter-Lake gives the following detailed account of the affairs:

J. J. Grant, deputy U.S. marshal and deputy sheriff of this valley, has proved himself to be more than an ordinary official. He has shown conclusively to the people of Missoula county, and Montana that he ranks among the best detective officers in the west. While Grant had in charge Antoine Finley, the Indian who shot Wm. Finley, he caught onto a slight thread that he thought might perhaps reveal a horrible deed committed by the Indians, and finally unraveled the following story in Finley's own language:

"Me goin' to die? Before me die, me want to tell where Kootenai Indian killed white man, on trail half way to Dayton creek, but me want to sleep first.

The Story.

Next morning (Thursday), Deputy Sheriff Grant summoned a few witnesses to listen to the Indian's statement. The Indian recited as best he could, in broken English that a white man was either coming into or going out of the valley riding a grey horse, and when on the summit of the divide, an Indian overtook the white man and asked for a drink of whisky which was given him. Soon afterwards the Indian fell back in the rear, drew his gun and shot the white man in the back, dragged his body into the brush, where he took his belt, which contained about $1000 more or less. A posse was at once summoned and under command of J. J. Grant, Charles Shepherd, acting coroner, C. O. Ingalls, Oscar Boos, Lou Schafer, Wm. Wade, Wm. Mumbrue, Dr. J. W. Sanders, Dan English, E. W. Burnham, Hospital Steward C. H. Dodge, of the 25th infantry, and Charles Therriault started with teams and guns to search for the remains of the deceased, taking Antoine Finley along to show the place where the bones were hidden. Upon arriving at the spot the skeleton of a white man was found together with remnants of clothing, all of which were gathered up and the remains were brought to Demersville, where an inquest was held.

Description of the Man.

From the remains found as near as can be got at the description is about as follows: Height 5 feet 10 inches, dark hair, slightly gray. He wore a half-wool light colored overshirt, all-wool butternut colored undershirt, all-wool drawers, a black and white pin check vest, good quality blue boss-of-the-road overalls. Any one who can give any information in regards the deceased should address J. J. Grant, Egan, or C. O. Ingalls, Demersville. There seems to be no one that can guess who the deceased was. Dan Bue thinks he might have been a man named Robert Turney, as he had been corresponding with him at Carlton, in the Bitter Root valley and was to have been here last fall, but never came, and he has been unable to learn why he did not.

In Antoine's statement before the coroner's jury he says that the Indian Pascale told him that he killed the white man because some white man killed Chief Eneas son in Demersville last fall.

The Verdict.

The verdict of the jury before Chas M. Shepherd, justice of the peace and acting coroner, was "that the unknown came to his death from a gunshot wound inflicted by a rifle in the hands of one Indian, known as Pascal, some time between Aug. 15th, and Nov. 15, 1889, at Angel Hill, about 25 miles from Demersville, on the road to Dayton creek, and about one mile in a southeasterly direction from the Little Meadows. The motive for which act we believe to be revenge. Signed, W. H. Munbrue, Oscar Boos, Dan English, Lou Schafer, C. H. Dodge and Wm. Wade.

Deputy Sheriff Grant started this afternoon with a party of brave and determined men for Pleasant valley, Wolf prairie and the Libby country, and will make a diligent search for the Indian murderer.

Document 3

Uneven Justice for Murder in Western Montana

August 1, 1890

Source: Peter Ronan, *Justice To Be Accorded to the Indians: Agent Peter Ronan Reports on the Flathead Indian Reservation, 1888-1893*, ed. Robert J. Bigart (Pablo, Mont.: Salish Kootenai College Press, 2014), pages 142-145.

Editors' note: Ronan summarized recent murders of white people by Flathead Reservation Indians and Indian people murdered by whites. He related the remarkable story of how Kootenai Chief Eneas was able to avoid open conflict with a white posse that surrounded his village, despite considerable aggression. Upper Flathead Valley whites lynched two Kootenai Indians who were accused of killing white men. At the same time white men who murdered Indians were not punished.

United States Indian Service,
Flathead Agency, Mont.
August 1st, 1890.

The Hon. Commissioner of Indian Affairs
Washington, D.C.
Sir:

Referring to my telegram to you dated at Arlee, July 21st, 1890, which called attention to rumored trouble between Kootenai Indians and settlers at the head of Flathead Lake, and to your reply by wire, of July 22d directing me to proceed to the Camp and investigate cause of trouble, and to use my best efforts to prevent a conflict between whites and Indians, I now have the honor to report as directed:

For a number of years my reports to your office have spoken of ill-feeling prevailing between the settlers at the head of Flathead Lake and a band of Kootenai Indians of the reserve that occupy land midway of the Lake and adjacent to the settlements of the whites. Whiskey has been sold to the Indians by the whites and resulted in several rows in which some Indians were Killed by the latter, and among them the son of Chief Eneas, of the Kootenais; two of the Chief's Indians were also hung by a mob of settlers for alleged murder, without trial or recourse to law. Pending an investigation by the Missoula

County Grand Jury, into the Killing of the son of the Chief, it adjourned three days before I was able to bring the Chief and his Indians witnesses into court. These unfortunate circumstances have shaken faith in the mind of the Indians, as to justice having been done them in the Courts, and murders and outrages have been Committed by the Indians in retalliation [sic]. I trust this state of affairs will be brought to a close by prompt arrest and speedy punishment of Indian, as well as white, law breakers.

The recent trouble which I was ordered to investigate may be stated as follows:

On last 4th of July, at a celebration at Eagan, some Indians got drunk and quarrelled among themselves. In the scuffle a gun went off in the hands of an Indian named Antoine, who was trying to arrest another Indian named Finlay. The slayer was arrested by the whites and taken to Demersville for trial. He became frightened, fearing that he would be lynched, and stated to a deputy sheriff who had him in charge, that he Knew he was going to be hung and had a confession to make. He stated that another Indian named Pascal, told him of the murder of a whiteman last spring, and pointed out to him where the body was concealed. Before a number of witnesses the Indian repeated his narrative. A party was then organized and taking the Indian with them proceeded to the spot where the body had been buried, and found the skeleton and clothes. Intense excitement was created among the white people at Demersville, when the crowd returned with the skeleton and clothing.

Antoine stated that the man was passing along the road on horseback and was met by a party of Indians. The Indians asked for whisky and the man gave them some out of a bottle. The bottle was returned to him and he started away, when Pascal shot him in the back, Killing him instantly. He also stated that the murder was committed in revenge for the previous Killing of the son of Eneas, the Kootenai Chief, by whitemen. A large sum of money, the Indian said, was found by the murderer in a money belt around the dead man's waist. A Coroner's jury was called and an inquest held over the remains and a verdict rendered that the unknown man came to his death by Pascal, according to the evidence of Antoine.

The citizens then organized to the number of about fifty determined to surround the Kootenai village and to capture Pascal and other Indian criminals that might be found there. It was arranged to start at seven o'clock, p.m. with a deputy sheriff and the citizens as a posse. A company of troops, under Command of Captain Sanborne of the 25th U.S. Infantry, who are encamped at Demersville, concluded to go to the reservation, with this party, as the Commanding officer has orders to arrest Pierre-Paul and La La See, two other reservation Indians accused of the murder of whitemen. On arrival of posse of citizens, the Indian Camp was surrounded and a demand made for the surrender of the murderers. Chief Eneas informed the leader that the Indians asked for were not there, and invited those who could identify them to search the camp. The posse then awaited arrival of the United States troops, who came about two hours after the arrival of the armed citizens. It being clearly ascertained that the Indians wanted were not in the camp, the troops and citizens returned to Demersville.

In accordance with your telegram of July 22d, I proceeded to the Foot of Flathead Lake by team, and from thence took steamboat. The high sheriff of Missoula County joined me on the steamer and we both proceeded to Demersville. On arrival there we found the town in wild commotion, and it was stated to the sheriff and myself, that an organization of two hundred men was formed, and that on Wednesday, the 30th of July, they would march to the Camp of the Kootenai Chief, on Dayton Creek, and capture the culprits even if it involved a fight with the chief and his band. If the Indians sought for were not found at the Kootenai camp then they would march to St. Ignatius Mission, where the Church and Indian schools are situated and where the annual feast of St. Ignatius would be celebrated on the 31st, and where a great gathering of Indians would be found. I informed some of the leaders that I was ordered on the ground to prevent a collision between the Indians and the whites; that a march of a mob of disorganized men would surely result in bloodshed, and would not accomplish the arrest of the outlaws, as it was evident as soon as warning came of the march the culprits would take to the mountains and escape while innocent parties would be made the victims, should a conflict occur.

The sheriff stated to the leaders that he would not take any responsibility for the action of the mob; nor would he authorize any of his deputies to do so. This settled their conclusion to give up the expedition for the present. But it was stated by the leader that a reasonable time would be given the authorities to capture the Indians accused of murder and their accomplices, or that the matter would again be taken in hand by them as they intended to hold the organization together and Compel arrest or a fight.

I sent a messenger to the Kootenai Camp and called Eneas, the Chief to meet me at St. Ignatius Mission, which he did. I demanded Pascal to be delivered up for trial for murder at Missoula, the County seat. After considerable discussion the chief said that, if Antoine, the accuser of Pascal for murder, would be brought to Missoula, as prosecuting witness, he would at once deliver Pascal to the authorities for trial. I readily acceed [sic] to this as sheriff Houston stated he would get Antoine for witness at once. I considered that by the arrest and trial of Pascal, the accused murderer of the traveller, that it would lead, in a short time, to the peacable arrest of every Indian for whom the Sheriff holds a warrant. I apprised the sheriff of the Chief's proposition, but did not yet learn if he acted upon it.

In order to settle the present difficulties between the white settlers at the Head of Flathead Lake and the Indians of this reservation, every Indian charged with crime should be arrested and tried and if guilt is proved, punished to the full extent of the law. The Indian Police are afraid to make the arrests as they claim the outlaws have a small number of followers who have given them warning that revenge on themselves and families will follow. The Chiefs are weak and afraid to act — in short the great majority of Indians who are peaceful and law abiding have been terrorized by a few gamblers and outlaws, who harbor and protect the criminals. It is my opinion, that those outlaws should be taken by the lawful authorities, no matter at what cost, or it will result in a conflict that will be ruinous to the civilized, the progressive and the inoffensive members of the confederation of Indians occupying this reservation and also, result in bloodshed of innocent white travellers and isolated settlers who will be made the victims of revenge, which is the Indian mode of warfare.

Very respectfully
Your obedient servant,
Peter Ronan
U.S. Indian Agent.

Document 4

Chiefs Taken Hostage and
Accused Murderers Arrested
August 1890

Source: "Cleverly Caught," *Missoula Gazette* (daily), August 5, 1890, page 1, col. 3-4; "One of Them Caught," *Missoula Gazette* (daily), August 7, 1890, page 1, col. 5.

Editors' note: Missoula Sheriff William Houston took Kootenai Chief Eneas and Pend d'Oreille Chief Michelle hostage to force tribal members to turn over Indians accused of murder.

Cleverly Caught.
Sheriff Houston Brings In a Trio of Bad Indians.
Pascale, Antee and Williams, Kootenay Bucks, Arrested for Murder.

Three supposed Indian murderers are in jail, placed there by Sheriff [William H.] Houston, who brought them from the reservation last evening. The bucks are Pascale, Antee and Williams, all Kootenais. Sheriff Houston a week or so ago became weary of listening to the wily reds who, whenever he went among them for the purpose of arresting men wanted for crimes, would promise to give up the men at a certain time and then fail to do it. Growing tired of Indian duplicity, and failing to secure assistance where he expected it the sheriff proposed to see what armed force would do, realizing that intimidation was necessary if he wished to accomplish anything, and organized a strong posse of sixty men, a small posse having failed to bring in Pascale.

Saturday morning last the sheriff and posse left Egan heavily armed, Ralph Ramsdell acting as guide and interpreter. The camp of Chief Æneas on Dayton creek was reached about 2 o'cloeck [sic] yesterday morning and surrounded. The Indians were taken by surprise but showed fight. Chief Æneas drew his knife but laid it down when Mr. Ramsdell told him that if he attempted to use it he would be a very good Indian in a brief space of time. Sheriff Houston informed him that he wanted Pascale, Antee and Williams, and would hold him as a hostage until they were given up. The old Kootenai tried to squirm out, but seeing he could not had Antee and Williams pointed out and they were immediately placed under arrest. Pascale was not in camp but Chief Æneas guided the posse to where he was, at the foot of the lake, and he was also arrested.

The Indians were very much excited and would undoubtedly have attempted a rescue of their companions had the posse not been as large and determined as it was. Sheriff Houston had a medicine talk with old Æneas. He told him the whites wanted no trouble with him or his braves as long as they obeyed the laws, but if he or his men transgressed they would have to pay the penalty, the same as white men. Æneas replied that he always the friend of the pale face and had no desire to do anything wrong. After the talk the sheriff left the camp with his prisoners, having first learned from Æneas that La-La-Cee and Pierre Paul were among the Pen d'Oreilles and that they belonged to that tribe.

Michel Taken.

Reaching the foot of Flathead lake Sheriff Houston sent word to Michel, chief of the Pend d'Oreilles, that he wished to see him and the chief came into camp when he was immediately placed under arrest and told that he would be held until La-La-Cee and Pierre Paul were given up. The chief said he was willing to do the best he could, but it was doubtful if he could induce his men to give them up, as he did not have much influence among them. This was found to be true, Mr. Ramsdell explaining that Michel was not considered much of a chief by his tribe; that his authority was frequently questioned and that he was obeyed only when it pleased his bucks to do so. It was thought best to take the chief along, however, and he was taken on board the boat with the other prisoners. Before the steamer left the wharf a vicious looking half-breed rushed on board and into the cabin where the prisoners were. Approaching Sheriff Houston, he said:

"Me want my chief. Me will have my chief."

The sheriff told him to go away or he would kick him overboard and the fellow departed swearing in all the lingo at his command.

Reaching the railroad the sheriff boarded the train with Pascale, Antee and Williams, and brought them to Missoula, leaving Michel and six deputies at Ravalli. Shortly after reaching here and placing his prisoners in jail Sheriff Houston received a dispatch from Ravalli which stated that a band of twenty-five Pend d'Oreilles had arrived at the station and demanded the release of Michel. The sheriff wired back that Michel could be released as he had no further use for him, and in any case not to make a fight. Shortly afterward he received a reply that Michel refused to accompany his men, and there was no danger of a fight. The sheriff returned to Ravalli this morning and will begin anew the search for La-La-Cee and Pierre Paul. He says he will catch them.

Who They Are.

The Indians under arrest are what is known as bad Indians and are suspected of innumerable crimes. Enough evidences has been secured to convict Antee and Williams of the murder of the two unknown prospectors whose bones were found on the Jocko last spring. It is said they have openly boasted of the murders and are known to have had in their possession the horses and accoutrements of the unfortunate miners. Pascale is the alleged murderer of a man supposed to be J. M. Dunn, of Ida Grove, Iowa, whose skeleton was pointed out about a month ago by Antonie, an Indian, who supposed he was going to die for having killed another Indian, but has since been acquitted of the crime. It was first reported that an Indian named Lame Louie was the one who killed Dunn but Pascale is the man. Pascale is lame in the same leg as Louie, but his leg bends outward while that of Louie bends in. Both being lame is what caused them to be taken for each other. Louie is said to be a good Indian. The evidence against Pascale is damning and he stands an excellent opportunity of gracing a gallows. If La-La-Cee and Pierre Paul are caught, and if convictions follow in all cases Missoula will have a hanging bee that will be worth witnessing.

* * * * * * * * *

One of Them Caught.
The Indian Police and Sheriff's Posse Get Pierre Paul.
He is Brought to Missoula this Morning and Jailed —
Lalacee and Others Certain to Be Captured.

Early this morning Sheriff Houston, Jim Conley and Ralph Ramsdell arrived from Ravalli, having with them the notorious Pierre Paul, the Indian murderer, and two other Indians. The sheriff and Ramsdell took the 6:50 train back to the scene of operation to endeavor to capture Lalacee, the other bad Indian wanted. From Mr. Conley the *Gazette* learned the particulars of Pierre Paul's capture.

The party of Indian police and the white posse that were after the murderers went from Ravalli across the country on horseback. When they got to the Pend d'Oreille river they saw an Indian and s.... on the other side of the river and going away from them. The boat in which the party had to cross was a small one, and only a few could cross in it at a time. Four of the Indian police, the interpreter and two of the whites went over in the first load, and when they got over the Indians recognized the buck ahead of them as Pierre Paul. He evidently knew that the party were after him and commenced to weaken. He gave up his rifle to the s.... and sent her back with it, at the same time starting up the mountain side with his pony. When the party started uphill after him he gave up entirely, getting off his horse on the upper side and throwing up his hands. allowing them to capture him without any trouble.

The other two men whom the sheriff brought in were two who had been in attendance at the council and who had slipped out from there and ridden on ahead to warn the murderers that the party were after them. Pierre Paul seems to take his arrest very well and does not appear to be much frightened. He says that both him and Lalacee were warned by these other two the night before, about 12 o'clock, that the poose [sic] were after them, and that Lalacee immediately struck out the same night. Their informants had told them, however, that the party would come in from Camas, instead of the way they did come. Paul seems to think that his time has come, as he told the party that they might as well have shot him, as he is going to die any way. He said he was going to Missoula, where he would get good clothes and soon after he would have to die and go and fly with the angels. Paul is a splendid specimen of his race, being tall, straight and intelligent looking. He was laughing and joking in the jail this morning when the reporter went in to see him.

Sheriff Houston and Ramsdell went back on the morning train. Conley says he thinks, in fact he is sure they will get Lalacee if they get any trace of him, that the fighting men the two generally had around them have apparently abandoned them, and left them to their fate. Conley left for Helena on other business on the 11 o'clock train.

Thomas C. Adams came over from the agency this morning and brought with him the Indian interpreter there. His main object in coming was to change the charge against Joe Brothers to the court of Judge Logan United States commissioner as the offense of selling liquor to Indians is a federal offense. Mr. Adams saw Sheriff Houston at Ravalli this morning and thinks he will get Lalacee inside of a day or two, perhaps today. He also stated to a *Gazette* reporter that he had telegraphed from here to the sheriff to try and get Pierre Paul's brother, Ambrose, as he is implicated with Paul and Lalacee in some of the murders committed by them. He thinks Houston will make a cleanup of the gang of bad Indians, which number about twelve, four of whom can be got at most any time at the agency.

The two principals in these murderers are supposed to have been concerned in the killing of at least ten men, Chinamen and whites. It is said that when the railroad was being built Paul and Lalacee would kill the Chinese laborers just for fun. They are also the men who killed a couple of white men in the Flathead country two or three years ago, and several others were implicated with them in this crime. From all accounts the Indians at the agency would be glad to have this gang exterminated, as they have been a terror to the Indians as well as to the whites. Word of the capture of Lalacee is expected at any time.

Several dispatches have been received from Houston this afternoon. The last one stated that he had great hopes of capturing Lalacee this evening. He also gives Ralph Ramsdell great credit for the capture of Pierre Paul, Ralph having been captain of the posse that captured him.

Sheriff Houston
Source: "Death's Decree: The Indian Quartette's Farewell to Earth,"
Missoula Weekly Gazette, December 24, 1890, page 1, col. 1

Document 5

Pascale Confesses — Pierre Paul Pleads Innocence August 1890

Source: "Confession of Pascale," *The Anaconda Standard*, August 13, 1890, page 5, col. 4; "Pierre Paul Talks," *Missoula Weekly Gazette*, August 20, 1890, page 5, col. 1.

Editors' note: Pascale confessed to having committed murder, but Pierre Paul maintained his innocence.

Confession of Pascale
He Admits Having Committed a Brutal Murder in the Flathead.
Details of the Deed as Learned From the Murderer's Confession
Special to the Standard.

Missoula, Aug. 12. — Pascale, the Indian murderer was arraigned before Justice Logan at the county jail this morning. He was questioned by District Attorney Webster, Antoine Findley acting as interpreter. For a while Pascale held that he had not shot the man, whose bones Antoine showed Deputy Sheriff Grant in the early part of July. Then he became silent and afterwards pleaded guilty. The story of the murder is as follows: The man, whose name is supposed to have been Dunn, was sitting down for a rest when Pascale came up. They spoke a few words, when Pascale asked for a drink of whiskey. The man gave it to him. Soon he wanted another drink, but the man refused it. Then he offered a dollar for a flask of the liquor, but this was refused also. The man got on his horse and said he was going to Demersville. Pascale said he would go too. Dunn was riding ahead when Pascale shot him under the left shoulder blade. The man dropped from his horse but held to the rein with a death grip. Pascale dismounted and cut off a belt which he wore, when the horse broke away and started into the timber. The Indian feared that the animal would run into the bounds of civilization and cause suspicion, so he started after him and in the chase lost his belt. He went to a camp of Kootenais and told them about the murder and got some of them to help him drag the body into the brush. Then they searched for belt but could not find it. That night, November 8, '89, snow fell, so the belt was never found until this spring. Pascale got about $700 of the $2,000 it contained and other Indians got the rest. After hearing the testimony Justice Logan remanded Pascale to jail to await examination by the grand jury on the charge of murder in the first degree.

The two Indians who compelled another Indian to give his horse to La La See to aid him in escaping, were also examined and remanded to jail to await the action of the grand jury on the charge of grand larceny.

* * * * * * * * *

Pierre Paul Talks.
The Pen d'Oreille Buck Says He Is Innocent.
He Says Lalacee, La La and Harry Finley Killed
the Two Frenchmen on the Jocko.

A *Gazette* reporter through the kindness of Sheriff [William] Houston has been ing [sic] allowed to interview Pierre Paul at the county jail, Harry Paul, the half breed, acting as interpreter.

Pierre Paul denies having had anything to do with the killing of the two Frenchmen. He says that La-la-cee La-la and Larry Finley, who is now serving a ten years sentence for the murder of the Indian Jocko, killed the men. They had asked him to join them in the job, but he would have nothing to do with it. The murder was committed at night in the spring of 1889, near Jocko station on the Northern Pacific railroad, at the point where Jocko empties into the Clark's Fork river. the men were of medium height and built, and about 35 year old. They came walking along the road and were shot down. Whether or not they had any money or valuables in their possession he could not tell.

When asked as to his reason for evading the officers all this time, Paul said that he had no particular reason to evade them or to go to them, that he at times saw the sheriff and other officers, but that he was not afraid of them. He does not believe that La-la-cee will stay on the reservation, but the will, if he has not already, cross over into the British possessions, and thinks that he has already got away.

Larry Finley, after being sentenced to Deer Lodge last spring told the *Gazette* reporter in an interview with him, that La-la-cee and Pierre Paul killed these men. That it always had been his intention to help the officers get them and that he would appear as a witness against them. He further stated that he killed Jocko in self-defense and did not think he ought to have been punished for it; now that he had been sentenced he would never open his mouth against these Indians. Sheriff Houston at the time Larry was convicted, felt somewhat discouraged as he had always depended upon Larry's being an important witness against La-la-cee and Pierre Paul in the event that he should ever capture them, and he his going to the penitentiary removes him as a witness.

Document 6

Lalasee Surrenders to Duncan McDonald
And Is Taken to Missoula Jail
August 1890

Source: "What Duncan Said," *Missoula Weekly Gazette*, August 27, 1890, page 5, col. 2; "Captured Pierre Paul," *Missoula Weekly Gazette*, August 27, 1890, page 5, col. 2; "Duncan M'Donald Gives Version of La La See Capture," *The Daily Inter Lake*, (Kalispell, Mont.), December 1, 1915, page 4, col. 2-4.

Editors' note: According to these accounts, Lalasee confessed to having taken part in the murder of two white men near the mouth of the Jocko River in 1888. He surrendered to Duncan McDonald, who escorted him to Missoula and jail. McDonald's 1915 letter gives more detail of the surrender and arrest. McDonald also commented on the problems involved with the reward for Lalasee's capture.

What Duncan Said.

Duncan McDonald was in town last Wednesday, having brought in Lalacee and delivered him to Sheriff [William] Houston. Mr. McDonald says that Lalacee confessed to him that he killed the two Frenchmen near the mouth of the Jocko, but did it because his heart was bad towards the whites over the death of his brother whom the whites had killed a short time previous. Lalacee said he was thinking over his wrongs, the tears were streaming down his face when he saw the two whites coming towards him. Suddenly the evil spirit entered his heart and he determined to avenge the death of his brother. He ran to his tepee and secured his gun and when the whites came up he shot them both. He was satisfied then because the earth had drank their blood.

Mr. McDonald does not consider Lalacee as bad an Indian as Pierre Paul. Before his brother was killed Lalacee was a good Indian. He has a family and little ones whom he loves dearly. Pierre Paul, on the other hand, has always been a rowdy and a ruffian, a desperate man with a desire to kill. The Indians were afraid of him. He was in the habit of bullying and terrorizing all with whom he came in contact, but is at heart a coward. Lalacee on the other hand is a quiet but determined man. He killed but never threatened to kill. He at one time wanted Pierre Paul to surrender but Paul would not do so. Mr. McDonald said that when Lalacee concluded to surrender he sent a messenger to him to come and get him as he would not surrender to the Indian police or the whites. The messenger on his way to Ravalli told every one he met his business, and when he reached there, a large crowd of bucks were in readiness to assist Lalacee's capture, hoping to get some of the reward, but McDonald would not allow them to go with him to the place appointed for the surrender. He had no trouble in bringing his prisoner to Missoula. He thinks that these murderers might have been captured before had officials used the same methods employed by Mr. Houston. The Indians had bluffed the whites so often they though the same thing would work on Mr. Houston, but found out their mistake. As soon as he began arresting the chief men they weakened and promised all assistance in their power. They kept their word. There is but one bad Indian at liberty now, Antonie, a partner of Pierre Paul and Lalacee, and perhaps the worst one of the lot. He is supposed to be in Washington somewhere.

* * * * * * * *

Captured Pierre Paul.

"There is the boy who got the drop on Pierre Paul and made him surrender," said Mr. McDonald, pointing to a young, good-looking half-breed dressed in citizen's clothes and evidently proud of an incipient moustache which shades his upper lip. The boy blushed but looked rather pleased at Mr. McDonald's remarks, "Antoine," Mr. McDonald continued, "was with the sheriff's posse after Pierre Paul and had the best horse in the party. When they came to Paul's camp he jumped on his horse and tried to flee up the hill, but Antoine pursued him so closely that he jumped from his pony and Antoine got the drop on him and made him throw up his hands. The others then came up and put the fellow under arrest."

Antoine was asked what he would have done if he had met Pierre Paul alone, and replied that if he had been looking for him he would have done exactly as he did. His gun made him the big warrior's equal. Antoine is certainly entitled to a portion of the reward offered for Pierre Paul's capture.

* * * * * * * *

Duncan M'Donald Gives Version of La La See Capture
Indian Said McDonald Knew the Ways of the White Man and Placed
Himself Entirely in His Hands
— Delivered Into Hands of the Sheriff at Missoula.

The story of the early days in what was originally Missoula county, as related by William Mooring in the Inter Lake recently has created considerable interest in the western part of the state.

Following is a communication from Duncan McDonald in the Missoulian, in which he disagrees with the version of the capture of the Indian La La See, as given by Mr. Mooring:

I have been much interested in reading the story in last Sunday's Missoulian regarding the capture and hanging of Pierre Paul, La La See, Pascale and Antley (correctly spelled Andre). The story in the main is correctly told and in passing I want to say that the action then taken by Sheriff Bill Houston in the capture and execution of those outlaw Indians was the best job that was ever done in this state. To my mind Houston was a typical sheriff and is entitled to the lasting gratitude of the people of western Montana for the work that he did in restoring law and order during the years of 1889 and 1890.

But in the article in question there is one serious mistake that in the interest of truth and historical accuracy should be rectified.

In his article Mr. Mooring, in speaking of the capture of La La See says, "in the forenoon La La See sent us word that he was tired of being hunted like a coyote, and if we would go back a hundred yards he would come out and ride ahead of us to Ravalli. We did so and reached Ravalli about sundown, and landed the prisoner safely in Missoula that night."

Now, the truth of the matter concerning the final capture or surrender of La La See is this: I was at that time living at my present residence just west of Ravalli station. The posse was in camp at my house and I was in a position to know the tactics of the white men and Indians. Now, all I ask is the true facts of the case.

An Indian by the name of Charles Simmo came to me at my house and said to me, "I am a messenger from La La See and he wishes to see you." I said to the messenger, "are you telling the truth," and he said "yes, sir."

I asked him where La La See was and he said he was down the Pend d'Oreille river across from where the town of Dixon now is and just across from the present new Indian agency. I then pulled out my hunting case watch, which I still have, and gave it to the messenger, telling him to give the watch to La La See and to have La La See meet me at 9 o'clock at a certain point on the hill southeast of Ravalli about a mile and a half, telling the messenger distinctly to have La La See on the top of that hill at 9 o'clock sharp and to watch for a man across the Jocko river riding a white horse, then he would be sure I was the right man going over to meet him and would tell him what was best to do. The messenger said, "all right," and took my watch with him to give La La See, so that he could tell the exact time when he should be at the place.

That evening the head men of the Indian posse hunting for La La See arrived at my house and asked me if I knew anything about La La See. I said, "no sir."

I had already fixed out a plan to meet La La See.

That night Joseph, head of the Indian posse, camped at my house. The next morning I went to my barn to get my horse, intending to go and see La La See, but I met the messenger, who handed be [me] back my watch instead of La La See keeping it.

I said: "What is this for? Didn't I tell you to give this to La La See so that he could tell the exact time and know when to meet me?"

He said: "La La See went to the mission to see the Fathers."

I said: "What is La La See going to do?" and he said "I do not know."

I then went upstairs in my house to my room and on coming downstairs again I saw La La See sitting in my hall with a sad smile on his face. I shook hands with him.

He said: "Duncan, I am ready, do as you please with me; you take me to Missoula or any other place, as you know the ways of the white man."

I didn't care about aaking [sic] a hand in this case and in about a quarter of an hour after he arrived some of the head men of the Indian posse and some of the Indian police arrived at my house, among them was Joseph. Joseph made a suggestion to take La La See and deliver him over to the United States Indian agent, Major Ronan. Just then La La See spoke up and said "I do not want any suggestion, I gave myself up to this man to take me where he pleases."

I did not care about taking the job, but the other Indians approved of what La La See had said, "that I knew the ways of the white man and he will do anything I tell him," so then we mounted our horses and La La See shook hands with the men and women, bidding them goodbye, leaving some of the women crying.

I went to the kitchen and asked my wife for a little lunch to take along and we then started for Missoula, traveling along the side of the hills on the west arm of the Jocko, keeping out of sight of the white men and the Indians. We stopped for lunch near a spring by the hillside, La La See wanted to tell me the whole story of the killing of those men, and I told him not to talk about it.

We arrived at Evaro station. Our horses were completely exhausted, so we dismounted and went over to the station and inquired for a train. The operator informed me there was no train, so we walked around the depot where a big gang of men were working on the railroad track, and as I was acquainted with some of the men they asked me if I knew anything about La La See and I said: "They are hunting for him around the Pend d'Oreille river."

During this conversation La La See was standing close by me, but I did not want them to know that the Indian who was with me was the real man. We walked across the flat from the depot and had supper at Alex Matt's camp. We then went back to the depot and waited around for the chance of a train coming to take us to Missoula.

Finally the operator told us there would be an engine at a certain time. Finally the engine arrived and the operator told us to get on. There were four of us on the engine, Joe Herman, the engineer, the fireman, La La See and myself.

We arrived at Missoula about 1 a.m. and both us rapped at the door and heard the voice of a woman from the second story asking what we wanted and who we were. I said, "where is Kid Houston, the jailer?"

She replied, telling us that he was somewhere downtown.

We then left the pail [jail] and walked down through the alleys and at some places I left La La See alone in the dark while I was hunting around for Kid Houston, who was a brother of the sheriff. However, I failed to find him and finally I came across a man I knew by the name of Billy Hawks and told him our troubles.

We then started to look for Houston again, Billy Hawks, La La See and myself, and still could not find him. Finally we went back to the jail and after rapping at the door we heard the voice of Houston, who asked what we wanted and I asked him to open the iron door where he kept the prisoners, which he did. La La See passed through the door and while doing so spoke to the other Indian prisoners in their native language, saying, "I have arrived," the prisoners answering said: "We are glad that you have come."

That is the last I ever saw of La [La] See and I sympathize very deeply with his family, as I felt very sorry for them.

There was a reward offered of a thousand dollars for the capture of Pierre Paul and La La See. At that time I thought I was entitled to a consideration of about $500 at least. I did not intend to keep this myself, but intended giving it to his children. I inquired about the reward several times, but was always told there was to be no appropriation, but I notice by Sunday's Missoulian that the gentleman who signs himself Mooring says the reward was given, and that was the first time I ever was enlightened as to the reward.

I hesitated answering this article but I would like to see the future generations read the true facts instead of imaginary ones.

I am not answering this article to pass off as a great hero, Indian fighter or warrior, but what I want is the "true facts."

It is ridiculous, from my experience, that any sane man in capturing a wild Indian in the mountains and woods to ride one hundred yards ahead of the posse. Why, the Indian could get away at any time he wanted to at that distance in this country.

I am accused to this day by the Indians that I got that reward and I wish to enlighten them that I never got one nickel of that reward, nor did Antoine Morregeau.

Duncan M'Donald
November 23.

Lalacee
Source: "Four of a Kind," *Missoula Weekly Gazette*, November 12, 1890, page 3, col. 1-3.

Document 7

Pascale Tried and Convicted of Killing a White Miner
October 23, 1890

Source: "He Will Be Good," *Missoula Gazette* (daily), October 23, 1890, page 1, col. 1-2.

Editor's note: Pascale confessed to murdering a white miner in the Upper Flathead Valley in 1889. He had a lawyer but was found guilty after a trial before an all-white jury. Some of the testimony against him was from Indian witnesses.

He Will Be Good.
That is After He Has Stretched a Hempen Rope.
Pascale, a Kootenai, Found Guilty of Murder in the First Degree
by the Jury.

The case of the State of Montana versus Pascale, a Kootenai Indian, on trial in the district court charged with the wanton and wilful murder of J. M. Dunn, a white prospector, whose home previous to his death had been at Ida Grove, Iowa, was terminated yesterday afternoon at 5:15 o'clock, when the jury returned a verdict of murder in the first degree.

The verdict was rendered ten minutes after the court had completed his instructions.

In some respects the case is one of the most notable that has come under the notice of the courts of Montana in many years, for it is the beginning of the law's official investigation into a series of Indian horrors that have long proved the bane of our citizens and darkened the records of our state.

From time to time, and with alarming frequency within the last few years, murders and rumors of murders have come to the ears of the county authorities that have caused a great shudder of dread in the unprotected homes of our isolated ranchers and settlers. But the authorities have been unable to apprehend the perpetrators; and until the past summer the Indian murderer, and thief, alike, has almost without an exceptional instance, escaped the penalty of his evildoing. But the time of retribution came at last, and the iron hand of justice threatens now to strike a heavy blow in avenging the many infractions of her majesty.

Of all these crimes the one for which Pascale now stands in jeopardy of his life is perhaps typical.

Pascale's Crime.

From obtainable information it seems that Mr. J. M. Dunn, the man murdered, left his home and family at Ida Grove, Iowa, in the spring of 1889, to come west for purpose of bettering his health and financial condition. A report gained some credence at Post Falls, Idaho, where the ill-fated man first stopped, to the effect that his family life had not been the most happy, and that after making provision for their support he had left his home with the avowed intention of returning to it no more. Whether this report was founded on facts or was merely a rumor is uncertain, but certain it is that he did not live to return, had he so intended.

Arriving at Post Falls, Mr. Dunn purchased some property there from a Mr. Scott, the proprietor of a hotel at which he was stopping. Shortly afterward he left that place for a visit into some neighboring mines, but returned after a short trip. Then it was that he determined on the trip that was to prove his last. Purchasing a horse and some camping utensils he prepared for the journey, telling Mr. Scott that he was going to Horse Plains, Mont., and from there on into the Flathead lake region. He left his trunk at the hotel, but was known to have considerable money in his possession.

That was the last heard of him until the following spring of 1890, when the postmaster at Post Falls received a letter from a hotel keeper at Horse Plains, stating that the bones and clothing of an unknown man had been discovered about sixteen miles from Demersville on the Flathead lake.

The rest of the facts as deduced from the testimony of the witnesses at the trial are substantially as follows:

Immediately on receipt by the postmaster of the letter, Mr. Scott, who suspected that the bones were the remains of his former guest, Dunn, proceeded to Horse Plains. From there he went, in company with Sheriff Grant and Dr. Sanders, guided by Antoine Finley, to the vicinity of Angel hill, about half way between Dayton creek and Demersville, and there experienced no difficulty in finding the skeleton of the murdered man. Scott at once recognized the clothing found on the skeleton as the same worn by Mr. Dunn at the time of his leaving Post Falls.

Prior to this time, however, Sheriff Grant, on evidence furnished him by Antoine Finley, who is a Pend d'Oreille Indian, had arrested Pascale as the murderer of the unknown man.

Antoine's Story.

Antoine's story was about as follows: During the course of a hunt on Angel hill he had discovered the bones of a human being; two days after the discovery he chanced to visit the camp of some Kootenai Indians who were also hunting in that vicinity, and during his visit there mentioned to Pascale, one of them, the fact of his discovery. Pascale at once told him that in the spring before he had killed a white man and hidden the body at that place. He said he had killed him just like he would a grasshopper. After hearing this Antoine had gone to Horse Plains and told Sheriff Grant about it, and the result was that Pascale was arrested. Soon after his arrest Pascale told the officer that in the spring of 1889 he learned that a lone white man was travelling through the Kootenai country on a large, fine horse. The idea took possession of him that he would like to own that horse, and he accordingly went to his chief, Æneas, and borrowed his pony and gun, saying that he was going hunting. Instead, however, of going hunting, he struck the trail of the white man, followed him as far as Angel hill, and there bantered him for a horse trade. The trade was made, but owing to the fact of the pony belonging to his chief, Pascale said that he afterwards concluded that he was not willing to trade, and asked the white man to give him back his pony. This the white man refused to do, and Pascale attempted to take it by force. The white man after a short scuffle drew a pistol and tried to shoot him, whereupon he himself raised his gun and shot the man in the breast, killing him. Seeing what he had done, he concluded he would take what money the white man had, as he might need it to pay for something he wanted. He also took a ring, but afterwards lost it.

Three months after this he guided a party of his people to the spot where he had killed the man, in order to prove them that he had done the deed. They thought he was lying. The party found that there was nothing left of the body but the bones and some articles of clothing, including a belt in which was found upwards of $1500 in bills, which had been laid bare by prowling coyotes.

What Was Proved.

The testimony of the state's witnesses at the trial has shown that the man was shot from behind, instead of in the chest, as Pascale claimed; while the confession made to Antoine Finley and other contradicts the story of there having been a horse trade. It was evident that he had ridden in company with Dunn for awhile and then fallen behind and shot him.

Clearly it was the Indian's plan to deliberately murder Dunn and take his horse and valuables. He hid the body to escape detection, but his love for boasting and his confessed pride in the deed itself caused him to betray himself.

Pascale is an Indian perhaps 40 years old, with as cunning and treacherous a face as one could imagine. He is lame in one leg, being caused, it is said, by being thrown from a horse several years ago. His reputation among even the members of his own tribe is very bad.

At the beginning of the trial Judge Marshall appointed Mr. I. G. Denny to defend the prisoner, with Messrs. Stiff and Nichols as assistant counsel.

Notwithstanding these gentlemen recognized from the start the almost hopeless nature of the case, they have labored indefatigably and conscientiously in behalf of their client.

County Attorney Webster and Mr. Jos. K. Wood have conducted the prosecution.

The verdict of the jury meets the almost unanimous approval of the members of the bar, for there is small doubt that Pascale is worthy of death on the gallows.

Pascale
Source: "Four of a Kind," *Missoula Weekly Gazette*, November 12, 1890,
page 3, col. 1-3.

Document 8

Antley Tried for Murder of Three White Men on Wolf Creek October 24, 1890

Source: "Antley's Crime," *Missoula Gazette* (daily), October 24, 1890, page 1, col. 4.

Editors' note: Antley had counsel but was found guilty of murder. The article does not indicate how much of the testimony against him was from Indian witnesses.

Antley's Crime.
The Case Given to the Jury Which Found Him Guilty.

The hearing of evidence in the trial of Antley, the Indian charged with murder in the first degree, was terminated at 11 o'clock this morning, and the cause given to the attorneys for argument. The jury was out but a short time and returned a verdict of guilty as charged in the indictment.

The crime for which Antley has been arraigned, was complicity, as a principal, in the murder of three white prospectors on Wolf Creek, in the fall of 1887, and the circumstances as developed at the trial are as follows:

A party of six Kootenai Indians whose names were Jerome, John Annen, Koosta, Antoine, Domini, and Antley, started from Pleasant Valley to go to Tobacco Plains, a distance of about 50 miles, to attend a sun dance which their tribe was to give at that place. At the close of their first day's journey, the Indians went into camp for the night in the neighborhood [of] Wolf Creek, where the murder was committed.

Shortly after they had settled down for the night they heard the tinkling of a bell near them, and on investigation they found that it came from the camp of three white men, who were passing the night in the same locality.

John, who appears to have been the leader of the party, proposed immediately on the discovery, that they kill the prospectors, for such they were, and although there was no good reason for doing so, the others agreed.

Leaving their own camp, the Indians crawled stealthily towards their prospectors' camp. When within about twenty paces John, who had the only gun in the party's possession, paused, raised his gun, deliberately, and fired. Two of the men fell.

The third started to run in the direction of the creek, followed by the Indians.

As soon as the first shot had been fired John dropped his own gun and seized one belonging to the whites. Jerome seized another, while Antley grabbed up the one that John had discarded. All three started in pursuit of the fleeing man, firing as they ran.

On the witness stand Antoine testified that Antley fired the fatal shot. However that may have been, the third man fell mortally wounded, whereupon the Indians dragged his body back to camp, loaded it, with the two others, on their horses, conveyed them across the creek and there attempted to burn them.

A short time afterwards the incensed miners in the vicinity captured John and Jerome and hanged them.

The others escaped capture, and it was not until the past summer that they were apprehended by Sheriff [William] Houston and posse, aided by Chief Æneas.

The Indians were all young, John, the leader being but 24, while Antley, the youngest, was only 16.

The latter is an innocent-looking fellow, there being none of the vicious features present that were so marked in Pascale, who had just been convicted by the jury for murder.

The attorneys for his defense were Murry, Musgrave and Moore, while Jos. K. Woods has led in the prosecution.

Antley
Source: "Four of a Kind," *Missoula Weekly Gazette*, November 12, 1890,
page 3, col. 1-3.

Document 9

Lalacee Found Guilty of Murdering White Men on the Jocko River October 30, 1890

Source: "Lalacee's Trial," *Missoula Gazette* (daily), October 30, 1890, page 1, col. 6; "Lalacee Guilty," *Missoula Gazette* (daily), November 1, 1890, page 8, col. 2.

Editors' note: Most of the testimony against Lalacee was from Indian witnesses.

Lalacee's Trial.
Another of the Indian Murderers Before the Court.

The whole afternoon of yesterday and this forenoon was taken up in obtaining a jury to try Lalacee, one of the Indians indicted for murder.

The first witness put on the stand was Pete Colwell, an Indian who was with the party when the alleged crime was committed. He testified that himself, Lalacee, Pierre Paul, Larry Finley and an Indian named John were at Lalacee's place on or about the 1st of September, 1887; that it was on the west side of the railroad, about five or six miles from Ravalli. Lalacee went out to water his horse and when he came back said: "Let's go and kill some white men." He handed witness a gun, a sort of needle gun. Witness thought he was joking. Three of the party had guns and one had a Colt's revolver. They went across the railroad bridge towards where two white men were camped by a small fire. Witness began to think that it was more than a joke and gave the gun to Pierre Paul. Finley asked the white men where they were going and one answered that they were going to Missoula, where he had a home. Witness heard behind him either Pierre Paul or Lalacee make a remark to the effect that they would never reach Missoula. One of the white men had his boots off. The other man said to him to come on and start. He said he would as soon as he got his boots on. The white men started towards the railroad, but before they did witness heard Lalacee say to Pierre Paul, "When I shoot you shoot, too." When the white men started to the railroad Lalacee hurried past them and then turned and shot at one of them, hitting him. At the same time witness heard a shot from near the camp fire. The wounded man jumped forward and grasped Lalacee's gun, but the latter jerked it away from him. The white man then turned toward

Finlay, who shot him also. He turned back toward Lalacee who fired again, when the white man fell, and then Finlay shot him again.

This was as far as the witness' testimony went up to the time of going to press.

* * * * * * * * *

Lalacee Guilty.
The Jury Renders a Verdict of Murder in the First Degree.

When court convened this morning the counsel for the defense took up the argument on the point raised by them yesterday that the court had no jurisdiction in the case. Mr. Moore argued for the defense and Frank H. Woody for the state. After hearing all the arguments Judge Marshall ruled that the right of way on which the crime was committed had been deeded by the terms of the treaty by the Indians to the United States government and was not a part and parcel of the Indian reservation, but was a part of the public domain, across which the government had granted the Northern Pacific a right of way. He ruled that therefore the court had jurisdiction in the case.

The case for the state here rested, and as the defense introduced no witnesses, Mr. Wood opened the argument to the jury on behalf of the state. He was followed by Messrs. Moore and Denny for the prisoner, and the case was closed for the state by Mr. Webster.

After being charged the jury retired and were out only about twelve minutes when they announced that they had agreed upon a verdict. The verdict is murder in the first degree. Judge Marshall announced that he would pass sentence next Wednesday at 10 o'clock. When Lalacee was told the verdict he seemed considerably affected, his cheeks twitching plainly. He evidently realizes that it means death for him.

Document 10

Agent Ronan Reports on Trials of Accused Kootenai Indian Murderers November 1, 1890

Source: Peter Ronan, *Justice To Be Accorded To the Indians: Agent Peter Ronan Reports on the Flathead Indian Reservation, Montana, 1888-1893*, ed. Robert J. Bigart (Pablo, Mont.: Salish Kootenai College Press, 2014), pages 170-172.

Editors' note: Ronan emphasized that Pascal and Antley received trials and were convicted mostly on Indian evidence.

United States Indian Service,
Flathead Agency,
November 1st, 1890.

Hon. Commissioner Indian Affairs
Washington, D.C.
Sir:

The month of October was very pleasant on this reservation. The weather was beautiful and the Indians succeeded in threshing one of the finest crops of grain ever raised on the reservation. The threshing machines are now housed and put away for next seasons work. The grist mill has run every day during the month of October, grinding Indian wheat, more of which is delivered fast as the flour is hauled away. The mill yard is also piled up with logs awaiting to be sawed, and as some of the Indians are clamerous [sic] for lumber to repair and build before winter, I shall probably shut down the grist mill for a short time during the month in order to get some lumber ahead.

At the present term of Court for this District, now in session at Missoula, Pascall and Antela, two Kootenai Indians belonging to the band of Chief Eneas, residing upon this reservation, were tried separately and found guilty of murder in the first degree. At 10 o'clock on the morning of October 27th, they were brought into Court for sentence. After reviewing the cases from the time of the arrests to the indictments by the grand jury, the trial and the conviction, Judge Marshall asked the two defendants whether they had any reason to offer why sentence of death should not be passed upon them according to law. Neither of them replied. The Judge then sentenced each of them to be hanged on Friday December 19th, between the hours of 10 o'clock in the forenoon and 2 o'clock in the afternoon. This is the longest time that the law allows in this State to be allotted to condemned murderers, it being eight weeks from the time of passing the sentence.

Pascall was found guilty by Indian evidence of having murdered a traveler to gain possession of his horse.

Antelay's crime for which he is to suffer the penalty of death, was complicity, as principal in the murder of three white prospectors, on Woolf Creek, in the fall of 1887. It was clearly proved, on Indian evidence, that a party of six Kootenai Indians, whose names were Jerome, John Annen, Koosta, Antoine, Domini, and Antelay, started from Pleasant valley to go to Tobacco Plains, where a band of British Kootenais camp, just at the International boundary line, to attend a sun dance which the British Indians were to give. While on their way they came upon a camp of three white prospectors on Woolf Creek. John proposed they kill the prospectors in retaliation for Indians killed by white men. Leaving their own camp the Indians crawled stealthily towards the prospector's camp. When within about twenty paces, John, who had the only gun in the party's possession, paused, raised his gun and fired. Two of the white men fell. The third started to run followed by the Indians. Soon as the first shot had been fired John dropped his own gun and seized on one belonging to the whites; Jerome seized another while Antelay grabbed the one John had discarded. All three started in pursuit of the fleeing man, firing as they ran. On the witness stand Antoine testified that Antelay fired the fatal shot. However that might have been, the third man fell mortally wounded, whereupon the Indians dragged his body to the camp, loaded it with the two others on their horses, conveyed them across the creek and there attempted to burn them.

Shortly afterwards John and Jerome were taken from the custody of a deputy sheriff, who had them under arrest, by a party of citizens, at the Head of Flathead Lake, and hanged them. The others escaped capture and it was not until the past summer that they were apprehended and brought to justice through the good office of Eneas, the Kootenai Chief, who arrested them and turned them over to the Sheriffs posse. There are two more Indians yet on trial, belonging to the Pend 'd Oreille tribe. Their names are Piere Paul and Lal-La-See, and are the desperados who terrorized this reserve for several years. At one time a reward of a thousand dollars was offered for their capture. Last summer I reported to your office that the Indians at last agreed to capture them which they did and turned them over to the Sheriff's posse. They were indicted for murder in the first degree and their trial is now proceeding in the District Court. The capture and conviction of those lawless Indians will have a good effect in awing and subduing the restless and savage spirit of some of the young would be braves. The Chiefs and the Indians generally are pleased that those outlaws have at last been brought to justice.

I have just received the news that Lal-La-See, was found guilty of murder in the first degree and will be sentenced on Wednesday the 5th of November. On that day the trial of Piere Paul, also indicted for complicity in murder with Lal-La-See, will be commenced.

Herewith I have the honor to enclose sanitary report and report of funds and indebtedness; also report of farmer and have the honor to be

Very respectfully
Your obedient servant
Peter Ronan
United States Indian Agent.

Document 11

Pierre Paul Convicted of Murdering White Men on the Jocko River November 12, 1890

Source: "Pierre Paul Talks," *Missoula Weekly Gazette*, November 12, 1890, page 5, col. 1; excerpt from "Paul Will Hang Too," *The Anaconda Standard*, November 9, 1890, page 1 col. 7.

Editors' note: According to these articles most of the testimony against Pierre Paul was from Indian witnesses.

Pierre Paul Talks.
He Says Witnesses Did Not Tell the Truth.
The Last of the Quartette of Indian Murderers Makes a Vigorous Denial.

The court had been nearly two days trying to secure a jury for the trial of Pierre Paul, the last of the quartette of Indian murderers to be tried. About 3 o'clock Sat[ur]day afternoon a jury was finally obtained, and the counsel for the state opened with their evidence. Pierre Paul already shows the effect of confinement. He has lost his healthy color, and no longer smiles and laughs like he did when first captured, but his face shows an anxious expression, he no doubt realizing that the same fate awaits him as that of the other three.

The first witness called was Pete Colwell, whose evidence was substantially the same as he gave on Lalacee's trial. A map drawn by W. A. Irvin, civil engineer, is before the court showing where the N. P. right of way is, the bridge across the Jocko, and the positions, according to witnesses, of the white men and the different Indians when the shooting occurred: The map shows that the crime was committed on the right of way.

The Indian John, was placed on the stand at 9 o'clock this morning, and he testified a good deal as he did on the former trial. He stated the conversation between the whites and Larry Finley; also to the remark made by either Pierre Paul or Lalacee, that the white men might think they were going to Missoula but they would never reach there. He says that he heard Pierre Paul tell Lalacee that when Lalacee shot the one white man, he (Pierre Paul) would shoot the one by the fire. That Pierre Paul and the white man stood about eight feet from each other, with the camp fire between them, while he (John) was about the same distance from Pierre Paul, and towards the track. The white man had been putting on his shoes and had not fully straightened up, when Pierre Paul raised his gun, pointed it at the man and shot. The white man fell back in a half sitting posture, with his hands on the ground partially behind him. John then ran towards the railway. When asked if he or some one else did not hit the white man with a rock or club he answered, "What was the use of hitting them when they were dead?" John helped to carry the body of one of the white men and throw it into the river and stood on the bridge to see it go down stream, but did not see it pass down. Saw some of the party take a little money from the white man's person. Neither of the white men had arms. All the parties staid at Lalacee's house that night. Did not talk with any one about the murder for a year after.

Joseph, a judge or head man among the Indians, testified that some three years ago Pierre Paul told him at the mission that he was afraid the white sheriff would arrest him; that he and Lalacee had killed two white men near Lalacee's cabin, that they had buried one, and the he heard the bones had been found.

At this point in the testimony Pierre Paul, who had been listening intently to the evidence, got up, and pointing to Judge Marshall with his arm extended and with his towering form slightly leaning forward, said the white judge should not believe what Joseph was telling, that it was all a lie. When asked by Interpreter Michele, Joseph replied that it was not a lie. Pierre Paul then pointed to Joseph and said that he was either lying or had dreamed it. Joseph answered that he had not dreamed it; that he saw Pierre Paul's lips move, and that the words came out of his mouth and entered his, Joseph's ears. The scene was quite a dramatic one.

Mrs. Coture was the next witness, and testified to the finding of the skull, backbone, ribs and hips of a human being while out fishing. The bones had been partially burned and partially buried. She also testified that after she had found the bones and told of it Pierre Paul came to her house and was very mad. That he told her if the sheriff came after him he would find her if the whites were thick about her, and would kill and burn her as he had the white men.

Pierre Paul was placed on the stand and allowed to testify in his own behalf. He denied that he had anything to do with the murder. He said he remained at the camp when the others went to kill the men. Before he testified he demanded that Pete and John be facing him, which request was complied with.

* * * * * * * *

Paul Will Hang Too
Conviction of Another of the Flathead Indian Murderers.
Threats of His Friends

. . . .

The case of the state vs. Pierre Paul was finished to-day. The testimony was finished at 4:30 o'clock. The attorneys then addressed the jury until about 6 o'clock. The jury stayed out about twenty minutes, then went to supper, and, after deliberating until about 8 o'clock, brought in a verdict of guilty of murder in the first degree.

Pierce Pane [Pierre Paul] has a number of relatives, some of whom are desperate men, and they have threatened that, if he is hanged, they will take vengeance on all the witnesses who appeared against him. Some of the witnesses feel some anxiety. But there is not likely to be much trouble, as the Indians on the reservation know Sheriff [William] Houston well enough to respect his authority.

Pierre Paul
Source: "Four of a Kind," *Missoula Weekly Gazette*, November 12, 1890,
page 3, col. 1-3.

Document 12

Agent Ronan Defends Trials of Accused Indian Murderers
November 13, 1890

Source: Peter Ronan, *Justice To Be Accorded To the Indians: Agent Peter Ronan Reports on the Flathead Indian Reservation, Montana, 1888-1893*, ed. Robert J. Bigart (Pablo, Mont.: Salish Kootenai College Press, 2014), pages 172-173.

Editors' note: Ronan argued that the murder trials were fair. The accused had legal representation and most of the witnesses against them were Indians.

United States Indian Service,
Flathead Agency,
November 13, 1890.

Hon. Commissioner Indian Affairs
Washington, D.C.
Sir:

Replying to your letter October 31st, 1890 – "L 26991 – 1890" relative to the arrest by the civil authorities of Missoula County, Montana, of Pascal, an Indian, for murder etc., I have to say that in my report for the month of October, I made reference to trial and conviction of Pascal, Antley and Lal-La-See and that the case of Piere Paul was on trial, all of whom are Indians belonging to this reservation. I may now report that by their verdict on Saturday afternoon, November 8th, 1890, in the case of the State vs. Piere Paul, a Pend 'd Oreille Indian, charged with murder in the first degree, have disposed of the last of the four Indians on trial for murder. They returned a verdict of guilty as charged in the indictment. On Tuesday, November 11th Judge Marshal sentenced Pere Paul to be hanged Friday, December 19th, the same day on which Lal-La-See, Antley, and Pascal are to be hanged.

Thus is ended the last of four trials which has continued to attract the attention and interest of the citizens of this State.

The prisoners were properly defended, as the best legal talent of the County and probably of the State, was assigned by Judge Marshall for their defence. The conviction rested upon the evidence of numerous witnesses of both races, and was of a convincing character.

The only hope that the condemned Indians now have left for their lives lies in the power of the Governor or supreme court to confer, and it is not probable, considering the nature of the crimes and the evidence against the defendants, that an appeal will be taken to the higher courts, or that the Governor of this State will commute the death sentence if applied to.

I am very respectfully,
Your obedient servant
Peter Ronan
United States Indian Agent.

Document 13

Petition for Commutation of Death Sentences

December 17, 1890

Source: "Asking for a Respite," *The Helena Independent*, December 17, 1890, page 5, col. 3.

Editors' note: This petition for mercy for the four convicted Indians showed there were some divisions of opinion within the white population in Missoula. Note especially that Agent Peter Ronan signed the petition. Some of the other signers were from prominent Missoula families.

Asking for a Respite.
Missoulians Petition the Governor to Save the Indians from the Noose.
The Petitioners do Not Believe a Strong Defense Was Made.
Pierre Paul, La-La-See, Pascale and Antley Must Die Next Friday
Unless Reprieved.

Governor Toole has been asked to prevent the hanging of the four Indians who are under sentence to die at Missoula next Friday. His excellency has not yet announced what action he will take. The request is in the shape of a petition from a number of prominent people in Missoula county. Major Peter Ronan, agent of the Flatheads signed the petition, so did Hon. W. M. Bickford, F. G. Higgins, Mrs. C. S. Marshal and Mrs. Eli Fisher of the Woman's Christian Temperance Union.

Mrs. McCormick, in a letter to the governor says:

"Your excellency has already been apprised that the people of Missoula have drawn up a petition asking commutation of sentence for the Indians to be hung on the 19th inst. We know that your excellency is ever inclined to the side of mercy when it can be exercised without loss of the equally necessary quality justice. Therefore we ask that the condition of these poor wretches be considered, their ignorance, the cruelty with which their white brothers have treated them in refusing to grant to Indian depredations against our law and order, the same leniency which is given white men who are equally culpable with regard to Indian rights both to property and life.

"Only a short time ago on the Flathead reservation an Indian was shot down in cold blood by a white man while walking with his wife. The effect upon her was such that after three weeks of insanity she died. The law in this (and countless other cases) merely winked at the crime, and the guilty party was never punished.

"Knowing these things and also being aware of the Indian peculiarity, revenge, if not upon his enemy then upon his brother or any other relative, falling them [then?] upon the first white man he meets. It is justice and right to him and instead of a crime he has done a commendable act. Do not hang them for what in their eyes is laudable. Rather condemn them to imprisonment that they may be taught proper contrition for their offences and show them that they possess, as well as the whites, the inalienable right to the full protection of the law, should they need such. In this petition we have rather sought quality than quantity. The names are few but they are representative and express the general sentiment in Missoula." Mrs. McCormick closes her letter with the hope that she will soon hear favorably from the governor.

The petition recites the incidents of the crime, the trial, and sentence to death. Continuing it reads: "Your petitioners further state in most solemn form that the punishment by death of a crime, is a most cruel and inhuman manner of meeting the ends of justice; that the object and aim of human punishment is, first, for the reformation of the criminal, second, to place him in a condition where he can do no more wrong, third, to deter others through his example.

"Your petitioners are in sympathy with those great lights of jurisprudence, Franklin, Livingston, Rush, La Fayette, Becciris, Grotus, Lord Brougham and Wendell Phillips, who demanded the abolition of the penalty of death until the infallibility of human testimony could be shown. We think it enough to discredit the gallows that men might be hung by mistake. There have been scores of such cases in the history of jurisprudence.

"Your petitioners further state in the most sincere manner that all the material witnesses for the prosecution were Indians, and it is very doubtful if they understood the nature of an oath. That during the trial of the four an interpreter was used, and in many instances two were used to translate Pen d'Oreille into Kootenay and Kootenay into English. That none of the four defendants can speak a word of the English language. In view of these facts we most conscientiously believe that it was utterly impossible for them to have made as strong a defense in their own behalf as white men could have made.

"Therefore, your petitioners most humbly ask that a respite may be granted in their behalf for such a length of time as will enable your petitioners to take the proper steps before your excellency and the honorable board of pardons to ask that their sentence be commuted from sentence of death to that of imprisonment for and during the term of their natural lives, or that if in time they are enabled to present to the governor and board of pardons such proofs and statements as will convince them of their innocence, they be pardoned."

Document 14

Convicted Indian Murderers Deny Their Guilt

December 18, 1890

Source: "Deny Their Guilt," *Missoula Gazette* (daily), December 18, 1890, page 1, col. 5.

Editors' note: All four of the convicted Indian murderers denied their guilt when interviewed by the white *Missoula Gazette* reporter.

Deny Their Guilt.
An Interview With the Condemned Indians.
They Claim the Whites Should Have Been Killed,
but They Did Not Kill Them.

A *Gazette* reporter this morning interviewed the four condemned Indian murderers at the county jail, through interpreters Alex Michel and Pete Irvine. The Indians were found on the lower corridor sitting on the floor in a group. At first they were not inclined to talk much, but after being given a cigar apiece and a dram of Bourbon, and being told that the reporter was an emissary of the big chief, they readily consented to the reporter's wishes.

Pierre Paul

declares his innnocence. He says that he had nothing to do with the killing of the white men, except that he was present at the killing. Larry Finley, the half-breed who is now serving a ten years' sentence for the murder of Jocko, committed the murders. He first shot the younger man of the two whites as he was walking away from the camp and then returned to the fire and shot down the other. He says that after he received his sentence he began thinking of the matter and thought it no more than just and right that the white men were killed, because the white men killed two of his uncles, and his mother died from grief over their deaths, and he believed it was right for the Indians to get pay for his relatives' death in that manner. He does not want to hang, but if he must be executed he will bravely face his fate.

Lalacee

says that he is not guilty; that Larry Finley, Colville Pete, John and Pierre Paul committed the murders. "I did not kill the white men, but after I received my sentence, and after being confined in jail so long, I began thinking over the matter, I believe it right that the white men were killed, because they killed my brother." Should the big chief commute his sentence to life imprisonment he would be very glad and thankful to him.

Lalacee shows the greatest signs of weakening, and he will without doubt break down completely when he is taken to the scaffold. He will show less bravery than the others. The long confinement has shown more on him than the others and he appears most down-hearted and to suffer greater remorse than the others.

Antley

says he is not guilty. Jerome and John, his two companions, killed the three white prospectors. Chief Æneas had told him not to tell on the other boys, as he would see that he and Pascale were cleared. The little fellow shows the least weakness; he keeps up spirits in a brave manner, and grinned and smiled throughout the interview. From appearances he will face his fate with more bravery than the rest.

Pascale

also denies his guilt. He did not kill the white man. William killed him and got all the money. When asked why he told Antoine Finley of his killing Dunn, he replied that he never told Antoine anything about it. He was informed that he must tell the truth, for the Big Chief wanted to know the truth, whereupon he replied that he had told the truth before, but that the white man would not believe him. This was all he had to say. He did not believe it would do him any good anyway, because the whites would not believe him.

They were told by the reporter to keep up their spirits, that it was yet time for the Big Chief to interfere in their behalf. After being thus informed they all seemed to feel somewhat better and the reporter left them in good spirits and a great deal more composed than when he entered the jail.

Later in the day, when the reporter returned to the jail, the condemned men were still in apparent good spirits. The final refusal of Governor Toole to interfere in their behalf had been made know to them, and they had accepted it without a word and without a sign of concern.

Pierre Paul, still a giant, still upright, and still with his murderer's look, was laughing and joking with a little white boy that stood at the grated window of his cell. Antley smoked a cigar and smiled, Pascale, sour and repellant, limped from one window to another and gazed through the barred openings out on the valleys and mountains to the east as if he realized full well that his moccasined velvet foot had trod them for the last time. Lalacee was not to be seen. Hidden behind the iron cage he has remained throughout the day in sullen and morose quiet.

Document 15

Two Kootenai and Two Pend d'Oreilles Hung in Missoula for Murder December 19, 1890

Source: Excerpt from "Death's Decree," *Missoula Weekly Gazette*, December 24, 1890, page 1 col. 1-4.

Editors' note: This is the most detailed account describing the hanging of four Indians in Missoula on December 19, 1890, for murder. Much color has been added, but notice that two Catholic priests and two Flathead Reservation judges were present at the hanging.

Death's Decree
The Indian Quartette's Farewell to Earth.
The Final Act in Missoula's Legal Tragedy.
Pierre Paul, La-La-See, Antley and Pascale Die on the Gallows.
The Murdered Whites Avenged!
Fitting Culmination of a Play Whose Opening Scene Dates Back to 1885.
The Devil Has His Due!

From Friday's Extra Edition.

Pierre Paul, La-La-See, Pascale and Antley are good Indians now. They were hanged this morning; by their deaths expiating their offenses against the law of the land — the brutal and unprovoked killing of men, the details of which are given in another chapter. They were given fair and impartial trials; their counsel did for them all they could possibly do, and the juries, uninfluenced by prejudice, gave their verdicts in accordance with the evidence adduced at their trials. In the recital of their brutish and hellish deeds, not one extenuating circumstance came to light, nothing by which the juries could be influenced to extend a sign of mercy to the guilt-hardened wretches, ignorant, it is true, but of venomous ignorance which made them more to be feared than the poisonous snake, or the fangs of a wild beast. They killed for the love of killing. Taught that the pale face was their natural enemy, they sought to redress the wrongs of their race handed down to them by tradition, except, perhaps, in the case of La-La-See, who had a brother killed some time ago, which led him to declare a vendetta against the white man; but even if this had not happened,

"Just Before the Drop," December 19, 1890.
Source: Redrawn by Corky Clairmont from damaged original in "Death's
Decree: The Indian Quartette's Farewell to Earth," *Missoula Weekly Gazette*,
December 24, 1890, page 1, col. 2-5.

his vindictive spirit would sooner or later have led him into killing, for he was a murderer at heart.

Sympathy has been expressed for these redhanded murderers, but it should not have been. The tear of pity should never flow for wretches vile as they were. Sentimentality for them, expressed or felt, is maudlin, unhealthy, unnatural, and has no home in a well balanced mind.

Mercy is a child of God; in every heart she should find a home, in every home a resting place; every door should be thrown open to her timid knock; but Mercy, gazing upon the deeds these wretches did, fled from the sight of man.

Their Last Look.

The braves met their fate with the stoicism characteristic of their race; departed for their happy hunting grounds, as if on a journey through the pleasant lands they roamed while in the flesh; thinking, perhaps, that over the range, which is life, lies the valley of death, peopled not with the grisly shapes and terrors the pale face fears to meet, but the land of the buffalo, the elk and the deer; where the chase is never wearisome and its fruits abundant; where the lakes and streams are clear and cool, and the shadows of the forest invite to rest; where their kindred and friends await and beckon for them to come. This, their idea of the life to come, afforded them more solace than the religion of the pale face, none of which they understood except the future state, and that had been taught them at their mother's knees and told them by the old men of their tribe; soothed and sustained by this belief, with no regrets expressed, if thought, they left. The light of this life was shut forever from their eyes. The lifeless lumps of clay once animated by their cruel spirits, God-given, if not God-recognized, are all that is left. The untamable nature in them is gone.

The Morning Light.

Day dawns late in this northern clime in the winter, and at 6 o'clock there are few people astir; but on this morning before that time men passed to and fro, by the square brick jail near the court house, making remarks about the coming execution. Inside there were lights burning and signs of life. Felt-footed guards moved noiselessly along the corridors. There was no sound of grating key, nor clanking of chains. The prisoners, other than the condemned men, were pacing their cells or standing by their grated doors, with whitened faces pressed against the bars, comparing their fates — restrainment of liberty at the worst — to the fate of the poor wretches who had slept their last sleep save the one eternal. A few hours only and they will have left their cells forever.

The morning, chill and shrinking, opens its eyes. The mountains seem to rise from their snowy blankets and gaze helplessly about. The skies are dull and sodden. A few flakes of snow are whirled through the biting air. The trees in the court-house yard stand erect, nodding slight recognition to the unwelcome, prowling winds, which frisk around through, up and down the streets and whistle by the jail, by the court-house, and scurry along over the valley.

Back of the jail and adjoining it is a rude board structure. Planks set on ends and nailed to a square wooden frame. The planks are about twenty feet in hight and are placed as close together as they can be. But not close enough to shut out the light. One might peep through the cracks, and, to avoid this, strips have been nailed over the interstices. The enclosure, about thirty feet square, would be dark as a dungeon if it were roofed, but it is not. Inside of it nothing of the outside world but the sky can be seen.

One end of the enclosure is the rear wall of the jail, close against which the gallows is placed. At the other end two cottonwood trees stand. They seem grim and silent sentinels. Inside, the ground is barren and cold. It has been tramped by many feet of persons whose curiosity has led them to inspect the grim engine of death. Outside, the grass is brown and bare, a tuft here and there emerging from its covering of snow.

Waiting for What.

As near the enclosure as deputies will allow them to stand, are gathered groups of boys and men, waiting; for what, they really do not know themselves, only that inside, where they cannot see, four lives are to be taken. They cannot see the gallows, but they know it is there. They will not know when the drop falls, but they know it will fall, and they strain their ears to catch the slightest sound. Perhaps a murmur, or an exclamation from some one inside will let them know that the execution has taken place.

Hoping for this, they wait.

Inside the enclosure are the officers who are to see that the law is executed. The sheriff and his trained deputies, sheriffs from other counties, present by invitation, newspaper men, physicians, spiritual advisors and others fortunate enough to gain admittance, drawn, thither by their curiosity to see the life of a fellow-man taken. They stand expectant and wait.

The end is not yet. The victims of Moloch are waiting at the feast. The banquet of death is prepared, but the honored guests have not made their appearance. They are being made ready. There is a deal of prinking and primping to be done at a carousal where Death presides. He is a host who demands that all the proprieties be attended to when informed beforehand that he will be called upon to do the honors. He does not grow restless nor impatient. He knows they must come when he summons, and he graciously waits their coming. They will not fail him. He would not allow such preparations for his benefit only to suffer disappointment, and while awaiting the coming of those he is going to entertain he inspects his messenger, the gallows, and smiles. A tree has done him as good and efficient service here in Montana, but he allows us to have our way.

The Gallows.

It is not a sightly structure, this gibbit.

It is rough and earnest looking, though.

Two upright pieces of timber are mortised into a crosspiece lying upon the ground, and at the top, fifteen feet from the lower crosspiece, is another crosspiece mortised and bolted into the uprights. At the bottom each upright is braced to about three feet from the ground, making a firm, steady structure. A chain could be thrown over the top crosspiece and a locomotive hoisted free from the ground. Adjoining the two main uprights are two other solid uprights holding up a platform seven feet in the clear from the lower cross-piece. The outer part of this platform, about three feet, is a trap, sustained by four heavy iron hinges, and held up by a strong rope passing through pulleys in each of the lesser uprights. Pulled up in place, it rests on a level with the other part of the platform, apparently two feet across. When the rope is severed the trap falls down, and swings against the end of the jail, in which is a spring and against which the trap falls, but not hard enough to make it rebound to any great extent.

Twelve steps lead up to the platform, and each step about one foot apart. The rope holding the platform is concealed by a casing, and in the fourth step is a button known to no one but the sheriff. When that button is touched, a knife severs the rope and the drop falls. The sheriff is the last man to descend the steps, and before he reaches the ground the trap has fallen.

From the top cross-piece dangle four ropes equi-distant apart, and in the end of each rope is a hangman's noose, with enough slack in each to allow a drop of seven feet, allowing for a stretch of a fraction of an inch.

Everything is in readiness.

In the eastern side of the enclosure is a door. From this door is a closed passage way to the east door of the jail, out of which the condemned men can be taken without having to run the gauntlet of curious eyes. The sheriff has been considerate of their feelings.

Perhaps the ghosts of the men they have murdered will walk beside them and jeer at them as they follow their last trail. Who knows? But if they do, they are hidden from mortal ken.

Preparations have been completed. There is a bustle in the jail, the creaking of doors and the shuffling of feet.

They are coming.

The door of the jail is thrown open and sound of footsteps grows nearer.

The door of the enclosure is opened and the little procession makes its appearance.

It is now snowing furiously.

Before the procession reached the door of the enclosure the snow suddenly ceased as if awaiting for what was to follow.

Sheriff [William] Houston was in the lead. Then came Father [Jerome] D'Aste with crucifix in hand.

Pierre Paul followed towering like a Saul among his fellows. His face was wreathed in smiles.

La-La-See followed. His face was bloodless, and his muscles twitched as if he were in pain. There was a wild look in his face, pleading and pitiful.

Pascale was next in the death march. He was sullen and gloomy. The bitterness and hatred of generations showed on his countenance.

Antley was smiling and pleasant as if he was going to a wedding feast. His teeth gleamed and his eyes sparkled.

Father [Gaspar] Genna brought up the rear, crucifix in hand.

Sheriff Houston supported Pierre Paul; Deputy Sheriff McClung, La-La-See; Deputy Sheriff Ramsdell, Pascale, and Deputy [Evans?], Antley.

While the prayers were being intoned and the straps being fastened about them, Pascale spoke to Baptiste (Kicashee) chief justice of the Agency, and to Chief Joseph (Standing Bear), both of whom were standing near the scaffold.

He said: I came here to this stand to die like a man. I will die like one. I did the crime for which I will have to die now. They tell me it is just. I have nothing to say about that. I am resigned.

Pierre Paul also spoke to the chiefs. ["]I will die like a man. I killed the men. But I do not regret it, but they tell me it is wrong. If so I am sorry. You see how I am here. Try and help my people. Tell them how I died, and warn them not to do as I did, or they may die as I have to die. Be kind to my people and see that they do not want. I am glad you came and I thank you for being here and for what you have done for me. See that I am buried with my people."

Seeing Mr. Denny in the crowd, the attorney who defended him, Pierre Paul said "Good night Denny," then changed to "Good by, Denny."

The priests kept intoning the prayers, occasionally calling the attention of the doomed men to them, when they would look up and respond.

Pierre Paul kept tolling his beads.

La-La-See was handed the crucifix and he pressed it ardently to his lips.

The men were quickly pinioned and the nooses placed over their heads.

Not one of them trembled.

The ordeal was passed by which their courage could be tested. They were ready.

The black caps were placed over their heads. The priests intoned their prayers and there were low responses.

Sheriff Houston gave the signal for all to leave the scaffold, and it was obeyed.

Father Genna stood upon the steps.

Sheriff Houston walked down the steps, and when he reached the fourth one a sharp chisel cut the rope.

The trap fell and the bodies shot downward with the rapidity of thought almost. The drop was sprung at exactly 10:47. Pierre Paul's toes came within an inch of the ground, but the recoil of the rope drew him up until he was clear of the earth his feet would never tread again.

Drs. Parsons, Hedger, Kneitle, and Billmyer were ready, watch in hands, and life was soon extinct.

The bodies were placed in coffins and this evening will be taken to St. Ignatius mission and buried.

Agent Ronan was present and will see that the wish of the Indians to be buried at the Mission is carried out. He says there will be nothing but religious services at the graves, and no Indian rites will be observed.

Document 16

Struggle for Justice for an Indian Murdered by a White Man
August 12, 1892

Source: Peter Ronan, *Justice To Be Accorded to the Indians: Agent Peter Ronan Reports from the Flathead Indian Reservation, 1888-1893*, ed. Robert J. Bigart (Pablo, Mont.: Salish Kootenai College Press, 2014), pages 317-318.

Editors' note: This is the story of Agent Peter Ronan and Flathead Indian Reservation tribal members struggling to bring a white man to justice for killing an Indian. It is not known whether Robert Philips was eventually punished.

United States Indian Service,
Sand Point, Idaho.
August 12, 1892.

Hon. Commissioner Indian Affairs
Washington, D.C.
Sir:

On the 9th of August I left the Flathead Agency, for Bonner's Ferry, Idaho in response to an urgent telegram from the Indians of that locality, which I quoted in my last report from the Agency. On arrival at Sand Point, found a telegram urging my presense at Hope, Idaho, to investigate the suspected murder and robbery of an Indian from the Flathead reservation by a whiteman by the name of Philips, who was then under arrest, and to assist in prosecuting the case. Deeming it best for the service to act in this matter before proceeding to the Kootenai Indian Camp, I returned to Hope. Here I found encamped Joseph Cathoulihou, one of the Judges of the Agency Court of Indian Offences, Duncan McDonald, a halfbreed, some of the Indian Police, the wife and sister of the Indian whose body was found, and several Indians from the Kalispel Country. At the Indian Camp it was stated to me that a well to do Indian of the Flathead reservation, called Felix Burns, left his home some time previous to the 4th of July, having on his person about two hundred dollars. On the evening of the 3d of July, Alto and his brother Alexander, Indians also of the Flathead reservation, arrived at Sand Point, in Idaho. While at the depot Robert Philips a whiteman, called by the Indians "Buckskin Shirt," approached them and told them that there was an Indian at his cabin and asked them to go there and see him. The Indians accompanied Philips to the cabin where they found the Indian Felix Burns. Philips had a large flask of whisky and the Indians and the whiteman commenced drinking. Philips went out at different times and bought whisky — three bottles were drank. In the morning when they recovered from their carrousal, Alto noticed Felix giving Philips money; after he went out Felix informed Alto that he had given the white man ten dollars to buy whisky. Philips came back with keg and a sack of provisions. They then gathered up the empty bottles and filled them from the keg with whisky. Philips then went after a boat, and returned with it. Their blankets, whisky and sack of provisions were put in the boat. Philips, Felix and Alto got into the boat the other Indian refusing to go. They landed at different times to drink, etc. At the last landing Philips held a conversation with Felix and the latter got into the boat alone, and was pushed off from the bank. Alto and Philips then started towards the Great Northern Railroad track, when Alto became so drunk by the whisky plied to him by Philips that he remembered no more, and finely [sic] made his way back to the reservation. The Friends of Felix Burns became anxious at his long absence and as Alto was the last seen with him Joseph Catholueluhu, the Indian Judge, McDonald, some of the Indian Police and the sister of Felix took Alto to Idaho to search for him. The body of Felix Burns was found by the Indians on the shore of the river running out of the Pend 'd Oreille Lake towards the Kalispel valley, below where he was shoved off alone in the boat by Philips. The Indians instituted a search for the latter, and warrant was sworn out for his arrest. His trial was set for three o'clock of the 10th, but I had it postponed in order to procure an interpreter from the Agency. At ten o'clock of the 11th the trial commenced, and the evidence given sustained the details in this report. The defence asked for a continuence until Wednesday the 17th of August. I demanded that the prisoner be placed under a heavy bond for his appearance on that day. The bond was placed at one thousand dollars. The Indians and Indian witnesses went into camp near Hope, Idaho, to await the trial. On the morning of the 12th I left again for Sand Point, on my way to Bonners Ferry over the Great Northern Railroad, from that place.

The case is a serious one, and if the man Philips is allowed to escape, or is not severely punished by the law for furnishing whisky which led to the death of the Indian Felix Burnes, it will cause great discontent among the Indians, particularly as they feel assured that Philips is guilty of the murder of the Indian. I informed the Indians that if they suspected justice would not be done to their side of the case to send a messenger to me at Bonner's Ferry, and I would leave my business there long enough to give attention to the prosecution of this outlaw Philips, who has made a business of the selling of whisky to Indians for years without punishment, although arrested and tried several times for the crime. A suspicion also of the murder and robbery of Felix Burns, demand that the case be sharply looked after, and give Indians confidence in the enforcement of the Laws of the whiteman.

Trusting that my action in this matter may meet the approval of the Hon. Commissioner of Indian Affairs.

I am very respectfully
Your obedient Servant
Peter Ronan,
United States Ind. Ag't.

Peter Ronan
Source: Montana Historical Society Photograph Archives, Helena, Montana,
photo MMM900-004.

Document 17

Reward Brings Out Many Claimants

February 23, 1895

Source: "It's A Very Funny Bill," *The Anaconda Standard*, February 23, 1895, page 6, col. 1.

Editors' note: Many people with dubious claims were trying to get part of the reward for capturing Pierre Paul and Lalasee, who had been hung in 1890. See also Duncan McDonald's reference to the reward in his 1915 letter regarding the arrest of Lalasee, reproduced above.

It's A Very Funny Bill
Such Is the Opinion of Some Missoula People.
Names the Wrong Men
In the Matter of the Reward for the Capture of Pierre Paul
and La-La-See, the Indian Outlaws.

Missoula, Feb. 22. — There is a bill before the legislature which has escaped general notice but which is, nevertheless, of considerable local interest. In substance it appropriates $1,000 for a reward for the capture of the Indian outlaws, Pierre Paul and La-La-See, who were hung in Missoula under Sheriff [William] Houston's administration for murder. The persons named in the bill as the beneficiaries of the appropriation are well known residents of the Flathead country, who took an active part in the pursuit of the outlawed Indians, but who had no part in their capture. The history of the seizure of these desperate Indians is a familiar one to Missoula people and it is a matter of surprise here that the men named in the bill in question should claim the honor of the capture.

La-La-See was brought to Missoula and turned over to Sheriff Houston by Duncan McDonald, the well known halfbreed merchant and ranchman of the reservation. The Indian renegade came to McDonald's place voluntarily and surrendered himself. He said: "I am tired of being pursued. I have hidden from my people and from the white men. I have been hunted like a rat. Take me." McDonald brought him to Missoula alone and on horseback and without pomp or ceremony gave him into the custody of Sheriff Houston. That was all there was to the capture of La-La-See. McDonald's is whatever honor attached to it. Nobody else had any hand in it and but few knew that he had been taken until he had been placed in the county jail.

Pierre Paul's capture was a different matter. He eluded the officers for a long time, but was at length discovered by two Indians, Chief of Indian Police Pierre Catullayeuh and Antoine Morrijeau, who came upon him in a secluded spot on the reservation and disarmed and bound him at the muzzle of a Winchester. After they had taken him prisoner he was turned over to the posse from the upper Flathead, among whom were some of the men named in the bill as entitled to the reward offered. He was brought to Missoula by these men, but the honor of his capture belongs to the Indian chief of police and his companion.

The renegades had many friends among the Indians, and the men who captured them have been very unpopular ever since. For that reason they have never claimed the reward which was offered at that time, as their people would look upon it as blood money and would be enraged at their acceptance of it.

Duncan McDonald is now in the city and an attempt has been made by a representative of the would-be recipients of the reward to induce him to sign certain affidavits regarding the capture of the outlaws. To-day McDonald refused to sign these papers and he says that he will not at any time do so. There is a very bitter feeling in the reservation against some of the men named in the bill in question, as the Indians claim that these men shot and killed a defenseless old Indian during the pursuit of the renegades, mistaking him for La-La-See.

It is not known here what strength the bill has in the legislature, but it seems unjust and unreasonable that the reward should go to men who are in no way entitled to it. The above account of the capture of Pierre Paul and La-La-See was given to the *Standard* reporter by a man who is familiar with the occurrence and who vouches for its truth.

Chapter 2

Salish Removal From Bitterroot to Jocko Valley

1891

Document 18

General Carrington Negotiates with Charlo and the Final Removal to Jocko July – October 1891

Source: Excerpt from Henry B. Carrington, "The Exodus of the Flatheads," manuscript, Carrington Family Papers, MS 130, Manuscripts and Archives, Yale University Library, New Haven, Conn., chapter 10, pages 3-14; chapter 11, pages 1-7; and chapter 12, pages 1-9.

Editors' note: This manuscript gave Carrington's view of the final negotiations with Charlo and the removal of the Bitterroot Salish to the Jocko Valley. The Indian people involved certainly had a very different perspective on many of the events he described. Carrington seemed to have failed to understand the deep pain and sorrow felt by the Salish who had struggled to develop a self-supporting Salish community in the Bitterroot Valley. He also probably magnified his personal importance in the negotiations and removal. The Salish-Pend d'Oreille Culture Commttee at St. Ignatius, Montana, is working on a tribal history compiled from oral sources which should give balance to Carrington's account. The Culture Committee has published a short brochure giving a preview of this part of their history book: "The Exodus of the Bitterroot Salish," (St. Ignatius, Mont.: Salish Culture Committee, 1998). Many of the quotation marks were not used consistently, but this version leaves them as they appear in the manuscript. Some typographical errors in the manuscript have been corrected.

Chapter X
Removal of Flatheads Delayed. Work Renewed in 1891

Arlee station, on the Jocko Reservation, was reached upon the 26th of July, The Flathead Agent had received no orders from the Indian Commissioner as to buildings, or special supplies for Charlos' Band, in anticipation of their arrival. About 400 pounds of bacon remained on hand, but no flour, coffee, tea, sugar, rice or hominy, and neither logs, lumber, nor nails were on hand to finish the jail which had been begun, and had been so greatly needed two years before.

At the Missoula Land Office, no instructions had been received as to advertising the Indian Lands, neither was there to be found a copy of the

Executive Document, which contained the Official Report, with Map of the Valley and full specifications of the Apraisement, and full description of lands to be offered for sale.

Mr. Ex-Assemblyman Blake, of Victor, in St. Mary's Valley, whose wife was of the Flathead people, as well as Major [Peter] Ronan, the Indian Agent, believed that the Indians would not, and could not be induced to remove to Jocko prior to sale of the lands and receipt of the purchase money. This deadlock at the very entrance upon execution of the Agreement of 1889, had a cause, and must have a key. It was soon learned that hard times for crops, and disappointing mining and building ventures had benumbed the maturing land boom which had anticipated great results for Bitter Root Valley so soon as its best lands could be redeemed from the lien of Indian possession. Missoula was especially feeling the re-action which affected the entire region. It had been supposed by the Indians as well as by citizens of the valley, that Stevensville would be selected for the sale-mart, so that access to the lands, with map and full field notes and proper guides, would realize for the Indians fair values and a corresponding influx of permanent settlers. Letters from both Missouri and Michigan, intimated that a fair emigration would flow from those States; but the decision that the Indian lands would be sold in the ordinary way, and at the Missoula Land Office only, added its weight, to depress values. All these facts had to be considered before meeting Charlos and his searching interrogatories, both as to delays and immediate prospects. Senator Powers, Ex-State Senator Fisher, Register of the Land Office, Rev Mr Tower, real estate agent, who preached at Stevensville in 1889, Colonel Catlin, partner of Mr Zeb Harris, of the Stevensville hotel in 1889, Rev Hugh Lamont, Ex-Judge Reeves and others who had been familiar with the legal proceedings and general work in 1889, were consulted freely. The current depression of all real estate values, had initiated a depreciation of the appraisements of that year, then favorably accepted. The press, in part, shared in this influence.

At a later date, Spokane was visited, and the same re-action was observed. That city, beautiful for location, and wonderful in the dynamic resources of its cataract river, had been rebuilt after its disasterous fire without regard to cost. Magnificent granite and brick buildings more than doubled the immediate demand for tenants. Thousands of out-lying building lots, coursed by electric cars, were simply so many pieces of durable but un-saleable merchandise.

Upon the conviction that the conditions of 1889 would be restored after the hard times expended their influence, the Secretary of the Interior maintained the appraisement as made, and as binding under the terms of the Act of March. 2. 1889.

Stevensville was reached on the 27th. John Hill and many Flatheads, quite a party, living near the town, awaited the Commissioner's return. As the Stevensville Hotel had been burned, the ground floor of the McLaren building was made headquarters, on the morning of the 29th, with additional accommodations in the vacant store-room of Mrs Hunt, close by the Indian cabins near the church. Eneos Francois, (pronounced "Fronsway" by the people) arrived from Jocko as temporary interpreter until Michael [Revais] could reach the valley. He came on horseback from Jocko, 56 miles, in one day and night.

Those who accompanied John Hill, were bright with paint, ear-ring blankets, moccasins and feathers, and he, as spokesman, at once asked food for many families, besides his own, a total in flour alone of 2150 lbs. Chief Charlos soon appeared, with other Flatheads, accompanied by their women and children. His first act was, to produce his "Almanack," which he began at parting in 1889. It consisted of two pine sticks carefully squared to the half inch, and joined at two ends by a buckskin tie. One notch had been cut in 1889, when the farewell interview closed. From that date, without omission, a notch had been cut, daily, with cross-marks, like X, for each Sunday, for Christmas, and other Feast Days, and upon arrival of the Commissioner in 1891, the record of the intervening days was found to have been accurately preserved.

"He had kept his word, and wanted his promised money, for his lands." "Everybody was starving and they would not leave until they had their money, and wanted enough to eat, until the money came." "He had been to Jocko and could get nothing, because there was not enough there for their own people."

Among those present, pitiable sights, and evidently needy, were "Big Mouth Charley, with his shaggy, tangled, iron gray hair, and Charley Bad Road, neither of whom ever worked more than at fishing, and old Stephen James, with his crutches, all "waiting for something to eat." Charlos, while solemn and apparently more grieved than angry, said "Charlos will talk no business until his people are fed. Ronan has no flour. The stores all around," (with a sweeping gesture) "are full of flour." White Chief says, "he will send to Washington by wire, to have supplies bought and sent, but the people will die before the iron horse can bring them food."

Answer. "Charlot, how many families are hungry?," and the interpreter announced the names, as a list was being prepared."

A messenger was sent to Amos B. Buck, Henry Buck, the Missoula Company's Office and others, and they were asked in Charlos' presence if they would furnish what Charlos' people needed by ten o'clock, the next day, if the s....s would bring ponies and load the stuff." All answered promptly, "Of course, whatever you say."

"Charlos. And they will come to Charlos when he gets his money and make Charlos pay.

Answer. "No. This is a present and will not be taken out of your money. Believe it Charlos. Eat all you want and let your people have all they need, and then we will talk about the lands and going to Jocko.

On the following day the village was filled with Indians. After 45 sacks of flour had been counted on the sidewalk as well as easily recognized packages of tobacco, coffee, and sugar, tea, rice Charlos appeared at headquarters with a pleasant face. His hair was carefully braided and he again wore his bright red vest, and a felt hat with an eagle feather in front. A copy of the Western News had been read to him, stating that the Indian Commissioner at Washington had some trouble with the Catholic Educational Bureau, and he insisted that some plot was on foot to get the Indian lands and not sell them at all." Assurances that General Morgan had directly interested himself, from the very first in his behalf satisfied him on that point. He then spoke of an Article in the Missoula Gazette, that told lies about the Indian lands." A published official reply to that article was then read to him, and he accepted that, "as honest." Unscrupulous men were evidently fermenting discontent, but his inherent honesty triumphed over all, at last.

On the first of August John Hill and Vandenburg came to announce that Charlos was coming back within three days, to have a big talk, but would not have Francois for his interpreter. "On the succeeding Sunday, the church bell rang and the floor as well as the benches was again packed with all ages; but this time, all were as well dressed as they had skill or apparel for the occasion. Charlos sulked in bed, near the church, for a while sending fresh gossip for explanation. "A man from Missoula told him that 'the lands had never been advertised:' that something was wrong: that interpreters lied; that they lied at Missoula and lied at Jocko; that he would not take words from Francois, or Matt" (who sometimes acted as interpreter) but have Mary Laumphrey interpret for him." In the afternoon, however, he came in with John Hill and a few others. Charles Laumphrey acting as interpreter. Neither Father [Jerome] D'Aste nor Michael had as yet been able to reach the valley to resume their former parts as confidential advisers and interpreters. Charlos' first request was that "John Hill and his friends should have plenty of flour and groceries." When shown the receipt of Mr Buck for flour furnished John Hill, quite liberally, he significantly turned to his companion, saying "John Hill, bad as white man. No more flour for John Hill."

He was suffering intensely from the toothache, and occupying an old decrepid rocking chair. When shown a set of false teeth "that never ached," he threw himself back with amused surprize, but with such violence that the chair and Charlos went with a crash to the floor. Being raised to his feet, he helped himself to cigars from the table and passed out saying pleasantly, "I guess, Charlos' heart is too heavy to-day, for talk." Some other day, just as good! Charlos' is going home."

For ten succeeding days Indians came and went, at will, all looking forward with pleasure for the arrival of Father D'Aste. During informal talks it was suggested that the young men and others who were good hunters should make their first hunt of the season, at once. When the 5th of October was announced as date for the first sales, the hunting trip was accepted as a timely diversion during the weeks of delay. It was difficult for Indians to understand that a certain period must elapse after the advertisement, in order to make the sale legal. A suggestion had also been made that some of the leading men should go to Jocko, pick out small patches of land and "put in some grub"; but Francois explained that men like La Moose, who had good farms at Bitter Root, did not dare leave them for fear that their fields would be stripped of fences and their cabins plundered during their absence.

On the 6th of September, Rev Alexander Diomedi, S.J. then in charge of the parish and Mission at Missoula, arrived to conduct religious service and advise with the Flatheads. Twenty seven Indians gathered at headquarters to meet him and consult as to the suggestion, to anticipate the sales by earlier removal to the Jocko Valley; and among that number and most influential were Chief Charlos, Louis Vandenberg, Joseph La Moose, Antoine Tibeo, Joseph Colluyer, Antonine Nine Pipes and John Fisher. The question submitted was simply this. "Do any families wish to go to Jocko before the lands are sold? The responsive Indian Inquiries were such as these, *viz*, "whether the houses were to be of logs, or frame, of how many rooms, to be built by white carpenters or by the Indians themselves; whether to have a fireplace, or stoves, or both?

Charlos, especially requested, that, "half-breed Flatheads should be wholly excluded from the Jocko Valley; that Frenchmen (from Canada) should be kept away; that the United States should buy out the claims of all who already hung about the Reservation, and that white men should not be allowed to graze their stock on the reserve. On the next day, the interview continued, with Mary Laumphrey again as interpreter. A letter from Washington was read, stating that "Major Ronan had been ordered to make arrangements for them at Jocko and he would have both money and provisions."

Question. "Would any of you like to go and help put up the buildings and get the same pay as white carpenters?"

Charlos. "Will Flatheads who work, be paid out of the Indians money?"

Answer. "No, but by the United States."

Charlos. "Will the old people have to walk" (putting his hand to his moccasin) "or will they ride?

Answer. "Just as they wish themselves. Have all your people who can work, got good lodges to live in until the houses are roofed?

Charlos. "Will tell you to-morrow, or pretty soon, how many will go and work. All are hungry now. (Rubs his stomach) "Big belly three years ago! No belly now!"

At close of the interviews 39 sacks of flour, with bacon, coffee, sugar, tobacco, rice, and baking powders were issued, and all dispersed to their homes.

Weeks passed during the absence of those who went on the autumn hunt; but all returned before the 5th day of October. Only four sales were affected on that date, and another day was announced for their continuance. Of the four sales, two enured to the benefit of very poor Indians and netted more than the appraised value. A telegram from the Secretary of the Interior, that the "appraisement would be sustained and that their lands would not be sacrificed" restored confidence, and the general wish among the Flatheads was, to remove as soon as possible and before cold weather.

On the 10th of October, after three days of close conference during which time Charlos, Vandenberg and the interpreters dined with the Commissioner for more familiar intercourse, Charlos announced that, at noon the next day, Sunday, he would decide whether he would move his people before winter, or wait until all the lands were sold. "A messenger from Arlee, had told him that there were no supplies at the Agency which could be sent to Stevensville for any Flatheads who should remain in the Bitter Root Valley," but, "he wouldn't believe any more stories. He had his paper, and his people were getting all they wanted to eat, and he meant to follow the paper, just as he said he would when he signed it."

Sunday morning was bright and clear; but no Indians appeared on the streets. The cabins about the church were unoccupied and silent. Nearly the usual number of dogs prowled about the dead embers of fires where the Indians had cooked their last meals: but all except two old tepees, had disappeared.

At 1 o'clock, P.M. a messenger dismounted at headquarters, to give notice "that the Indians had been in conference since daylight, had been saying prayers at Vandenberg's cabins, two miles away, and were already starting for the village." At 2 o'clock, Charlos, Vandenberg, La Moose, Antonine Nine Pipes, and the Laumpreys, Delaware Jim, John Hill, and all the leading and most prosperous men of the tribe, arrived, soon followed by old men, women and children, speedily filling the room, the platform in front, and the adjoining street. The interview was brief. Charlos alone spoke, though all in turn shook hands. He spoke with dignity, calmness, and evident sincerity and feeling. As expressive of his character and wisdom, his exact words are memorable of the occasion."

"I could not sleep, at first, last night. I remembered my father Victor and that his people expected me to do what he would approve, for their good. I told everybody to come together in the morning as soon as the sun was up to say prayers to the Great Spirit. That made me feel better, and I could go to sleep. Then, the Great Spirit gave me these thoughts." 'Charlos, go with your people. They will starve, or freeze here. Nobody will buy your land if you stay. Go and pick out good land and build houses before winter. Shut your ears to lies which bad people tell you.' "So I come, to say, we will all go, and go together. We dont want any soldiers with us, or any other whiteman except, White Chief and Joe McLaren. Tell us when to be ready, three days, two days, one day. How many? What you say, we do."

It had been understood that an ambulance from Fort Missoula with a sergeant and the necessary men had been tendered for the Commissioner's personal convenience on the march, and this led Charlos to feel, that "if the white soldiers went with the Indians, it would appear to his people and to other Indians and to the white people, that he went under force and not because he wanted to keep the treaty." McLaren was an estimable citizen, a carpenter by trade, and had not only been a kind friend of the Flatheads, but was accounted by them as "honest."

The following Thursday, at 8 o'clock, A.M. was designated for the time of departure; and Wednesday afternoon was selected for a general rendezvous near St Mary's Church, where a farewell service would be held.

As after signing the Agreement in 1889, Charlos brightened as if relieved of a great burden. Wagons were promised for the old, the infirm, and the sick, and a special car, if necessary. The interview was short, and the Indians swiftly away as if preparing for a grand frolic or hunt. The decision was the more impressive and significant because it was known through confidential Indian advisers, that some who lived at Jocko, particularly such as might fear the advent of so many would restrict their own privileges on the Reservation, had advised members of Charlos' Band not to leave until they received cash for their lands." But, as the proceeds of all sales were to pass into the United States Treasury, and afterwards disposed of for the benefit of the respective patentees, such advice was clearly unwise, even if sincere. As a matter of history, arrangements had not been perfected by the government for preparing the Reservation for an early arrival of Charlos' Band. The officials at the Agency doubted whether the removal could be secured, with Charlos' consent, before spring. Even the venerable

Father D'Aste, feared lest the slowness of the government in meeting Indian demands, might be repeated in the case of the suffering Flatheads. The prompt action of the Secretary of the Interior, instructing the Commissioner to carry his agreement with Charlos to complete fulfilment, secured a corresponding good faith on the part of the Flathead Chief.

As the Indians mounted and dashed away in all directions, to put their moveable property in readiness for the march, Charlos, Vandenburg, La Moose and John Delaware, (Last of the Delawares) watched them from the platform with pleasure and pride, and all passed as smoothly as if there had never been any doubt as to duty.

Morning visits to their tepees and cabins showed that all were in earnest in sorting their effects and getting ready. For the period of a complete generation, this removal had been the subject of controversy and fatal to all systematic improvement of lands occupied by them in the Bitter Root Valley. Never did a group of children find more difficulty in selecting toys for preservation, or abandonment, than did this people. All were cheerful, and in some cases, such as the tepee of Tibeo and the cabins of Vandenberg, the whole families turned out in their best attire, to ask what they might take with them. Each group, as photographed, better describes than words can, the neatness and variety of dress and adornment which were displayed in preparing for their departure. Such motley accumulations of antlers, skins, strung-heads, old guns, worn-out agricultural implements and household utensils, could never have been kept together except in the wonderful hiding of places of an Indian cabin or lodge.

Chapter XI
The Exodus of the Flatheads Begun.

As early as 8. o'clock on Wednesday morning, clouds of dust in various directions indicated that the Indians were in motion, and herd after herd of scampering ponies gradually emerged from the obscurity, to be placed in a secure, enclosed pasture between the church and the river, so that none might be missing at the fixed hour for departure on the ensuing day. Before sunset, all cabins near the church were crowded and twenty tepees had been erected to accommodate the gathering families. A steer had been furnished for fresh meat and four hundred pounds were distributed by Charlos for a night feast, their last supper in the ancestral valley.

Many, singly, or in groups went first after their arrival, to the church, where they remained awhile in silent, or low-murmured prayer. Others first visited the burial grounds and gathered grasses from the graves they must leave behind. Mary Laumphrey, Charlos' favorite interpreter, who buried a bright child on

Henry B. Carrington (left of tepee) and Bitterroot Salish Indians before removal. Photograph by Chase Carrington. Source: Penn Museum, Philadelphia, Penna., image 143362

Food distribution before removal march to Jocko Valley. Photograph by Chase Carrington. Source: Penn Museum, Philadelphia, Penna., image 142689.

the previous Friday, walked three miles, carrying a babe, but two days old, to deliver a message from Charlos.

Camp fires, within and without tepees, and within cabins, where all windows and doors were left open, blazed brightly. A large canvass, nearly ten feet high, formed an enclosure between two connecting cabins and at 9 o'clock, the dull Indian drum beat the call for the all-night feast. Here the men marched, leaped, and danced, keeping time to the music, chanting war songs and recounting the deeds of their people in olden times. In some of the quarters, as nearly all were visited, for a pleasant word or hand-shake, the women and children were mending, sorting, and packing, or selecting choice finery for the next days march. Two old women, one entirely blind, and another a helpless cripple, rocked back and forward, plaintively moaning of old times and calling over the names of departed ones now under the sod. One of these had buried every blood relation, but weeping, said, "It is all right. We will go where the Flatheads can all be together, but we will not ride in cars and get hurt." But "dont let anybody hurt the graves we leave behind. Tell me what you told Charlos, and Charlos said you promised to take care of the graves of our people." One old man, on crutches said, "I will ride my pony once more. It is my last march. Me cant hunt — die soon, — want plenty to eat, — no work, plenty."

A few, had small packages of mink, otter, beaver and deer skins, but most of their furs had already been sold to white men, or traded for guns and ammunition for hunting trips in the mountains about Jocko. Even in these hours of haste, exchanges were made of many articles, and even "Big-Mouth-Charley," was on hand, to get anything the best way he could. Above his shoulders, he appeared with his usual disregard for his ample hair, to which no justice can be done except by a picture taken one morning at sunrise when he was surprized at a gambling camp four miles below Stevensville. He had never admired the picture, but none of his people refused it recognition.

Just as the sun rose on the 15th of October, the camp sprang into life as by magic, awaiting the signal "to break up." The stores were all open and crowded for small purchases in the expectation, not often disappointed, of some farewell present from old friends. During explanation of the plan and order of march, one wide awake Indian hoisted the stars and stripes upon his wagon, having secured it from a store, and he was promised a place in the center of the column when ready to start.

At 7 o'clock the first signal was given and a great scattering ensured. Boys and girls raced with each other, lariat in hand, among the herd of more than five hundred ponies to find each their own pack horses. During their absence, tepee-covers were unwound, stripped off, and rolled, disclosing in concentric circles around the poles, carefully arranged packs, ready to be loaded upon horses or wagon, in regular order. The tepee poles were then equally divided and tied, with suitable cross-bars added for the transportation of such effects, including cooking utensils and provisions, as could not be loaded in packs.

Charlot, bearing in his right hand and across his breast an eagles wing, badge of his chiefship, directed the strange medley to the broad street of the village where rations were to be drawn for the march, and where the incongruous combination was to be drawn out into some thing like marching order. Mounted and dismounted warriors, with rifles or shotguns: s...s, children and pappooses; pack ponies, wagons and loose stock were for a little while in seeming and inextricable confusion. But a list of families and an order of march had been prepared which Charlos said, "he could make all right." Michael, when asked if it could be carried out, answered with, his invariable reply to all questions which he knew he could answer, "You bet." Mingling with the crowd, or on porches, and at windows, the citizens appeared in full numbers to bid a kind goodbye to the kind people who once been their preservers, and the saviours of the valley settlements.

When the last flour sack went into a wagon, and the last presents of tobacco and crackers had been distributed, Charlot laid aside his eagle's wing, saying with friendly dignity. "Charlos and his people are ready. Tell Charlot what to do." He was placed in charge of the advance division and Vandenburg brought up the rear. La Moose was in charge of a third division on the west side of the river, to join the main body at the first fording place. Selected young men, who had donned their best equipments and with paint and feathers were most conspicuous for their fine horses and complete outfit, formed a party of scouts to accompany the column and bear messages between its divisions. Gradually, under the management of Charlot and Vandenburg, the great mass of horses, wagons, and people melted into a column, more than a mile in length, but in breadth varying according to the excentric activities of the hundreds of loose ponies that shared the Exodus.

Curious incidents, ludicrous or serious, as they were taken, attended the march. Occasionally a horse broke into a wild dash over tepee-poles against packs, or into the rear of loaded wagons, with now and then a genuine runaway or some unsophisticated colt unused to such systematic restraint. Cradle-boards would slip loose and the cry of a dropped papoose would be heard, in the dust, right under the heels of loose ponies that mixed themselves up with the train just where they were of the least use to themselves or anyone else.

Two fordings of the St Mary's furnished episodes, with no more serious an incident than expended plunge baths. Horses, cows, and calves would persist in taking to deep water instead of following the guides through the [shallow?]

places. Tepee poles would float on the surface and swing down stream, to
the complete astonishment of the horse who had been accustomed to have
them trail behind. Packs would slip and appear beneath the ponies, when,
as both front and hind feet could not kick at once, and enforced halt had to
be administered by the women who always proved equal to the emergency.
Lodge poles would also [sliliy?] slip out and gradually scatter behind, until the
rider, missing their rattle, plunged back with desperate haste, to dismount,
re-load, and start again. One patient young woman had the difficult task of
managing two babies and three packhorses, while riding a spirited two-year-
old colt which hauled twenty lodge poles; and all this, in spite of the shouts
and cracking whips of half a dozen young men who multiplied indefinitely,
until checked, their tests of her capacity and patience. But the first ford was
safely made, and the third division, under La Moose, was found to be awaiting
orders.

It was three o'clock. After a brief delay to tighten girths, packs and poles,
the column was again in motion. Less than fourteen miles had been made. A
hot sun and choking dust had been the test of strength, order, and endurance.
Suddenly a cloud rolled down from the snow clad peaks, and in almost less time
than this narration, a cold driving rain set in, mingled with hail, drenching
everything and everybody, besides starting innumerable pools along the way.
Neither people nor animals had eaten since starting, and few, since day break.
A halt was ordered without waiting to reach the anticipated camping ground.

With marvellous dexterity the lodge poles were set in the form of a double
street and thirty women with axes and hatches started in search of fuel. Nearly
six hundred head of stock found a good pasture, well fenced and watered,
belonging to Mr John Mc Clay, after whom the camp was named. His family,
one, his sister, a teacher from Michigan, and all, agreeable and hospitable,
were duly compensated for all favors extended to the command. By six o'clock
all had eaten supper, and were rested and dry enough for sport. Twice on the
march the young warriors had distributed, paper packages of cigarets though
the entire column, and this was repeated when the evening gave leisure for
their enjoyment. At 8 o'clock, as agreed upon with Charlot, the drum beat,
and in spite of deep mud in the street, two social hours were permitted. Songs,
dances, and stories mingled with stacatto war whoops and vagrant yells, until
10 o'clock, when silence was enjoined. No garrison taps ever more quickly
subdued the noise. Only the incorrigible chorus-choir of discordant Indian
dogs denoted the existance of an Indian encampment.

The next morning was clear and cold. Charlot rang a bell, which he had
taken from the church sacristy, as a call to prayers, and before every tepee,
the responding Indians bent the knee before beginning the duties of the day.

This people had been taught to ask God's blessing, with thankfulness, before partaking of His gifts, and the fatigue, the exceptional incidents and the license of a free marching column did not interrupt their morning duties. That pecularity of the Flatheads had been frequently noticed. Upon asking Michael, what he meant by "grace before meat," he answered, "you bet, I know. We say this, and think it too. This is what we say."

"God Almighty, Father of all mercies, bless the food I now use. In the name of the Father, Son, and Holy Ghost."

At 7 o'clock, as arranged in advance, the signal was given to drive in herds, load packs, strike lodges, and be ready to start at 8. o'clock. A few ponies, in spite of care, had started to their old grazing grounds, but at twelve minutes past eight, the last of the rear guard was on its way.

The day proved pleasant, and the march was urged forward so that the night's camp could be made beyond Missoula and beyond reach of its saloons. Upon approaching the Fort, four miles south from the city, a brief call was made upon General Wilcox, commanding the 25th Infantry and the Post, to thank him for courtesies so frequently tendered during two different years, and to advise him of the Indian movement, already opposite the fort. Several sergeants' parties were usually in the city; but the absence of all military influence was desirable, and Charlos entered into the plan with wisdom and promptness. Vandenburg and a select party of mounted young men were made a guard of honor and stationed at the bridge across the Missoula River, to let no one pass, whether Indian or white man, until the rear had fully closed up and the column could be re-organized for a compact march through the city.

A brief halt, with permission to replenish thirst and take such food as was at hand, with another liberal supply of the Indian's favorite cigarette, and tobacco for those preferring pipes, was made, and the advance began.

Chapter XII
Reaching the Promised Land.

The march through the broad streets of Missoula at mid-day was a novel incident never to be repeated. The trailing lodge poles in parallel files, with ample space between for the pack-horses, loose cattle and ponies, and the great variety of doges, all in bunches, were under such quick control as only skilful Indian herders could accomplish. Some of the old men and women as well as the younger, were now mounted the better to see and be seen. Many had never before seen a white man's great city; and few had even visited Missoula. Little children were strapped between packs and furnished with whips which they continually applied to animals that trotted steadily along unmindful of the innocent stimulant. Cradle-boards, taken from wagons and hung to saddlebows, allowed the out peep of many a staring pappoose. Gay blankets, feathers, necklaces, ornamental leggings and moccasins, with faces freshly painted in the morning, had full share in this display of the Indian's personal treasure.

Even the packs, themselves, often made up of well tanned and brilliantly painted skins, were so skilfully adjusted for their best display, and withal, so admirably arranged for a halt, or re-loading, that any Army quartermaster might well envy the celerity with which the work was done.

Never was there a "Wild West Show" so dramatic and at time pathetic in its slow and steady procession. The streets were lined and the windows were crowded with lookers on. To the casual observer, the silence of the march, the close order observed, the inquisitive glances of the surprised Indians, and their rapid disappearance as the rear guard wheeled out of Main Street and took up a quick step so as to reach camping ground, before night, with wood and water at command, gave no hint that many were weeping and longing to get away from the gaze and criticism of the white observers. There were no stragglers from the line of march. The young Indians, finely mounted, who guarded at every cross-street, did their duty with commendable fidelity and spirit. Even although three young men, and one of them the Chief's son, did slip back during the night for liquid refreshment, they returned so promptly to the next camping place, that their hard night-ride, one lame poney, and the reported loss of a good Winchester, were considered a sufficient penalty for the diverting escapade which they managed so shrewdly, if not profitably.

When actually clear of the town and its people, the spirits of all revived. They seemed more like children with plans for the future already within reach, when the Flatheads should all come together, beyond the pressure of the white man's immediate surroundings. At Camp McLaren, named in honor of the faithful, honest, and worthy friend and confident of the Flatheads, a careful inspection showed that all were present and that not even a pony or cow was unaccounted for. John Hill, the Nez Perces, who visited Washington with Charlos, missed a horse, but it strayed before the march from Stevensville began. Close by the camp, was the Rail Road station "De Smedt," named after the Flathead's great friend of early times, and the story of his deeds was retold during the evening by one of his most enthusiastic admirers, in the cabin where headquarters were established for the night. Some white herders, near by, were so solicitous lest their stock should be mingled with that of the Indians, though a fence separated, that their clumsiness of action, prevented their successful smuggling of whiskey among the Flatheads, to the great disappointment of the mutually interested parties. The night passed, in general quiet. The days march was through Mc Kean's deep canyon and over the high mountain range which separates the Missoula and Jocko valleys. Cliffs, ravines, thickets, noisy brooks, and sudden torrents, as well as tangled woods and broken ledges of sharp rock, furnished constant incentives for ponies, cows, and calves to go astray and become hopelessly lost. The shouts of the mounted herders and the crack of rifle when a missing head was found, were almost constant. Now and then, half a dozen warriors with rifles in hand, with blankets and feathers streaming behind, and disappearing at full speed, only to come as suddenly again in sight at some unexpected moment, vividly recalled the memory of other days when such whoops and demonstrations were warnings of a life-and-death struggle, and the speeding horsemen were hunting for human estrays.

Even at 10 o'clock, the tall peaks upon the right and left, shut out all sunlight, adding a shade of lonesomeness to the march as if all were lost in some inextricable labyrinth of Nature's worst confusion. In one deep gorge, before reaching the summit, when the entangled and struggling animals were distributed through a long an strange perspective, the Atlantic Express of the Northern Pacific, whistling fiercely, turned a sharp curve and swept eastward parallel with the march, but at least five hundred feet above its course. The half crazed and impetuous ponies seemed determined to rush into the very course of danger, as if they snuffed wild game in the rush of the iron monster, and the dash of boys, women and girls, as well as men, to head off and control the affrighted stock, and control the struggling, snorting, and kicking wagon-teams, can be freely imagined, but never described.

At last the "summit" was gained and the descent towards the Jocko Valley commenced. Wagons slipped from one shelving ledge to another. Fallen trees compelled circuitous conduct of the wagons, many of them heavily loaded, while the steepness of the descent, and the looseness of countless splinters from the shattered, laminated rocks, made the footing of the every poney dangerously uncertain. A sudden scream, repeated by a score of female voices was followed by a rush to the headquarters wagon. If a grizzly or cinnamon bear had been their pursuer, their faces could hardly have expressed more terror. Laumphrey's wife, bearing a babe at her saddle-bow, lost control of her stumbling pony and he fell, bearing her to the ground with great force. Consternation became universal. An examination showed that she had broken her hip bone, and was in great agony. A handy army case with cloroform, paragoric, bandages and other appliances for sudden frontier emergencies, served a good purpose. A few springy and slender, small pine saplings, interlaced and placed across a wagon bed, quickly emptied for that purpose and covered with blankets, furnished a sufficient couch for temporary relief. Clothing was offered on all sides to be torn into bandages, and the simplest possible adjustments secured the limb in place until surgical aid could be obtained. It was one of those incidents, where the Indian, wholly dependent, even as a little child, exhibits the utmost gratitude for the smallest service rendered, and under the terror of this seemingly fatal injury, until advised to the contrary, to appease their alarm, very touching expressions of gratitude were not wanting. And these were even more tenderly renewed, when under the skilful hand of Dr [John] Dade, it was found at the final parting with this people, that the injury was not beyond his skill. The men were no less sympathetic than the women. Twenty Indians dashed forward through the woods, leaping fallen timber, and hallooing to those in front to "clear the trail" so that the only spring wagon in the outfit might be hurried to the Reservation for the assistance of the surgeon in charge. And then, already within a few hours of the Agency the column pressed forward, for one more brief halt before concluding the Flatheads Exodus from the Garden Valley. The injured woman slept quietly, well-packed in shawls and blankets, so that she ceased to be a matter of urgent concern. Knowing that all possible relief would soon be at hand, both young women and young men, asked permission to rest, take food, and get ready to enter the Reservation in full array, and this was granted.

In the curve of a bright, swift stream, where open ground and a good [sward ?] permitted all to assemble, the last meal was cooked and the last scenic preparation for a triumphal march into the Valley of the Jocko, took place. Three tepees were erected by the water's edge. Surely, no dressing room of some eastern banquet hall could have exhibited a fuller development of toilet mysteries, or one more deftly and expeditiously manipulated, then did these enclosed tepees.

Additional strings of beads, ear-rings, armlets, anklets, and ornamental belts, were quickly donned. Fresh vermillion and ochre restored the brilliancy of painted brows, cheeks and necks, which the exercise of the march had dimmed, or marvellously confused. The young men and a few of their elders, appeared with most startling war paint, and speedily remounted their horses as if triumphantly splendid! Although few in numbers, they made a creditable show. As a view of the Jocko Valley opened, less than five miles distant, and its amphitheatre of mountains and precipitous bluffs disclosed the Agency buildings in full sight, a request was made that they be permitted to advance "like white soldiers." Of course, this was granted. The flag was seized by one horseman and transferred to the center of a fairly formed line-of-battle. All care of teams and loose stock was left to women, boys, and girls; while the men advanced at a gallop, firing their rifles in the air, with war-whoops and shouts as if charging upon a hostile village. It was probably the happiest hour ever known to this people!

The heavy sense of dependence upon the charity of the whites which had despoiled the old home-valley of its chief charms for the red man, gave way to a conscious pride of independence, in reaching a country where they hoped to live, labor, and hunt in peace, without the white man's presence in the rivalries of the farm and the chase.

Although the arrival near the Agency was earlier than had been anticipated, and even the success of the march before Spring had not been fully realized, the tidings of the accident, followed by notification of the temporary halt so near the valley, aroused the post and the resident Indians to immediate and enthusiastic activity. All gathered at once, to extend a most cordial welcome. Just outside the main gateway was the church where the Flatheads had so long worshipped. Here, had been the first interview in 1889; and now, the farewell, in 1891. The officiating priest had skillfully raised the "Banner of the Sacred Heart" upon a long pole, to lead the procession. At the request of Major Ronan, the Indian Agent, the advance was halted, and all who so desired, were permitted to alight and to enter the church in good order where a solemn "benediction service," of genuine thanksgiving, was to be celebrated. Vandenburg, finding that his people were extremely tired and hungry, and remarking that "they could attend service on the following morning which would be Sunday," declined to dismount his division and his family, as a whole. Chief Charlos, with quick perception of the proprieties of the occasion and the fulfillment of pledges made to him before leaving the Bitter Root Valley, spliced the short flag-staff, which had been borne throughout the march, to his cane, and bore the "Stars and Stripes," to the church entrance, holding it aloft while the men deposited their arms at the portal, and then followed the priest within.

Two very happy Flathead Indians joined in the universal welcome, with illuminated faces and eyes filled with tears of joy. These were Michael Revais and Eneos Francois, alike descendents from the earliest known stock of the tribe. Both were pious men, who ever since visiting Washington had never ceased to pray and labor for the consummation which they had been spared to witness. They had also been the tireless and trustworthy advisers and companions of the Commissioner during the years 1889 and 1891, and from the date of the Garfield Agreement, had never ceased to long for and expect the union of the Flathead people in the Jocko valley, even as the Hebrews of old longed for entrance into ancient Canaan. Along with them, came Louicon, the Indian Police Judge, a man rich in cattle and horses, and on this occasion brilliantly combining rare Indian ornaments with the military blouse, brass buttons, stove-pipe hat and other emblems of his judicial, military and police dignity. Big Sam, the largest man of the tribe, was equally happy, if less sentimental. Major Ronan, ever the patient, considerate and reliable friend of this people, with his entire family, took prominent part in the religious service, and with the surgeon, Dr John Dade, a veteran of the Mexican war and an old comrade of Captain May, of the 1st U.S. Dragoons, did their utmost to welcome and accommodate this large accession to the many under their charge.

At the close of a brief service, very impressive in its simplicity and evident appreciation on the part of all participants, all remounted wagons, or ponies, to pass through the Reservation grounds to the designated camping place. Crossing a bight clear stream they pitched their lodges upon a small level tract at the very foot of the pine-clad mountain which climbed from its base to the upper sky. A few cabins, including the home of Old Felix, accommodated some of the more aged. The injured woman, was already under careful medical care. Fires along the stream soon burned brightly, and so soon as packs and tepee hauls were un-loaded, the ponies were set loose for their freedom, at will. Suitable garments for culinary and other manual labor were soon donned, and the dignity and show of a dress-parade were quickly exchanged for the freedom and simplicity of a frontier Indian village, with its people, "perfectly, at home."

Shortly, three rifle shots rang out, to announce the fate of three steers which Major Ronan had furnished for their supper. It was not a notable feast in its enjoyment, for all were too tired and hungry and too glad to throw of[f] all care, for dances and jubilations, the journey accomplished. Gossipping with friends was short-timed, and long before midnight the camp was silent as if no unusual event had transpired during the three days of passage. Even the dogs seemed to combine their appreciation of "enough to eat," with the instinct of keeping their mouths shut when too tired to keep them open.

At the hospitable home of Major Ronan, a few assembled to exchange congratulations and compare thoughts for the future. The EXODUS of the Flathead Indians from their ancestral home in the Bitter Root Valley, the Garden Valley of Montana, had brought them safely, at last, with un-broken numbers, and without the loss or estray of a single head of their stock, to the Jocko Valley, their PROMISED LAND.

Document 19

Charlo Consents to Move to Jocko

October 12, 1891

Source: "He Dreams a Dream," *Missoula Weekly Gazette*, October 14, 1891, page 7, col. 1.

Editors' note: Some color has probably been added to this article, but it seemed that Charlo had reluctantly been forced by events to consent to move to the Jocko Valley.

He Dreams a Dream
Chief Charlos Tells His Braves to Go to the Reservation.
The Bitter Root Indians Will Pack up Bag and Baggage
and Leave Thursday.

Stevensville, Mont., Oct. 12. — [Special to the Gazette.] — Much to the surprise of everyone, the Bitter Root Indians for whom the government has of late been endeavoring to dispose of their land, but so far without success, have suddenly decided upon picking up their traps and with bag and baggage strike out for the Flathead reservation where the government has assigned them quarters. They will number some 200 and under the guidance of their chief — Charlos — will start for their new home on Thursday morning. They will go in wagons, on horseback and on foot, carrying with them all their worldly possessions, leaving their lands to be disposed of by the government in the future as best it can.

Charlos gives no reason for this summary action, saying only when asked about it that he had a dream wherein the big Indian spirit told him it would be best to move. The natives were hungry and thought it best to go on the reserve where Uncle Sam would feed them. In view of the fact that they have all along refused to vacate until their lands were sold, this decision on their part appears singular, unless explained by the knowledge that a season of severity and hardship is impending, and which they wish to avoid by going on the reservation.

Chief Charlo.
Photograph by John K. Hillers,
Bureau of American Ethnology,
Washington, D.C.
Source: Montana Historical Society
Photograph Archives,
Helena, Mont., detail from
photo 954-526.

Gen. Henry B. Carrington
Source: National Archives,
Washington, D.C.,
photo 111-BA-867.

Document 20

Bitterroot Salish Leave Stevensville for Jocko Agency October 15, 1891

Source: "The Natives Gone," *The Western News* (Stevensville, Mont.), October 20, 1891, page 1, col. 3-4.

Editors' note: This article describes the scene as the Bitterroot Salish left the Bitterroot Valley for the Jocko Valley.

The Natives Gone.

On last Thursday at 11 o'clock a.m. about one hundred of our noble red men and their families congregated on South Main street, some with wagons and teams and some riding on horseback and a large number of their ponies packed with tepees and dragging their lodge poles, ready to take up the line of march to their new homes on the Flathead reserve. It was a grand sight to the person who was unacquainted with the Indian custom of traveling, and, although most of our citizens have seen so much of the red tribe, yet their curiosity was aroused and they stood on side walks and in store doors to see the starting of this grand march. The public school took a recess and about ninety pupils came down to bid the copper colored youth and their ancestry a farewell adieu. While the Indians were standing in the street with their outfits, photographer O. M. Baldwin and L. J. Knapp were out with their cameras and took several different views from different positions, which will mark a place in the history of the farewell departure of the Flatheads from the Bitter Root valley. At about 11:30 o'clock, after several sacks of flour and other provisions had been placed in different wagons, General H. B. Carrington and J. R. McLaren got into their buggy, and taking the lead, the procession took up the march and moved slowly toward the north, en route to their destination at Flathead.

While it was gratifying to witness the accomplishment of so many long years of hard labor in getting this removal effected, yet there was a feeling of sympathy touched the hearts of our citizens, for the noble red men who at one time saved the people from the tortures of the tomahawk of the Nez Perce who made a raid through this country several years ago.

For many years past Stevensville has been the assemblage place for winter quarters for these Indians, owing that the first Indian mission for education and civilization of the Flatheads was established at this point in 1853 [sic], which has made them feel that this was their home ever since.

The Indians of this valley have from the first settlement of the white people here, been peaceable and quiet and had become very much attached to the American citizen. Many of them have been educated in agricultural pursuits and have gained wealth. Fifty-two patents to lands were issued to them several years ago, forty-six tracts of which are now open for sale to the white man, six having been disposed of already. The removal of these Indians gives place to a more energetic class of people, and as many of the tracts of land held by them are valuable, being rich in agricultural productions, we see no reason why prosperity should not crown the prolonged efforts in getting these lands into market. Many good homes now await the purchasers of these lands and the future prospects of our valley indeed look very bright. We hope our red brothers may get comfortably located in their new quarters before winter sets in, and that they will be contented and become attached to that country as they were to this.

Document 21

Bitterroot Salish March Through Missoula on Way to Jocko October 16, 1891

Source: "On the March," *Missoula Weekly Gazette*, October 21, 1891, page 1, col. 2.

Editors' note: The Missoula newspaper described the transit of the Bitterroot Salish through the city of Missoula on way to Jocko.

On the March.
Charlos and His Band Pass Through Missoula en Route to the Flathead.

A novel sight was witnessed by Missoulians today, the occasion being the exodus of Bitter Root Indians en route to the Flathead reservation where they are to reside in the future, Chief Charlos having so decided. The band numbers forty lodges, numbering about 250 souls, and is followed by some 400 head of horses and ponies and about 100 wagons. The command is in charge of General H. B. Carrington, who accompanies the body in person to the reservation. The distance to the agency is about forty miles, which will be traveled by easy stages, covering about twelve miles per day. At the reservation they will be provided with comfortable homes now in course of preparation by Indian Agent [Peter] Ronan, who has received orders from the government to care for them in similar manner to the natives now under his charge. The travelers are apparently pleased with the change, if one is to judge by the many grunts of satisfaction expressed along the line and they feel that they are going to meet friends and will be well cared for. They are in appearance an average body of Indians with the usual number of papooses. There is a noticeable absence of young s....s. One or two of the bucks are blind and ride led horses.

Gen. Carrington says the sale of the lands which these Indians are leaving in the Bitter Root will commence again on October 19, and continue from day to day. The lands are not included in the Northern Pacific company's claim of alternate quarter sections and the government undertakes to give clear title to all purchasers. Gen. Carrington has been unremitting in his efforts concerning this removal and sale, and is meeting with great success.

Document 22

Bitterroot Salish Arrive at Jocko Agency

October 17, 1891

Source: "Arrived Safe," *The Western News* (Stevensville, Mont.), October 20, 1891, page 2, col. 1.

Editors' note: Charlo and the Bitterroot Salish arrived at the Jocko Agency. This particular article gave much credit to Carrington, who may also have been the source of the information.

Arrived Safe.

The Flathead Indians that left here accompanied by Gen. H. B. Carrington and J. R. McLaren on Thursday morning last, en route to Flathead Agency, reached that point on the following Saturday at 2 o'clock p.m. all safe, with the single exception, that of Joe Lomprey's wife receiving a broken limb by her horse stumbling and falling with her. No loss was sustained among their four hundred head of horses or one hundred wagons. Just before they got to the Agency the Indians wanted to camp but Gen. Carrington ordered them to move and complete the journey that day, they stopping long enough, however, to paint and attire themselves in Indian style. Charlos caused the whole march to be made under the American flag, and when arriving at their destination the Catholic priest had the flag of the "Sacred Heart" raised, and forming a circle under this flag he began receiving them, when Charlos patriotic to his country, walked steadily up to the flag's staff and raised the stars and stripes — though but a small Fourth of July flag — as high as the stick on which he had it tied would permit, being only a few feet above their heads. With this he walked to the church and planted it at the door.

Now the Indians are there and seemingly satisfied. Gen. Carrington deserves much praise. He has accomplished a work that our government has had in progress for twenty years, several different officials attempting to effect a removal of these Indians, but failed. His untiring efforts and keen wisdom has caused that to be accomplished which others could not. Our people are under many obligations to him and are beginning to see the advantages of getting the Indians on the reservation. The Bitter Root lands that have been tied up in these Indian patents are now open for settlement and a larger population and increase in business in our valley will be the result. J. W. Noble, Secretary of the Interior, is to be congratulated for his wise selection in placing Gen. Carrington in charge of the removal of these Indians, who had so successfully made the treaty with them in 1889. The whole has been a complete success of prudent, patient and untiring labor.

Document 23

Arrival of Charlo and the Bitterroot Salish at Jocko Agency October 17, 1891

Source: "Removal of Charlos," *The Spokane Review*, November 29, 1891, page 3, col. 5-6.

Editors' note: The information in this article may have come for a letter written by Mary Ronan to her children at school in Spokane.

Removal of Charlos
How the Flatheads Were Taken to the Jocko Reserve.
The Welcome at the Agency
The Transfer Took Place on the 17th of Last Month — Strange Scenes.
Written for *The Review*.

We have already acquainted our readers with the fact that in the latter part of the month of October the Flatheads of the Bitter Root valley were removed to the Flathead reservation. The following is an interesting description of their arrival at the Indian agency.

The autumnal season, with its faded, falling leaves, mellow tints and suggestions of sad partings, seems a fitting time for a subdued though proud chieftain to bid adieu forever to the lands that he and his followers have loved so well. This is the reason that Charlos, hereditary chief of the Flathead Indians, chose to remove his faithful adherents from the land of their forefathers to the Jocko reservation. October 17, 1891, has witnessed a unique and to some minds pathetic spectacle, Charlos and his band of Indians, numbering less than 200 souls, marched into their future home, the Jocko reservation. Their coming had been heralded, and many reservation Indian had gathered at the agency to give them welcome.

When within a mile of the agency church the advancing Indians spread out, forming a broad column. The young men kept constantly discharging their firearms, while a few of their number, mounted on fleet ponies, arrayed in fantastic Indian paraphernalia, with long blankets partially draping the forms of warriors and steeds, rode back and forth in front of the advancing caravan, shouting and firing their guns until they neared the church, when a large banner of the Sacred Hearts of Jesus and Mary was erected on a tall pole. Near this sacred emblem stood a valiant soldier of Jesus Christ, Rev. P. Canestrelli, S.J.

With outstretched hands the good priest blessed and welcomed the forlorn looking pilgrims. Chief Charlos' countenance retained its habitual expression of stubborn pride and gloom as he advanced on foot, shaking hands with all who had come to greet him. After the general handshaking was over, all assembled in the agency chapel to benediction of the most holy sacrament. The "O Salutaris" and "Tantum Ergo," chanted by those "untutored children of the forest," told better than any other words could of the patient teachings of the noble Jesuit fathers. Every word of the beautiful Latin verses sounded as distinct as if coming from cultivated voices. if the poor creatures reflected on the meaning of the words:

> "Belia premant hostilia
> Da nobus fer auxi ium,"

they must have felt that the touching sentiments truly expressed the feelings of their hearts.

After benediction the good and learned Father Canestrelli, who has spent years laboring among the Indians, striving to enlighten their minds and purify their souls, addressed them in their own language, the Kalispell. The goods words seemed to console and comfort them, if the peaceful expressions their countenances wore indexed aright their minds.

On leaving the church ponies were mounted and wagons driven through the agency grounds to the place selected for their encampment at the banks of a rippling brook that flows down from the great mountains back of the agency. Major [Peter] Ronan, United States Indian agent, had provided a feast for the Indians, the "menu" consisting of three large beeves, a quantity of flour, sugar, tea, etc.

Document 24

Whites Vandalize Bitterroot Salish Farms

October 30, 1891

Source: *North West Tribune* (Stevensville, Mont.), October 30, 1891, page 3, col. 2-3.

Editors' note: This note is both a sad commentary on the honesty of some of the Bitterroot Valley whites and an important endorsement of the honest and friendly conduct of the Salish while they were in the Bitterroot Valley.

Gen. Henry B. Carrington who has been an active energetic worker in the removal of the Indians to the Flathead reservation, started for home yesterday morning. The talented gentleman takes with him the kindest regards of the good people of this community, for his future welfare. His work here will be felt and appreciated by the generations to come.

General Carrington informs us that some of the Indian huts have been broken into during their absence and timothy seed and other things which they could not take have been stolen; some of their fences thrown down and hauled away, and windows broken. Such work is not conducive to the health of the parties committing the same. The Indians have never been known to have molested a white man's house in the whole history of the valley and now some cowardly whelp is guilty of work as described above.

Document 25

Carrington's View of the Bitterroot Removal

April 23, 1892

Source: "The Catholic Flathead Indians," *The Pilot* (Boston, Mass.), April 23, 1892, page 1, col. 3.

Editors' note: The information for this article was compiled from Carrington's letter to the Secretary of the Interior at the conclusion of Carrington's work in Montana and a later interview with Carrington after he had returned east.

The Catholic Flathead Indians

The Pilot referred nearly two years ago to General [Henry B.] Carrington's official service among the Flathead Indians, and although without consulting him, published extracts from one of his private letters as to the labors of the Society of Jesus at the St. Ignatius Mission. It was his disinterested and frank tribute to the efficiency of the school among that tribe, under Father [Jerome] D'Aste, successor of those pioneer missionaries, Fathers [Pierre] De Smet and [Anthony] Ravelli, who, more than half a century ago, founded the St. Mary's Mission in the Bitter Root Valley.

Since his recent return from his second trip to that country, and his removal of the entire band to the Jocko Reservation, where the whole tribe is now concentrated, we took occasion to learn more of the details of the removal, and particularly to get from him any facts as to their religious condition.

The Secretary of the Interior, Gen. John W. Noble, in his annual Report, quotes from a personal letter of General Carrington as follows: —

"A remarkable incident will show the inner confidence of Charlot (the chief) in the Government. Just outside of the Agency inclosure is the Catholic church. As the column drew near, the banner of the Sacred Heart was upheld by two men, and the priest conducted a procession of men, women and children, who were dismounted for the purpose, into the church, where a service was held. The Indians, of their own volition, had borne the Stars and Stripes on the centre wagon. The mounted men came down the slope to the Agency with a "good front," the flag in the centre, firing their guns in the air. When formed by the priest under the banner of the Sacred Heart, Charlot (chief) stepped to the wagon, spliced the flag stick with a cane, bore it to the front, and planted it at the church entrance, where his warriors placed their guns. He wanted the flag which protected his people to be with them all the time. It was done so promptly, and with an instinct so happy, that it reveals the trust he felt in our good faith.

On the march, herding, packing, unpacking, striking lodges, and all details were done as prearranged. No regiment could have more implicitly obeyed every order. Even fence rails were sacred, cold and wet as our march was. Tepees were pitched as a street, in two lines, so that the whole camp was under my eye constantly. Every lodge was visited from time to time, so that there was no chance for scattering or confusion.

There were many scenes and incidents of even thrilling interest in the exodus of the Flatheads from their ancestral home. The old people wept, but felt that "they could trust the Great Father at Washington, and all would be well."

The Secretary's Report, by use of General Carrington's friendly letter, discloses much that is too often lacking in formal official documents, and stimulated our desire to learn more. The following facts, which we gleaned from a brief interview, are of interest, and we wonder that some one of our leading magazines has not, before this, illustrated the extraordinary movement of this tribe to a new, a "promised land."

It seems that although St. Mary's Mission Church still stands in the Bitter Root Valley, service was seldom held, perhaps monthly, after the removal of Father [Jerome] D'Aste to the St. Ignatius Mission. The Indians themselves, however, met for prayers, and on the Sunday before the march began, Chief Charlot gathered his people and spent the entire morning in religious worship, seeking Divine guidance as to his duty. He finally decided, as he expressed it, that the "Great Spirit" had answered his prayers, and would go with them, if they went with the "white chief." Among the interesting incidents of the march was his taking with him the hand-bell from the church and calling the camp together for prayers each morning before breakfast.

We asked General Carrington if any of the soldiers from Fort Missoula, or any other officers went with them. His prompt reply was, "Of course not. Our confidence was mutual. I did not even take a revolver with me. The glad faces of all, men, women and children, as I daily looked after their wants, glowed with pleasure, and not a jar of insubordination occurred. They had nearly six hundred head of loose ponies, children of all ages, fords to cross, a storm to face, and many adventures, some funny and some trying but none lost their temper. None straggled beyond permission, and the recollection of the experience will ever be pleasant. When I went out in 1889 I went with the purpose to do the fair thing for this tribe. When put in charge of the execution of the treaty then made, two years later, I went with the same purpose, and fulfilled the agreement to the letter. Every man, woman, child and pony was safely moved, and when I bade them good-by it was with mutual regret, marred by no incident to impair the friendship which was and ever will be mutually sincere."

We have taken this much pains in this matter because it is an illustration of what can be done by conscientious dealing with the Indians on the frontier, and to further show how the training by the missionaries had prepared the Flathead Indians to appreciate fair and truly Christian treatment and respond to it with equal confidence.

Chapter 3

Documents of
Salish, Pend d'Oreille, and Kootenai
History Between 1890 and 1894

Document 26

Allard Stage Line

1890-1891

Source: "Tales of Montana's Early Days: The Allard Stage Line," *The Anaconda Standard*, November 26, 1899, page 19, col. 1-7.

Editors' note: In 1890 and 1891 travelers headed for the Upper Flathead Valley took the Northern Pacific Railroad trains to Ravalli station. Passengers and freight then headed north by stage to Polson and by steamship across Flathead Lake. Allard's stage line was a major business on the Flathead Reservation in the early 1890s. Traffic on the line was especially heavy as the Great Northern Railroad was being built through Northern Montana at the time.

Tales of Montana's Early Days
The Allard Stage Line

There stands in a neglected corner of the barn yard at the Allard ranch on Mud creek on the Flathead reservation an old stage coach. It is dilapidated as to cover and boot; its upholstery is in tatters; the paint is gone from its wheels and running gear; its body is defaced and worn. Weeds and vines grow among the spokes of the wheels and the pole furnishes a comfortable roost for poultry. Motherly hens nest in the corners where once passengers sat during the fast drives from the Northern Pacific station at Selish across the reserve to the foot of the lake, and there is little about the old stage at present to indicate that it was at one time the crack turnout of the Allard stage line that used to do such a big transportation business on the line that furnished the only inlet to the Flathead valley in Northern Montana and its phenomenally rich country. Yet this is the stage that was in demand when the road across the reservation almost an unbroken line of wagons and stages while the country in the northwest corner of Montana was being settled. Old travelers across the reservation sought eagerly for seats in this coach and were disappointed if they found that they had to ride in some other.

Those were the days when Arthur Laravie held the lines over six horses on this trip and this was the stage that he drove. "Young Joe" Marion was another of the drivers and Andrew Stinger a third. The list of those who handled the baggage and freight wagons is a long one, but they were all good reinsmen and the rivalry between them was great. It was intensified when an opposition line of stages was put on and the patrons of the road will readily recall the exciting races that these drivers indulged in in their efforts to be the first at the steamer landing at the foot of the lake. These men knew the road perfectly and they knew their horses. There was one thing that they did not know, and that was fear. They drove like demons and many a timid passenger has wished that he had walked, as the line of stages tore down the hill that marks the end of the drive to the steamer landing. It is a long, steep slope, and it was always taken on the run. The horses knew what that hill meant and they were always ready for it. The moment that they felt the load come over the brow of the hill they were off. They needed no urging by the drivers. They knew by experience what was in store for them and they entered fully into the spirit of the race. Once started, there was but one thing for them to do, and that was to keep on the jump. With the heavy load behind them and no disposition on the part of the driver to use the brake, they had to hit the road hard to keep out of the way of the rocking coach that swayed and swung behind them. But, with all of this reckless driving there were no accidents on the hill. Often there would be passengers aboard who thought that the ride down the hill would be the last they would ever take, but in some way or another they always got safely to the bottom.

On the other end of the road, approaching the railway station, there was another steep and dangerous hill. The road has been made over since then and is comparatively safe, but in those days, instead of circling around the hill, it led straight down the coulee that affords an entrance from the Jocko valley to the broad fields that lie in the shadow of the Mission mountains. It is related that Arthur Laravie at one time drove his stage with its six horses for two weeks down this hill with the brake broken, so that it would not hold the wheels. He let the horses go and guided them down that steep pitch of half a mile with only his sublime confidence and knowledge of the road to prevent the instant death of his passengers, for that would have been their fate had the heavy stage ever gone over the bank into the rough gullies that bounded the road. When Charles Allard discovered what Laravie was doing he reproached him for not reporting the break and having it repaired, but Laravie only laughed.

When the stage and steamer line from Selish station — Ravalli it was called then — was first started, the Allard line had things all its own way. This line had the mail contract and had a practical monopoly on the passenger business. It is not alleged that Allard ever abused this privilege or extorted heavy fares from his passengers on account of the fact that he had things in his own hands, but it looked like a good thing and an opposition line was inaugurated. Then

Top: Charles Allard, Sr.
Source: Montana Historical Society
Photogaph Archives, Helena, Mont.,
photo 940-336.

Bottom:
Charles Allard's ranch, 1890s.
Source: Toole Archives,
Mansfield Library,
University of Montana, Missoula,
photo 75-6054

was when the real excitement of the trip across the reservation began. From the moment that the passenger aligated [sic] from the railway train at Selish, when he was pulled and hauled about by the agents of the rival lines, till the steaming horses pulled up at the station at the foot of the lake, the experience was one that will never be forgotten by those who passed through it. It was first a struggle for patronage and then a race for the boat landing. There was no time lost anywhere and it was a whirl of excitement from start to finish.

When the rival line was established Allard sent his agent east as far as Evaro to meet the westbound train and to secure passengers. This worked well for a couple of trips, but then the rival line put a similar agent at Evaro and then the two fought it out on the train. Tickets were sold before Selish was reached and all that the stage men had to do was to pick out the passengers that had been ticketed to them on the train. Once in a while the rustling runner of one line would land a passenger who had been sold a ticket on the rival stage. Then there would be a row. The poor passenger would get the worst of it by the time they were through pulling and hauling him to land on the right seat and in the right stage. They tell of a poor Chinaman who alighted from the train one day with his possessions tied up in a bundle. All he had on earth was in that sheet. There was his pipe and his dope; there was his joss and his paper prayers. His clothing, too, and all that made him a man of means were stowed away in that capacious package. As he stepped from the train and looked about him he was seized by the runner for the new line and led toward one of the new stages. That was all right. He liked the looks of the stage and was willing to go. The proceeding had been observed by Arthur Laravie, who stood near by and, as the opposition agent passed him with the Chinaman in tow, Arthur reached out and jerked the bundle from the Mongolian. Before anybody could interfere the bundle was stowed in the boot of the Allard stage and the Chinaman was informed that if he wanted to ride with his bundle he must climb into the Allard vehicle. That was a hard pill for the opposition to swallow, but Arthur's 200 pounds were too much for the losing agent and he regretfully surrendered.

It was half a mile from the railway station to the top of the hill that overlooks the Mission valley. That was a slow start, but when the top of this descent was reached there was no time lost. Down the long slope to Mission creek and across that stream on the run; then up the gradual rise to the divide between Mission and Post creeks; another dash down the hill to the latter stream and across it, and then the dash over the smooth road to Crow creek. Here was the racing ground. Fours and sixes knew that there was work ahead for them when they started on this part of the journey. There were shouts and the crack of whips, the rattle of wheels and a cloud of dust and the race was on. It was most exciting sport. The Allard horses were the best that could be obtained and his drivers were as good as ever held lines over any team, but the opposition horses were fresh and had not been worn by service on the road, so that the race was an even one. The Allard men claim that the score of victories was largely in their favor and their line certainly was the favorite. From Crow creek to Mud creek and then the swing into the lane that leads to the Allard ranch house. There the passengers were fed. The opposition line fed back at the other creek and also changed horses. Usually, by the time that the meal was ended and the new team brought around, the opposition stage would be seen on the main road passing the ranch. It was quick loading then, and out through the pasture, where a gap in the fence afforded access to the road, swung the coaches, the fresh horses on the gallop. Then up the hill that rises high and steep above the foot of the lake. Here is where good driving counted. The man who knew how to get the most out of his team was the man who won this uphall [sic] race. It is a difficult pull — a steep grade and heavy sand to go through at first and then a steep, heart-breaking ascent over rocky soil. But that last steep rise brought the stage to the end of the last climb. The final two miles of the ride was down grade and a good steep grade, too. Here is where occurred the awful runs that have already been mentioned. The stages swung up to the landing and passengers and baggage were speedily transferred to the steamers. The excitement of the stage race was ended and the pleasant lake ride was ahead.

While the racing business was exciting, it was hard on livestock, and Charlie Allard decided that there was a better way than this to kill off the opposition. He cut rates. The cut was speedily met by the opposition and another reduction followed, only to be met again by the rival line. Then Allard offered to carry passengers and baggage for nothing. The other line met this, but failed to offer any bonus and Allard had the trade. It was not profitable for three weeks, but by that time the rival line had surrendered, and the Allard line was alone in the business once more. Matters settled down into the old ruts and the service continued till the opening of the railway line of the Great Northern through Flathead county destroyed the business of the stages and the steamers were taken out of service.

It is told of Charles Allard that he was riding over the road one morning and came to the brow of the hill that overlooks the big flat where the drivers used to race. The rival line had been driven out of business at that time and there was supposed to be no more racing, so Allard was amazed to see two six-horse teams and two fours racing like mad across the flat below him. They were all his own teams. Laravie had the big stage with six horses; Stinger also had six; an old driver had four and Joe Marion had four on the baggage wagon. These were putting up as pretty a race as ever graced a Roman circus. The fine teams were skimming over the ground, with the big stages rocking and creaking behind them; the eager drivers were urging the animals to their utmost and the passengers were cheering as first one and then another had the advantage. Finally Laravie pulled his team into the beaten path a safe winner and swung the big stage along well in the lead. Allard had watched this performance with all the interest of the sportsman that he was. When it was over, he rode on after the stages and as he overtook them he roasted the drivers in unmistakable language. He told them that it was all right to race when there was another line to beat and that he had been proud of them at that time, but he did not propose to have his horses ruined by racing among themselves. He didn't want to see any more of it and he would fine the first driver that he caught racing against his stable companions. "But," he concluded, "I was glad to see Laravie win. He has the best team all right."

Allard was an excellent manager. His men all liked him and were anxious to see him win out. There was one other time when he waxed indignant with his drivers, however, and that was when he found that they had been accepting extra pay for the box seat. That was, of course, the most desirable seat in the coach in pleasant weather, and the drivers had taken advantage of that fact to make a little pin money on the side. On some occasions as much as $20 premium had been received for that seat. Some kicker finally learned of this and told it to Allard. Then there was a blue atmosphere surrounding the stage stable for a few hours. The driver who confessed to having received a bonus for the box seat was fined $20 and informed that a repetition of the offence would result in a heavier fine. This settled the premium business, but the drivers later fell into a bad habit (for the line) of holding the box seat for lady passengers — that is, for presumable ladies. They were females, anyway. Some of them, however, were of well defined sporting proclivities and when one of them got upon the box seat the passengers inside were sure of a quick trip. One day Allard overtook one of the stages that was making about 20 miles an hour, and, as he galloped his horse past the front of the stage, he saw that the woman passenger on the seat was holding the lines. That settled the pleasant pastime in which the drivers had been indulging. The order was made that no woman should be allowed to ride outside. That made the staging business rather prosaic, but the prospect of a $20 fine was not calculated to cause the drivers to forget that such a rule was in force and effect.

All of the old stages of the Allard line have been sold and are now in service on other lines in the state, but this big one remains in its corner on the ranch. The owner refused to sell it while he was alive, and since his death there have been no opportunities to dispose of it. So it holds quiet state in the corner of the barnyard and it is too bad that it cannot speak to tell of the exciting scenes in which it has taken part. It was the crack stage of its day and it has made as good time, it is said, as any stage that ever ran in Montana. From the railway to the foot of the lake the road measures 24 miles, and some of the way the hills are steep and in other places the sand makes travel slow. Still these stages used to cover the distance in about three and a half hours with their heavy loads. Those were the last days of lively staging in Montana. The drivers are now quiet farmers or stockmen, whose only indulgence is an occasional horse race; the horses have gone to the last haven of all good steeds — the old stage is the only remaining monument of the days when the stage ride across the reservation was one of the exciting incidents in Montana travel.

Document 27

Ursuline Nuns Start Indian Kindergarten on Flathead March 18, 1890

Source: [Mother Angela Lincoln], *Life of the Rev. Mother Amadeus of the Heart of Jesus: Foundress of the Ursuline Missions of Montana and Alaska* (New York: The Paulist Press, 1923), pages 113-114, and 118.

Editors' note: This is a highly idealized account of the founding of the Ursuline school by Mother Amadeus in March 1890. The supposed willingness of the Indian mothers to give up their children raises some questions.

The year after Mother Amadeus had celebrated the twenty-fifth anniversary of her consecration to God, Our Lord sent her two more Missions. In March 1890, she opened St. Ignatius Mission. This was to be a kindergarten for the children of the Kalispel, the Flatheads and the allied tribes. The Very Rev. Father [Joseph] Cataldo, who was then Superior of the Jesuits of Montana, called upon her for this experiment. He felt that the conversion of those Indians could be best affected by training the little ones from the cradle up, and right glad was Mother Amadeus to plant the banner of St. Ursula in the historic soil of the Bitter Root, the field sanctified by the first labors of the pioneer missionary. Father [Pierre] de Smet.

So Mother Amadeus with a new colony of Ursulines, was soon under way again.

Two passes, McDonald and Priest, cross the continental divide, the great Northern Pacific Railway following the later. Butler, Montana, on account of its position, is called the "Backbone of the Rockies." The railway enters the famous Mullan tunnel, debouching at Blossburg, and wends its way westward over the O'Keefe and Marent trestles, 112 and 226 feet in the air, respectively — this latter the highest in the Northern Pacific system — revealing below a wealth of mountain streams, of luxurious pine trees and fertile valleys. Even a less pure, less poetic soul looking down upon the splendid deep might well be filled with awe, but when soon afterward, the name Ravalli greeted Mother Amadeus' ear, amazement made room for gratitude and love. What a life of heroic and enlightened charity the name Ravalli recalled! Here the travelers exchanged their seats in the railroad for one in the Mission coach, and a ride in the shadow of peak McDonald. . . .

On the day of the opening of the Mission, the very Rev. Father Cataldo gathered the Flatheads about the great Mission cross and spoke to them, telling them to send their little ones to the Ursulines. The chief woman gave her baby to Mother Amadeus who wrapped it tenderly in her choir mantle, and carried it to the kindergarten. Then Mother went about among the other women and stretched her arms to each one. Not one of them could resist the ineffable maternal attitude, the smile, so beautiful in its trust, its goodness, and the kindergarten was soon full — the first kindergarten every heard of among the Indians, for never before had an Indian woman trusted her baby to another. Carashee [Kakashee] was looking on in silence. "The Father hath spoken well," at last he said, "but the Mother hath spoken better." Mother Amadeus had not opened her lips.

Document 28

The Jocko and Mission Valleys in 1890

July 1890

Source: Palmer Henderson, "The Flathead Indians," *The Northwest Illustrated Monthly Magazine* (St. Paul, Minn.), vol. 8, no. 8 (August 1890), pages 1-3.

Editors' note: This is one of the more detailed accounts of Indians and Indian life on the Flathead in 1890. The descriptions of Henderson's visits to the farms of Antoine Moiese and Francois Saxa and the Jocko Agency church service were especially valuable.

The Flathead Indians.
A Visit to their Agency and to the St. Ignatius Mission.

I was never more sleepy in my life. All the other passengers slept as if there weren't a guilty conscience aboard. Even the train's roar had subsided into a low grumble at its ceaseless round of toil. The hours wore like Scotch plaids; so long were they that I had sullenly begun to feel that I might as well resign myself, that we should never arrive anywhere, but just go on forever and ever as we were. At this point I switched off the Northern Pacific for a train of thought which spun along, I trying to imagine how a soul would feel journeying, solitary and awed, from star to star, when terrestrial lights twinkled merrily and a train man hoarsely yelled "Missoula." So we were somewhere. The hour to Arlee was easily passed fussing with my belongings and at something like one of the clock I stood in the cool night air and followed a tall figure, through a darkness which was palpable, to a carriage. Five miles of mystery and Montana's electric air, then the barking of dogs from an Indian's tepee, then the cheery lights from the agency, then the cordial voice of Maj. [Peter] Ronan himself welcoming me to the Flathead Indian Reservation; lastly a homey room, strewn with the beautiful, long-haired white skins of the Rocky Mountain goat, with white curtains at the windows swaying invitingly, and an old-fashioned feather bed to whose embraces I yielded myself with a sigh of content and immediately lost myself in that unknown which is ever so near us. This was the beginning of it all, a week so novel and delightful that — "Lord keep our memory green."

The next morning was Sunday. Just as the sun ray had laid its fingers across my eyes with "Guess who — it is the day," the sweet little brown-eyed daughter of Maj. Ronan brought me in some hot water, and the sunny haired one timidly handed me a bouquet of the exquisite wild flowers which grow in such profusion thereabouts. Afterwards, I found those two little acts to be the keynote of the household harmony — "Helpfulness and courtesy."

What New York club man sat down to a better breakfast? Mountain brook trout just out of the icy water and venison, not to mention plenty of gay conversation and fun over Wong, the Chinaman, who was constantly rushing in and out noiselessly like a celestial Mercury. "Wong likes meals conducted on strictly business principles," laughed Mrs. [Mary] Ronan; "hold to your plate until you are done, or he will whisk it off while you are talking. I cannot break him of the habit. Often in the midst of a story he will swoop down on the Major's plate and before you realize it his cue [que] is disappearing through the door." "Clough?" broke in Wong at this juncture. Yes, we were and went out on the porch to view the land scape o'er.

Where is there a lovelier one? Agent Ronan's house stands in the center of the large fenced enclosure and there are cottages for the doctor, the head farmer, and the clerk of the Reservation, barns, the storehouse, and the saw mill, all painted white, neatly kept and flower-surrounded, an object lesson to the Indians who are constantly about. Without, near at hand on a little eminence, stands the little white mission church, the embodied reason for the difference between the dirty tepee near by and homes within the gates. Before the agency spreads the beautiful valley of the Jocko, level as a floor, green carpeted and almost covered with wild flowers. Seems to me no where else in the world are there so many as just there, and so various, and so brilliant. At the right runs the energetic Jocko, leaping hastily over the rocks and singing all the time. His name just suits him. You cannot see the river at all till you plumb up to its steep bank. Evidently old Earth is growing warped and the Jocko tries to fill up the crack. Shutting in the valley on every side are the mountains, ever changing in their beauty, snow capped in the distance, with deep lakes resting in their hollows and cold streams leaping down their sides. How beautiful it all is.

As we sat there, Indians began to gather for service. They came afoot, the s....s carrying their papposes on their backs, or on the small Indian ponies which they tethered here and there. They all wore the brightest yellows, purples and reds obtainable and the braves, especially, strode along wrapped in their striped blankets, their long hair in tiny braids, with all the superiority of mind that a consciousness of being well dressed confers. As well be out of the world as out of the fashion. There was no stopping to gossip on the way, not meeting of friends and inquiries as to the health while the braves discussed stocks for a moment or the s....s made mental notes on bonnets. Every one went straight to the little meeting house in singleness of purpose, glancing neither to right nor left, and thither, when the bell had stopped ringing, we followed them. "I shall be dust when my heart forgets" that service. The priest was away, so it was lead by dear old Michel [Revais], the half breed interpreter, though he looks full Indian. In white man's dress he sat up in front, his earnest face almost saintly, and stamped with a life of peace and good will, his sightless eyes turned upward as he sang. We had chairs near by, but all the Indians knelt or squatted on the bare floor. I must admit that I did little but watch the swarthy faces. I never saw a congregation so earnest and attentive. All the men were at the right, kneeling immovable, wrapped in dignity and blankets, looking straight ahead, not a glance toward the belles on the other side. Such of the braves as felt they could sing with the spirit and the understanding did so, but all the women sang. Among the latter were many who had children and little babies with them. The youngsters sat gravely on the floor, cut up no monkeyshines, whimpered never a whimper, and, in short, were so exemplary that I wondered if it were real inherent Indian piety or the fact that they wore no scratchy starched white gowns which they "mustn't muss up" or stiff broad collars which make life on Sunday a burden to the American small boy. Only one youngster was at all restless, and he would have been a model of propriety to most white children at church. He fingered his beads and twisted his bracelets and occasionally hitched about. Then would his mother, without ceasing her chanting in Latin or changing a muscle of her face, calmly lean forward and punch him once, twice, thrice. He took it in the same way it was given and would reform for a moment, but the flesh is weak.

One of the young girls was really pretty. She wore a bright red calico gown, an orange silk handkerchief knotted about her neck, and her hair in two long dusky braids. She sang the prayers in a very musical voice, but her eyes were constantly wandering to the blood-red cut glass vinaigrette which hung at my waist. I'm afraid she was cornally [carnally] minded. It was a touch of nature that made us kin. Next to her was a hideous old s... with mournful eyes and a hare lip, who would have had small patience with the young girl's thought, yet she herself kept her shawl tightly drawn across the unsightly mouth lest I should see it. Poor old thing, so would I.

Those untutored Indians can do something I can't. They can sing the whole Roman Catholic service through in Latin without a slip, and they wound up by chanting some prayers in Indian, weird music that roused all the underlying barbaric in me. After service some of them sat down upon the grass, mothers standing their babies near them by driving the sharp ends of the cradle-boards into the ground. This custom of fastening children on these boards and lacing the buckskin flaps around them has undoubtedly much to do with the high death rate among them, beside being responsible for their growing up "pigeon-toed." Going among them, we saw a rather fine looking young fellow, tall and well built, who is the grandson of Clark, the great Montana explorer, with Lewis, in early times, who, you remember, married an Indian wife. I rather think this Clark considers his white blood a stain on the family escutcheon. He is very proud of his bright little three-year-old boy, however, who was attired gorgeously, his moccasins and clothes gaudy with bead embroidery, his neck hung with many necklaces, a brass political badge on his hat and row of what appeared to be gold coins for bangles across his shoulders behind. Examining them, I found them to be "drink checks," each bearing the legend, "good for one drink."

Monday was one of those perfect days never seen, seems to me, out of the Rockies; and Major Ronan took me out driving to see the Indians in their homes. First we crossed the Jocko and followed along the irrigation ditch. This is Agent Ronan's pride and I don't wonder. He it was who planned and put through the whole thing and it cost but $5,000, six miles including the flume. The water is obtained from the Jocko, and it falls three-fourths of an inch to the rod. From this ditch the Indians can irrigate their farms during the dry season, turning the water directly into the fields. "I hired the Indians for the work, and how they did work," said Major Ronan; "I paid them so much a rod. One of a family would dig till he was exhausted, then another would jump in. They'd keep it up all night. I don't suppose there ever was another government job pushed like that one. About two years ago the commission came down to see it; Holman, 'the watch-dog of the treasury,' Cannon of Illinois, Ryan of Kansas, Peel of Arkansas, chairman of Committee of Indian affairs, Maj. Maginnis, Leedom, Sergeant-at-arms, and the financial clerk of the Senate. They were right pleased with the work."

Everywhere we went were dogs. "Yes," said the major, who's about as entertaining a talker as one meets in a day's journey, "when I first came here there was half an acre of wheat to two acres of dogs. I've got it down to half an acre of dogs to two acres of wheat and hope to get the proportion smaller yet.["]

From all the major told me that day I've arrived at the conclusion that the Indians have what is popularly known as a decided snap. In this Flathead reservation are 1,300,000 acres of the most fertile land in the world, well watered, hemmed in by mountains rich with minerals. About 3000 Indians live on this immense tract. If an Indian wants wood, all he has to do is to cut it and take it to the government sawmill at the agency to be sawed. If he wants a farm, all he has to do is to select the most beautiful spot he can find and fence in all he wishes. "But that's the great trouble with Indians," said the major, "they seem to have no conception of owning in severalty. They are genuine communists, have always held, and probably always will, that the earth is theirs as a tribe. When an Indian builds a fence he's made considerable advance towards civilization." Well, perhaps, major; I don't suppose there's a man in the country who has given more study to the question or knows any more about the Indian. I suppose fences are a sign of that meum and teum which is the basis of our boasted civilization, but the cry against capital from labor strikes against that fence like the sea against a stone wall. But to return; having his farm, the noble red man goes to the store house and obtains his farm implements, free, to work it. He pays no taxes, he has a physician furnished him, a perfect luxury of woe we would think, who, all through an illness, are confronted by doctor's bills which rustle so as to disturb our fitful sleep, and say ominously, "We'll sit heavy on your soul to-morrow," when we waken. No man prospects in the Indian's mountains — the gold and silver are his also. But curiously, he seems to have a superstition against digging into the depths, or else a lofty disregard for filthy lucre, for an Indian is seldom a miner. The mineral lands are rich, too, on the Flathead reservation. One Indian came to the major not long ago with some good gold specimens. The Indian, too, has schools furnished him, religious instruction, even earthly food if he is unsuccessful with crops or too lazy to work. These and many other things incline me to cry out:

> Oh to be an Indian
> And with the Indians stand,
> His "wrongs" to make life easy,
> And a little of his land.

Three tribes inhabit the Flathead reservation — the Flatheads, Kootenais and Kalispels. The first are called so, I suspect, for the same reason that Mark Twain named his dog Spot, because he hadn't any. I had heard about the heads of young children being placed between boards till they flattened, as Egyptians of old made dwarfs, and I revelled in the prospect of a novelty. Wisely, I did not refer to this nor to my half notion that I was taking my life into my hands when I went there. Riding from one well kept farm to another, I laughed quietly to myself and even joked with "Francois" about his past scalping days, remarking that my hair was so long as, I feared, to prove quite a temptation. How he laughed! Talk about the solemnity of the Indian, its absurd. Many that I saw gigglen like school girls.

Francois had a well cultivated farm and left his horses to come up to talk. "Flathead never killed a white man," said he. I asked him if he had any scalps left of those I heard he brought home from the last fight with the Blackfeet. His natural Indian pride struggled with his acquired Catholic horror, but he said, "Oh no." However, I think if no one had been around, he might have skirmished up one, and I do want a scalp awfully. "What is that queer kennel-like place," queried I. "The sweat house." It was long enough to lie down in and quite low, When an Indian has rheumatism he constructs one near water, covers it closely with skins, crawls into it and stays till he streams with perspiration and then plunges into the ice cold river. It is said to be a sure cure. I should think it might be — of all ills that flesh is heir to, including "the fever called living." Francois had a tepee, or "lodge" as they are called in Montana, near his little house. "The Indians always move into them at the first approach of hot weather," said Mr. Ronan.

As we drove to another farm, he told me something of the government on the reservation. It is mostly by the Indians. From among them are appointed three judges who are greatly respected, for authority has great weight with Indians. Seldom is a decision appealed from to Major Ronan, who shows his clear-headedness in making much of the judges. Fifteen Indian police bring offenders to justice. They are very faithful and, mounted upon their ponies, will run a man down much more persistently than St. Paul officers of the law.

By this time we had reached Antoine Moise's house. He is a son of the chief and one of the men who went to Washington a few years ago to make a treaty. He has the most beautiful farm I ever saw and is worth several thousand dollars in horses and cattle. Elk skins hung outside the door and within the little house sat his young wife embroidering some moccasins. She was really pretty, with the loveliest of shy black eyes and courteous manners. She spoke no English, but needed none to express her hospitality as she waved me to a seat as on the manner [manor] born. In the universal language she told me her head ached. I loosened my vinaigrette and, trying to explain that she must not put it too close to her nose, handed it to her. What a whiff she got of strong ammonia! The tears rolled down her face. I showed her again and she seemed to enjoy it all the time we stayed. Antoine himself came in with a string of trout. "I got him," said Antoine triumphantly. He talked good English. Presently she said something, both glanced at me, and laughed. "What did she say, Antoine?" "She says how pretty you are." I never had a compliment please me more. "Tell her," said I, "that I can honestly return it."

They showed us over the little house proudly. It was papered with odd bits of wallpaper, a few dishes, which seemed their special pride, were piled on a shelf. Antoine's Sunday vest was hanging from a branch of large antlers, a cross of fancy stones ornamented a shelf and a small clock ticked cheerily. His wife returned to the floor and her bead work, and I felt like a child who had to go home when I wanted to stay and play house too.

Judging from all I saw that morning, I say decidedly the Indian problem is being rightly solved on the Flathead reservation where the Indians are taught

St. Ignatius Mission, Montana, 1895.

Source: Montana Historical Society Photogaph Archives, Helena, photo 950-722.

to depend on themselves. Everywhere we went, too, I could see the really affectionate feeling they bore toward Agent Ronan and am glad to know since my return that he stays another four years.

I wish I had space to tell you of the glories of the next day, when alternate rain and sunshine made the mountains too changeful and fascinating to allow me time for watching anything else; or of the curiosities shown me by the agency clerk, Mr. [Thomas] Adams, nephew of Senator Blackburn, including the jewel box Emperor Iturbide gave his father on the days of the former's execution; or of all the Indian legends blind Michel told me as I sat in his doorway and looked at the mountains. All these must wait.

The next day we drove twenty miles over the mountains, along the Jocko, which becomes fairly riotous when he thinks himself out of sight, through changing scenes of beauty which make me happy whenever I close my eyes, with meadow larks welcoming us on every side, and flowers fairly tumbling over on another in their haste each to be first to say "The Spring is here." And at last we came to St. Ignatius mission, the oldest in Montana. Here is a picture which at best can be but a mockery. The buildings are fine and large and white. They cluster in the beautiful valley, encircled by the Mission Ridge like a protecting arm. Still behind are the main Rockies in all their grandeur, which you can see near at hand even forty miles to the north where they suddenly pitch down to the Flathead Lake, as beautiful as any of the Swiss lakes of world-wide fame.

One ought to devote a whole article to the mission, it is so interesting, and yet must be slighted. We first visited the girls' school in which there are now 118 pupils. It is conducted by seven sisters, and eight lay sisters of the order of Providence. The house is like wax from turret to foundation stone. The Indian girls are taken when small children and kept till they are quite grown up when, as is hoped, marriage often occur between them and the boys from the Jesuits' school. They are taught to do all sorts of housework, sewing, weaving, etc., beside books. They have their recreation, their annual camping out under the sisters' care, their flower gardens, their music, for they are fine singers, and even their corsets, dear to their womanly hearts, each pair hung in the girl's individual closet with her card and name, which by the way is not Romona, nor Juanita nor Alfaretta, but invariably, alas, Marie Something. Pillow shams, I regret to say, have struck the Indian nation. As with the boys, each pupils is paid for, to the order, by the government, $125 a year. Indians, you know, are wards of the nation. As I came away one of the sweet-faced nuns accompanied me to the gate with an invitation to share their hospitality in their guest room for a week and gave me all the pansies I could carry.

Across the street are four Ursuline nuns who have started a kinder-garden and already have thirty little Indian children under their care.

The largest academy building in Montana is the one seen in this picture of the Jesuit school for boys, now numbering ninety. It cost more than $60,000 and is complete in every particular. Attached to it are small buildings for the various trades, and a boy may be apprenticed to any that he chooses, so giving him a good start in life. Two are now apprenticed as printers, three as shoemakers, etc. The boys have formed a base-ball team, — so do the vices of civilization engraft themselves upon the noble red man — a fire company, and a band of eighteen pieces. They are taught the theory of music and specially trained by one of the Brothers, and they meet for practice every week. I had shrunk from the thought of a band more than a German street band, but they really play well and enjoy it hugely. They have also got together a very creditable museum of Montana animals, birds, minerals, early relics and Indian curiosities.

A very novel entertainment was given by this school last Easter, so novel, especially considered as an Easter celebration, that I will give the program complete. It was printed by themselves.

Program.

Music — Bull Dozer Quickstep .... St. Ignatius Band.

Reading — Resurrection .... R. McCloud.

Song — Climbing up the Golden Stairs ... St. Ignatius Glee Club

Dialogue — The Secret of Content ....M. Ripley M. McLeod

Song — The Farmer.. The Wee Wee Tots

Recitation — God is Good ....Ignace

Duet — Music...M. Irvine A. Bell

Song — I'm going far away .... F. Matt J. Blodgett J Morrigeau.

Recitation — What not to do...................................L. Couture

Reading — Easter ....W. Finnigan

Dialogue — A Comical Incident................................ The Girls

Song — There's Something to do .... The Junior Songsters

Recitation — The Little Bird....................................E. Lacourse

Solo — Why does mother stay so long ....A. Carlin

Reading — Miss Pussy .... O. Morrigeau

Dialogue — The Little Rebels ....Nine Boys

Song — Little feet so White and Fair .... S. Lanctot

A farce in Two Acts.

Scene First.

(*Office Room.*)
Scene Second.
(*Lunatic Asylum.*)

Characters —

Pompey .... R. McCloud
Chas. Squeezepenny .... Plasoa
Doctor .... L. Paul
Cloudy .... T. Bell
Pump .... P. Trudo
Old Squeezepenny .... B. Marengo
Finale — Marching Through Georgia .... St. Ignatius Band

One of the courteous fathers gave me this picture of the mission as I came away and accompanied me to the little burying ground with its modest stones and quaint memorials. "Oh, they're dying off fast," said he, "this Indian people. Here are forty new graves this Spring. There was much suffering during the Winter and many ate their dead cattle. Pneumonia and scrofula and nursing their children till they are three and four years old. Yes, the Indian is passing away." But say, can anything more be done for them?

Palmer Henderson.

Document 29

Scenes at Arlee and Jocko Agency

September 1890

Source: "Among the Reds," *Missoula Weekly Gazette*, September 10, 1890, page 12, col. 3-4.

Editors' note: The correspondent noted that the delay in removing the Salish from the Bitterroot Valley to Jocko from 1889 to 1891 left them impoverished. He also described his meeting with Michel Revais, the blind interpreter at the agency.

Among the Reds.
A Visit to Arlee and the Flathead Agency.
How the Noble Red Looks When He Is Engaged in Threshing Wheat.

Arlee, a few white houses hedged round by a white paling, shining in the sun at the foot of the mountains, is the headquarters of the Indian agency. It can be seen from the depot four miles to the east, and looks like a snow flake dropped out of the skies in its spotless garb. Your correspondent headed for it this morning, with an armful of *Gazettes*, though he concluded before he came back that the *Gazettes* might as well have been left at home, for nothing but soft Flathead syllables saluted his ears outside of the paling. Inside this fence are Major [Peter] Ronan's residence, Dr. [John] Dade's, Mr. Thomas Adams, a blacksmith shop, a carpenter shop, a mill and a house with some Indians. Outside stands a church with a cupola on one end of it, an apology for a steeple. We met two of the Fathers who were industriously sawing boards and building a barn. "Both a preacher and a carpenter," I said. "Yes; and farmer, too," replied one, laughingly, which reminded me that the missionary to the Indians must be not only a dispenser to the soul, but a healer of the body, and a trainer of the muscles. Surely no very light task. But these Fathers, many of whom came direct from Europe, are fully equipped for their work, and cheerfully shoulder the physical as well as mental burden imposed upon them.

Congress to Blame.

I found Major Ronan at home, a quiet thoughtful gentleman, who told me during our short conversation that he didn't consider General [Henry] Carrington to blame in the matter of the Bitter Root Flatheads, but that the delay was owing to congress. It is true, however, that the Indians have been considerably inconvenienced, selling their stores, wagons, harness, etc., with the expectation of going to the reservation this spring. The high valuation placed on the land, it is feared, will prevent few if any bidders. That the general was authorized to tell them to sell their personal property is doubtful. The major has had a long experience with the Indians, and a ready test of his efficiency is found by asking any Indian or half-breed on the reservation how he likes Major Ronan. "Good," he replies. I have heard that the major could do much better by traveling for the Indian department, but he is a home-loving man, who prefers quiet, and his home among the Indians he has so long supervised. I wandered around aimlessly till I poked by heard into a neat room, where sat an Indian.

"Do you read English?" I asked.

"Yes, I could read English, but I am blind," he said.

His eyes had no appearance of a physical defect whatever. So sound did they seem that I fancied he was shamming. He devised my thought, for he said:

"They look good, but it is the nerve that is affected."

For Ten Years.

"How long have you been blind?"

"Ten years."

The walls of the rooms were ornamented with pictures of biblical life, which had no meaning to him, for he was blind. Yet patience was expressed in every line of his face, and his manner was cheerfulness itself.

I saw an interesting sight as I returned and that was a threshing machine run by Indians. On the horse power stood an Indian, caroling to the horses and snapping the whip as they trudged round. At the feeder stood two Indians in blankets, shoving in the grain, and on the straw stack nearly buried to the neck stood Indians, their black heads covered with dust and chaff, pitching up the straw. Squatting around were a circle of admiring Indians, one of whom would occasionally jump up and relieve one of his exhausted brethren. It was amusing but somewhat saddening to see these hunters of the forest and plain making an effort to conform to the teaching of the whites, for, can you make a silk purse out of a sow's ear? The Indian is admirable in his element but almost a caricature trying to farm, unless he is educated from infancy, and not allowed to sleep too long in the tents of his fathers. An Indian who talked some English, asked me if I had seen Lalacee.

An Indian Talks.

"No," I said. "He was a bad Indian, was he not?"

"Not so bad."

"Do you think he was as much to blame for killing as a white man would be?"

He shook his head.

A half-breed who was sitting near said:

"No; it was revenge."

The question suddenly presents itself to one: Is an Indian as responsible a being as a white man?

I can hardly think so. His whole training in life and his disposition by inheritance is to kill those who wrong him. You may say, "But he knew the law." Yes, but has he not more to contend with in keeping it? However, this is a question for jurists which your correspondent will not make bold to arbitrate on.

At the station it is very lively, nine or ten freights passing every twenty-four hours, besides the regular passenger trains. The usual number of tie travelers and box car passengers are around. I encountered one crew who claimed to be horsemen, followers of the races, but from all appearances this sounded flattering. There is one store and restaurant here run by Alex Dow, around which the Indians sit and jabber.

There is everything in the store that can attract the color loving eye of the Indian — red blankets and tobacco galore. Alex is almost a chief, whose word is his bond.

The weather is chilly, an "eager and nipping air" being abroad that savors of winter, but let us not borrow trouble, for it lies over beyond three months yet, and it is now but September — "Season of mists and mellow fruitfulness."

W.

Document 30

McDonald's Hotel and Restaurant and Allard's Stage Line May 12, 1891

Source: "The Flathead Country," *The Helena Independent*, May 12, 1891, page 8, col. 1-2.

Editors' note: This account has considerable detail about Duncan McDonald's hotel and restaurant at Ravalli and Charles Allard's stage line from Ravalli to the Foot of Flathead Lake. Freight and passenger business were booming in 1890 and 1891.

The Flathead Country.
The Big Monopoly Which a Half-Breed Is Enjoying at the Ravalli Station.
Scenes Along the Way From the Railroad to the Steamboat Landing.
Demersville Fast Assuming the Air of a Genuine Frontier Boom Town — Kalispel and Columbia Falls.

"Have you been to the Flathead country?"

"Are you going to the Flathead country?"

For several weeks these two questions been leading ones, not only in Helena, but also in other portions of the state. Many answer yes to the first, and those who do not are almost sure to do so to the second. Outside of hunting parties but few people have gone into this section until the last year, the rush now being occasioned by the fact that the Great Northern extension will run through the country and the probability that somewhere in northern Missoula county a new and prosperous town will be started. Leaving the question of speculation aside the trip is one well worth making by any person who has never witnessed boom times on the frontier. You leave Helena by the Northern Pacific at 1:50 p.m., buying a ticket for Ravalli — cost, $8. At 9:15 the same night you are at Ravalli, when the first intimation of what is in store for you is given. The station is on the Flathead reservation, and the only stopping place is kept by Big [Duncan] McDonald, a half-breed. The accommodations he has to offer guests are comprised in a two-story log cabin, which is nicely furnished and lucky is the traveler who is assigned to quarters in the cabin. Beside the cabin the hay sheds and some smaller cabins are used for lodgers, while the proprietor and his wife, a full-blood Indian, sleep in a tepee. McDonald's receipts have been from $40 to $50 a night for the past two weeks, and this is gradually increasing. For a place to sleep one dollar is the charge, while meals are 50 cents. A half dozen Chinamen attend to the restaurant business for the proprietor, and they feed every day from 350 to 500 people. The majority of the guests are freighters, engaged in hauling merchandise from Ravalli to the lake. Besides McDonald's place, the only other buildings are the store and the postoffice, and the half-breed has one of the best paying monoplies [sic] in the state to-day.

Some idea of the amount of goods of all kinds which is going into the Flathead country is gained by the traveler at Ravalli. There are forty loaded cars on the track all the time, and though 750 head of horses, with enough men to handle them, are engaged in freighting to the lake, there is no appreciable diminution of the vast quantities of freight brought by the railroad. Besides the freight at Ravalli, there are other cars always at Helena and Missoula, simply waiting the chance to get them on the Ravalli sidetrack. It costs from 40 cents to $1 a hundred to get goods from the station to the lake. Five miles from Ravalli is the mission farm, in a high state of cultivation. The work is all done under the supervision of the Catholic fathers and the sisters, and the government has furnished all the improved farming implements and men to handle them, and to show the Indians how to farm successfully. In the school at the mission are 124 girls and 149 boys, including those in the kindergarten. As the stage leaves Ravalli at five o'clock in the morning, but few of those now going to the Flathead take the trip to the mission and thus lose one of the most interesting sights in Missoula county.

After a night spent at the Hotel McDonald, at five a.m. the fortune hunter is aboard a four-horse Concord coach, on his way to the foot of the lake. The fare is $3 and by 11 o'clock the same morning you are ready for the boat-ride. The journey across the reservation at this season of the year is a very pleasant one. The country is level, the road good, while the scenery is magnificent. The first glimpse of the big lumber country is had on this trip, the trees ranging in diameter from eighteen to forty-eight inches and from forty to eighty feet in height. The country is well watered by half a dozen creeks, from three to five feet deep, and flowing swiftly. During the trip the Mission range is in plain view, with its snow-capped peaks glistening in the sun. These peaks are 5,000 or 6,000 feet high, and are among the sights of the country.

Twenty-four miles from Ravalli is a relay station, kept by Charley Allard, a half-breed, and the owner of the stage line. Allard is a bright business man, the owner of 2,000 acres of land, occupies a nice house comfortably furnished, has 600 or 800 horses, 5,000 head of cattle, and is taking in $200 a day from his stage business. But what Allard values most highly is a herd of buffaloes,

Top: Duncan McDonald
Source: Montana Historical Society Photograph Archives, Helena, Montana,
photo 943-624.
Bottom: Duncan McDonald's hotel at Ravalli
Source: Toole Archives, Mansfield Library, University of Montana, Missoula,
photo 77-280.

fifty-six in number. He has been offered $16,000 for the herd, and $500 for single animals, but has refused all offers, perferring [sic] the glory of being the owner of the largest herd of buffalo in North America, to adding a big sum to his bank account. The ride across the reservation is of one the pleasantest parts of the journey to the Flathead country, if one will but keep his eyes and ears open. Along the road humanity of all sorts and conditions is seen, from the well-to-do business man in his own conveyance, to the tramp, trudging along with his belongings done up in a handkerchief. They are of all nationalities, and of all ages, and all bound for the Flathead country. The large majority do not know what they will do when they get there, but they are going anyway. Some say they will stop at Demersville, other believe Kalispel is to be the great town, while yet others pin their faith to Columbia Falls.

Arriving at the foot of the lake at 11 o'clock the traveler has three hours to wait for the steamer. During the interval he may get his dinner at one of the three log cabins owned by half-breeds, for 50 cents and spend the balance of the time sizing up the freight pile, of which there is enough on the shore to fill fifteen or twenty cars. There is no system in handling freight at the lake, and the freighters simply unload one lot on top of the other and pile it all together indiscriminately. The result is that merchants who want their goods keep a man on the ground to sort their stuff out and forward it. Unless this is done the chances of getting it through within sixty or ninety days are very meagre.

Up to date the Tom Carter has been the only steamer plying on the lake, but soon two others will take her place. The Carter, built to carry at the outside thirty passengers, makes room for 100, and in addition tows a barge loaded with 100,000 pounds of freight, besides carrying 40,000 pounds herself. The Tom Carter is owned and run by Capt. Kerr, J. W. Cheney and Wm. Houston, and takes in for her owners every day in the month, Sundays included, $700. The boat to take the place of the Carter will cost $20,000, be 170 feet long and twenty-six feet beam, with a number of staterooms, and will carry 100 tons of freight. The Columbia Falls people are also building a boat to cost $18,000, 140 feet over all, twenty-six foot beam, fitted with staterooms, of big freight capacity, to run from the foot of the lake to that town. When these boats are completed traveling will be much more pleasant and convenient than at present. The steamers are constructed on the lake, the builders and all the machinery being imported from the east.

Flathead lake is one of the most beautiful sheets of water in the country. The lower bay is five miles across and from twelve to twenty feet deep, the water so clear that the bottom is easily discernible. From the lower bay the entrance to the lake proper is through a cut dotted with beautiful islands. Here the character of the water changes, and has the greenish tint of the eastern lakes. It has been sounded, to the depth of 400 feet and no bottom found. In the hottest weather the surface is barely warm, while at the depth of eighteen inches it is ice cold. Thirty miles long, it varies in width from five to twenty miles. The scenery along the lake is of the grandest discription [sic]. Fringed with big trees to the west lie the snow-capped peaks of the Mission range and to the east another chain of mountains of different formation, clothed with verdure. From the head of the lake to Demersville by road is twelve miles, but owing to the circuitous course of the Flathead river, when you leave the lake you still have a ride of twenty-eight miles on the Flathead river before your destination is reached. The shores of the river are skirted with cottonwood trees and back of these come tamarack, pine and beech. This is the heavy lumber district and the country of big trees.

It is nine p.m. and the second day since we left Helena, and here we are in Demersville, a quiet half-asleep trading post till a few weeks ago, and to-day the typical hurrah, pioneer boom town, with thirty saloons, dance and gambling houses, 800 to 1,000 inhabitants, the arrivals each twenty-four hours averaging 100, and everybody on the make. While there are tough characters in the town they by no means control things, the large majority of the arrivals being people bent on legitimate business. At the leading hotel, the Cliff house, a place to sleep costs $1, board and lodging being $3 a day. In every room there are two beds and as many cots as can be jammed in, it being a cast-iron rule of the house to let no rooms to one person only. No one has as yet attempted to figure how much the proprietor is making, but he takes care every night of from 200 to 250 people and yet cannot accommodate them all. A building which cost, with the lot, $500, rents readily for $85 or $100 a month, and in consequence many of the saloon men have bought lots for about $250, put up a thach costing as much more, and thus for $500 have a place of their own. The Flathead Banking company and W. C. Whipps, formerly of Helena, do the banking business and the Missoula Mercantile company runs the big store, the latter's receipts running about $8,000 per week. There are a number of smaller establishments, all doing a rushing trade.

Three and a half miles from Demersville is Kalispel, one of the coming great towns of the state, according to those interested. You can get to Kalispel easily, many walking from Demersville. The townsite company owns about 1,500 acres, 400 of which have been platted, corner lots on the main street are held at $1,200 and inside are at $1,000, the lowest priced being $800. Hon. Charles E. Conrad is the vice-president and general manager of the townsite company, is a good rustler, and manages to work every day from 8 o'clock in the morning to 12 o'clock at night.

Twenty miles from Demersville is Columbia Falls, at which point the Northern International Improvement company, under the management of Frank Langford, is operating. the stage runs twice a day to the Falls, and on arrival at Demersville the speculator or sightseer can take his choice of towns. Each town has a fine location, water, lots of natural resources, and each has its champions. The genuine speculator, after hearing each place discussed, is, as a rule, all at sea, and settled the matter by taking a "flyer" in each.

If you don't want to buy town lots, you can have lots of fun fishing for trout, which abound in all the streams. The Flathead Rod, Gun & Improvement company, composed of Helena men, has excellent quarters in the Flathead, close to good fishing and shooting. A week spent in the Flathead will give the Helena man an idea of the great natural wealth of that section, and just now will show him how a genuine boom acts when under full headway.

Document 31

White Tourists Meet Kootenai Indians
on Flathead Lake
August 1891

Source: James Ollason, "Canoeing on the Flathead," *Outing* (Albany, N.Y.), vol. 19, no. 3 (December 1891), pages 187-188.

Editors' note: The friendly interactions between the white tourists canoeing across Flathead Lake in 1891 described in this article suggest many Indian-white dealings in the 1890s were amicable. The Indians Ollason met were probably Kootenai.

Canoeing on the Flathead.
by James Ollason.
Second and last paper.

Our life in the wild seclusion of Flathead Lake and amidst its picturesque and enticing scenery might have excused a longer tarrying, but the call of duty was imperative, and with longing backward looks we took a homeward route which enabled us to cut off several miles at the northeast corner of the lake. Shortly after daybreak we paddled past the river's mouth and landed on a strip of brush-covered beach to the west of it. Up under the shade of a clump of bushes we lay down and slept, until the sun on his western course discovered us and drove us out of our nook and into the water.

The water was much warmer here, being shallower than on the eastern shore, and we found to our great delight that a long swim was once more a possibility. I was lazily moving along a few yards in front of Ned and looking across to where the islands near the southern shore lay half hidden in the purple haze of the hot summer day, when an exclamation from him made me turn.

As I did so a whoop from a group of mounted Indians on the beach reached us, and before I had recovered from the surprise which their unexpected appearance occasioned into the water they rode, their little cayuses apparently enjoying the prospect of a swim.

There were seven Indians in all, but only three swam their ponies out to where we lay waiting to witness their manner of disporting themselves. These we saluted with the customary "How" as they checked their animals alongside of us.

"You swim good?" asked one, nodding to Ned as he spoke.

"A little," answered Ned; "not very good."

The other two grinned at something Ned's interrogator said in Indian, and, speaking fast and earnestly, seemed to be prompting him to give an exhibition of his prowess. This apparently accorded with our dusky friend's humor, for patting his pony on the neck, he raised himself slowly on his hands until he gained a standing posture on its back; then, with a light step on the animal's haunches, he plunged head first into the water. The other two followed his example, and all three swam close up to us, laughing and spluttering, and making motions to us to entertain them in return.

"I'm going to try to fool them," said Ned to me in a low voice, and accordingly, shouting excitedly to them to look at the deer on the bank, with a swift upward movement of his hands, while they glanced ashore to see the imaginary deer, he silently disappeared beneath the surface. Turning around an instant later and seeing me alone they lost no time in looking for and discovering him as he struck out vigorously beneath the ponies in his effort to get out of sight. The youngest of the bucks immediately gave chase, and to Ned's intense disgust seized him by the ankle and brought him a prisoner to the surface.

This little incident created a good deal of merriment, and our painted friends made much of their superiority to the white man. Born and raised as they have been on the shores of the lake, they are without doubt splendid swimmers; but later in the afternoon when we visited their tepees we beat them ignominiously at shooting. They were blazing away at a mark on a tree when we strolled over to their camp. We were requested to try our skill and did so, balancing accounts by putting several holes through the target which they were unable to touch.

We fell in with several parties of these sons of the forest on our way south along the western shore. The majority of them were Flatheads. We met a few Jockos also, but, although feeling not the least enmity toward each other, they never mix together in their social life. They are all inveterate gamblers. We landed one evening near by an encampment and finding them very sociable and friendly, took the liberty after a while of crawling into a tepee, from which issued a short rapping, accompanied with a monotonous "ugh, ugh, ugh." Five young bucks were ranged in a row, on their knees, along the right side of the tepee. Each one held in his hands two sticks, with which he was thumping a board before him, keeping time to the rattle of the sticks with the guttural "ugh."

Seated in front of the line was another buck, whose place it was to name the one who had in his possession a small piece of polished wood, which was being rapidly passed from hand to hand, with much feinting introduced to confuse him in his efforts to detect it. Each one, as he was caught, gave up his place to the seeker and paid a certain sum to the rest. Several dollars were lost and won in this manner while we sat and watched them.

Next day, as we paddled down past where our Indian friends had slept, we saw them striking their camp, making ready to travel in search of that variety of scene and surroundings which their restless nature demands. Two or three miles farther south we went ashore. It was a perfect day for fishing, a soft gray sky overhead and a light breeze blowing down the lake from the north. On this occasion my former luck deserted me. Three times did Ned land before I hooked a fish, and when hunger compelled us to abandon the sport he had sixteen to his credit, just double my catch.

All the next day we paddled steadily southward, running our bark ashore on a little island in the twilight. We spent one day sailing out and in among the straits which separate these charming little evergreen rocks; and on the next, which was the fifteenth of our cruise, we steered across the four miles of water which lie between them and the foot of the lake.

The stockman in whose keeping we had left our ponies undertook to have the bear skin cured for us, and in return we made a present to him of the *Sprite* [their canoe], feeling very sorry to leave the little craft in which we had made so enjoyable a trip.

Document 32

Accidental Killing of a Buffalo
on the Flathead Reservation in 1891
September 14, 1891

Source: "Killed a Big Buffalo," *The Anaconda Standard*, September 14, 1891, page 6, col. 1-2.

Editors' note: The Pablo-Allard buffalo herd on the reservation gave Duncan McDonald and many retired buffalo hunters a chance to relive the old days.

Killed a Big Buffalo
Exciting Scene Witnessed on the Flathead Reservation.
His Heart Was Broken
An Event Which Recalls the Thrilling Days in Montana's Early History
— A Genuine Buffalo Run.

The great heavens
Seem to stoop down upon the scene in love —
A nearer vault and of a ten lever blue
Than that which bends above our eastern hills.
As o'er the verdant waste I guide my steed,
Among the high rank grass that sweeps his sides,
The hollow beating of his footsteps seem
A sacrilegious sound. I think of those
Upon whose rest he tramples. Are they here —
The dead of other days? And did the dust
Of these fair solitudes once stir with life
*And burn with passion * * * * a race*
*That long has passed away? * * The red man*
Has left the blooming wilds he ranged so long,
And nearer to the Rocky mountains sought
*A wilder hunting ground. * * In these plains*
The bison feeds no more. Twice twenty leagues
Beyond remotest smoke of hunters camp
Roams the majestic brute in her is that shake
The earth with thundering steps — yet here I meet
His ancient footprints stamped beside the pool.

Twenty-five muscular Indians and half-breeds mounted on swift ponies, pursing a herd of 63 buffalo, was a sight it was my rare good fortune to witness on the Flathead Indian reservation about three weeks ago. A buffalo hunt in Montana 10 years ago would not have been considered a very novel or interesting event. To-day it is decidedly novel, and it is possible that the hunt or "battue" which took place last month is the last that will ever be witnessed on the plains of Montana.

Charles Allard, a wealthy half-breed living about midway between the foot of the Flathead lake and the Mission, is the owner of the only large herd of buffalo in the world. A few years ago when the noble animals had nearly all been slaughtered Allard rounded up a small herd and kept them for a time in a stockade on his ranch so the would be safe from the hunters who roamed the prairies shooting the animals for their skins. When the buffalo had all disappeared from the surrounding mountains and plains Allard turned his herd loose once more, and from that day to this they have roamed the vast prairies and threaded the mountain fastnesses of the Flathead reservation unmolested. Everyone knows that they belong to Allard and woe be unto the hunter who would dare to molest the splendid animals.

Starting with a herd of half a dozen, year after year they have increased and multiplied until at the time of the recent run there were 63 of the magnificent brutes in the herd. This season's calves number 16, and Allard has already refused $75,000 for the herd.

Allard wanted to corral one or two old buffaloes recently, and he requested the Indians in the neighborhood of his ranch to assist him in surrounding the herd and driving them in. The buffaloes in this herd are quite as wild and sensitive to the presence of man as were the thousands that roamed these plains in early days. The horsemen located the herd feeding quietly in a ravine away to the east of the prairie which stretches from the foot of the lake to the Northern Pacific railway, a distance of about 40 miles. With alacrity the breeds and braves responded to the summons to the "run." They had all participated in the buffalo chase in the days of the regretted past and wistfully they recalled the loved scenes of their former life. With their faces painted, their many-colored blankets wrapped around them, their long black hair flying in the breeze, the band of hunters presented a scene that would have delighted the heart of the old time trapper. They cautiously surrounded the ravine where the buffaloes were browsing leaving unguarded an avenue in the direction they desired the buffaloes to run. When the word was given the horsemen quickly advanced from all quarters to the brow of the hills surrounding the herd.

One noble old bull, one of the finest specimens of his splendid race ever seen, was peacefully feeding on the hillside near the top when suddenly an

Indian dashed over the crest of the hill. Instantly this king of the plains threw his head and tail into the air, and with a roar that made the surrounding hills tremble, dashed down into the center of his fellows at the bottom of the ravine.

And now the chase was on. Over the ridges swarmed the shouting hunters. Every side was surrounded but one. For that opening, towards the west, the frightened animals dashed bellowing and blowing like ten score of runaway locomotives. The thundering of their hoofs could be heard five miles away. With the shrewdness and ease that told of experience the Indians kept the herd surrounded on all sides except the direction they desired the animals to go. The ponies, though the best of their kind, with difficulty could keep up with the maddened brutes.

Before they had been running far a great bull with his muzzle protruding straight forward and horns thrown back upon his powerful shoulders, bellowing like an infuriated fiend, made a break from the line and rushed through the cordon of horsemen on the side and was soon unsurrounded upon the prairie, stamping and bellowing in a most terrifying manner.

Duncan McDonald of Ravalli instantly gave chase and no more exciting run was ever witnessed. Over the level brown prairies they shot, the bull frightful with rage and terror, hunter and horse alike intoxicated with the excitement of the chase. McDonald knew too well that soon the noble brute would fall exhausted and die broken-hearted upon the plain. He desired to capture, not to kill the animal, so he shouted to the horsemen who followed him to bring a lariat in order that the brute might be dragged down before he exhausted himself. But some of the other hunters were not as familiar with the buffalo as was McDonald and his advice to lasso the snorting animal was unheeded until the splendid creature tottered and fell. Then he was lassoed, the lariat being thrown around his neck. In a few moments he struggled to his feet and once more attempted to evade his pursuers. But this time he was hampered by the cruel rope which pressed upon his windpipe until he was choked to earth again.

"You must remove that rope from his neck or he will never get up," said McDonald to the other hunters. But they laughingly replied that "the buffalo is tough," and there was no danger.

There was danger, though. McDonald was right. In a few moments the great brute, which had all the time bellowed piteously, resumed its fierce struggles for liberty. But his efforts lacked strength; his huge black eyeballs began to glisten with an unnatural light; his elephantine sides heaved and fell with unwonted frequency; his beautiful black horns tore up the prairie and gored his own flashing sides that shone with an unpleasant polish in the sunlight; the thick, powerful muscles of his ponderous shoulders twitched convulsively. Suddenly he arose upon his haunches, shook the dust and grass roots from his shaggy hair, struggled as if to rise, then, with a roar that gradually merged into a heart-melting moan, he fell back — dead. His great heart was broken.

Sorrowfully, almost reverently, the astonished hunters approached the fallen monster and patted his massive body. Years ago they had killed many a bull as great as this one and not a pang had arisen in their hearts to mar the pleasure of their success. But times are altered. The death of this poor brute seemed to reproach them. They felt they had slaughtered a friend, a companion. It is said savagery is civilization's childhood. Perhaps that is true, but I could not help reflecting at this hour that too often we have made the noble savage an ignoble brute. The Indian is a sentimentalist. He weeps when moved with all the emotion of his white brother. Gazing upon the carcass of the dead buffalo tears glistened in the dusky eyes of more than one. It was an impressive scene.

The day was merging into evening. The hot sun, whose rays had contributed to the burdens of the poor dead brute, was dipping like a ball of fire below the western hills, throwing a flood of red light indescribably magnificent upon the illimitable waving brown prairie, the colors blending and separating with the gentle roll of the long gras[s]es, seemingly magnified toward the horizon into the distant heaving swell of the parti-colored sea.

"This makes me long for my breach-clout and blanket once more," said Duncan McDonald to me, as his bright eye scanned the recollection of departed days and the memory of the long ago past came flooding back upon him.

"In those days we were happy," he resumed. "We realized the charm of living in nature's boundless solitudes away from the restraints, the worries, and the conventionalities of a corroding civilization, amidst the surroundings that contributed to build up a healthy physical frame and a happy heart. Is it any wonder that I grow sad when I think of the days that are gone? I have stood upon the peak of yonder mountain and looked out upon these prairies when 10,000 of these noble beasts were feeding peacefully hereon. I had a good gun and plenty to eat and my liberty then. Now I look upon the same landscape but a changed scene. Not even a coyotte [sic] greets my eye to relieve the desolateness of the plain. We are all struggling after the almighty dollar, and our methods are surely not less savage than those we once employed to gain our livelihood upon these hills and plains. I must confess there are times in my life when I question the civilizing influences of civilization."

The speaker, Duncan McDonald, is a highly educated half-breed. In conversation, manner and mode of living he is a gentleman. He is wealthy, too, and has therefore all the advantages that civilization can bestow. Is it not singular you ask that he should pine for poverty and the past?

We came to the Indian, not the Indian to us. We were the aggressors. We invaded his territory and "made of it an aceldama of blood." With one hand we held before him the cross; with the other we cut him down with the sword. While we showed him that Christ's kingdom was peace, we showed him that man's mission was war. So far from bringing him the olive branch, we have brought him firearms and fire water and what was worse, the diseases of lust and an example of morals he has not been slow to follow. We speak of the failure of efforts to civilize, but we do not boast of the failure to exterminate. It may be that it needs but little familiarity with the actual, palpable aborigines to convince one that the poetic Indian, the Indian of Cooper and Longfellow, is only visible to the poetic eye. But while we divest the child of the woods of these fictional fascinations that have made him an interesting and picturesque figure in the world of our western humanity, we should not feel called upon to paint him in the pigments of the pit, or to endow him with the attributes of fiends. In mental characteristics the Indian differs from the European race. He is essentially a creature of instinct, a child of nature. In his native state we have proved him an hospitable, honest, faithful, brave, warlike, cruel, revengeful, relentless yet honorable, contemplative and religious being. They have learned their worst vices from contamination with Europeans and they deserve our sympathy as a people who are dying of broken hearts and who can never speak in the civilized world a word in their own defense. Is it any wonder that those present at the hour when Allard's buffalo fell grew sad and longed for the days that are gone forever?

> *An inexpressible sadness at thought of the homes they were leaving*
> *Hung like a cloud above them and shadowed the path before.*
> *Swift in their veins ran the hot vindictive blood of their fathers.*
> *Deep in their hearts lay a hatred strong and cruel as death.*

                                                                  J. M. K.

Anaconda, Sept. 12, 1891.

Document 33

Kootenai Indians Allotted North of Reservation

October 1891

Source: "Outside the Line," *Missoula Weekly Gazette*, October 7, 1891, page 1, col. 4; Peter Ronan, *Justice to Be Accorded to the Indians: Agent Peter Ronan Reports on the Flathead Indian Reservation, Montana, 1888-1893*, ed. Robert J. Bigart (Pablo, Mont.: Salish Kootenai College Press, 2014), pp. 248-252.

Editors' note: The Kootenai Indians had long used a meadow north of their village at Elmo for grazing and hay for their stock. They understood that this land was on the reservation, but the official survey ran the boundary line south of where the Kootenai expected. The official survey turned out to be in error in the tribes' twentieth century U.S. Court of Claims case, but in 1891 the Kootenai meadow land was considered public domain. Agent Peter Ronan made off-reservation allotments to Kootenai farmers north of the reservation and the Kootenai proceeded to improve their allotments. However, see the newspaper articles below for December 13, 1891, and August 10, 1892, about white trespassers forcing the Kootenai farmers off their improved farms. See Peter Ronan, *"A Great Many of Us Have Good Farms": Agent Peter Ronan Reports on the Flathead Indian Reservation, Montana, 1877-1887*, ed. Robert J. Bigart (Pablo, Mont.: Salish Kootenai College Press, 2014), pages 219-222 for more information on the boundary problem.

Outside the Line.
The Indians North of the Flathead Reservation.
They May Acquire the Lands on Which They Have Settled
by Proper Application.

It was discovered last year that a number of Indians in the Flathead country were located upon lands lying outside of the northern boundary of the Flathead Reservation. Major [Peter] Ronan wrote to Washington about it, saying that according to the survey the boundary would run close to the Kootenai village or settlement on Dayton creek, and that it would take from the Indians land which they claimed on that creek ever since the Stevens treaty, cutting in two a large meadow where the Indians cut their winter's supply of hay for their stock. Major Ronan suggested that, in order to avoid trouble between the Indians and whites, the northern boundary be placed where it had always been considered to be by the Stevens treaty, instead of where the survey actually determined it to be. The department, however, found it impossible to comply with this suggestion and requested the major to explain the matter to the Indians. This the major did and urged on such Indians as were north of the line, the necessity of securing their claims to the lands occupied by them by fencing and improving the same. Upon a recent visit to these Indians the major found that his advice had largely been followed and that some seventeen heads of families over twenty-one years of age of the Kootenai tribe had fenced and improved their ground and planted small crops of grain. The major then wrote again to Washington, asking to be advised as to the proper steps to take in order to save these Indians their homes and to assist them in acquiring title to the same.

The reply to this request from Major Ronan is that as the lands in question are non-reservation lands, and as the Indians were residing on them at the date of the approval of the general allotment act, February 8, 1887, they should be allotted to the Indians under the fourth section thereof, as amended by act of February 28, 1891. By this act each Indian, whether adult or minor, married or single, is allowed, if entitled to an allotment, eighty acres, unless it is valuable only for grazing purposes, in which case allotments may be made in double quantities. In accordance with these instructions Major Ronan has presented to the land office here nineteen applications for the lands in question which will be forwarded to the general land office and allotments made. The major completed the work of preparing and presenting these applications day before yesterday and they will be passed upon at once.

* * * * * * * *

United States Indian Service,
Flathead Agency,
October 30th, 1891.

Hon. Commissioner Indian Affairs
Washington, D.C.
Sir:

Referring to "Land 31598 — 1891," dated at Washington, September 7th, 1891, in which it was stated that my communication of the 25th of August, received your attention, wherein I reported that I visited, at the request of chief Eneas and his head men, the Kootenai Indians residing at Dayton Creek, on the Flathead reservation, in order to fully report to your office, upon their request, in regard to certain lands which they honestly considered as rightfully belonging to them under treaty stipulations and which they have always occupied.

You referred also to the fact that I stated that the decision of your office, rendered November 10th, 1890, relative to the boundary of the reservation was announced January, 1891; that it was fully explained to them that it was impossible to accept other boundaries than those clearly defined in the treaty of July 16, 1855; that I endeavored to convince them that the line as run by Deputy Surveyor Harrison, was in the strictest accordance with the provisions of the treaty; that I then urged upon the Indians the necessity of securing their claims to the lands occupied by them by fencing and improving the same; and that they believed they were entitled to the lands lying West of Flathead Lake and North of Clarkes Fork of the Columbia river, segregated from the reservation by the survey of the said Deputy Surveyor, under his contract dated April 18, 1887.

I further stated that in obedience to my request, seventeen heads of families, over 21 years of age, of the Kootenai tribe of Indians commenced fencing and improving the lands claimed and occupied by them outside of the reservation boundary as designated by the Harrison survey; that upon my recent visit to these Indians I made personal investigation in regard to such claims; that I found the Indians whose names I furnished had not only fenced to some extent the lands claimed, but had also, on some tracts, planted small crops of grain and were then engaged in harvesting the same; that they were anxious to be assured that their lands would not be taken from them by either the Government or the whites who are now ready to "pounce" upon them.

In accordance with my request to be advised as to the proper steps to take in order to save these Indians their homes and to assist them in acquiring title to the same you have to State:

"1st. That you will at once forward a description of the lands claimed by the said Indians to the local Land office of the District in which the lands are situated, and call attention of the local Land Officers to the General Land Office circular relative to lands in the possession of Indian occupants, issued October 27, 1887, whereby Registers and Receivers are every where instructed to peremtorily [sic] refuse all enteries [sic] and filings attempted to be made by other than Indian occupants upon lands in the possession of Indians who have made improvements of any value whatever thereon (copy furnished[)].

"2d. As the lands referred to are non-reservation lands, and as the Indians were residing thereon at the date of the approval of the General Allotment Act, February 8th, 1887, they should be allotted to the Indians under the 4th Section thereof, as amended by Act of February 28th, 1891 (26 Stats., 794.)

"You will therefore at your earliest convenience proceed to that locality for the purpose of assisting these Indians in making applications for allotments under the said Acts, (copies enclosed[)].

"I enclose also for your information and use in connection with this work, copy of circular issued September 17th, 1887, by the Department, showing what is necessary to be done, how to proceed, and the proof required under the Act first named, and copy of circular issued by the Department July 2d, 1891, setting forth the amendments to the General Allotment Act as made by Act of February 28, 1891.

"You will observe from the Act and circular last referred to that each Indian whether adult or minor, married or single, is allowed, if entitled to an allotment 80 acres each, and furnishing the proof required, if there is sufficient land subject to allotment in that vicinity. If there is not enough land for that purpose, you will first allot to heads of families, in tracts of eighty acres each, and next to worthy and industrious young men, then if there is still land left you will pro rata the same among the minor members of the families referred to in tracts of not less than forty acres each, and aid them in making application for allotment of the same.

"As above stated if the lands applied for or any legal subdivisions thereof are valuable only for grazing purposes, the same may be allotted in double quantities, and you will carry out this provision of the Allotment Acts, if it is ascertained there is enough land to do so.

"If the lands are unsurveyed, the applications should contain a description of the same by metes and bounds beginning with some natural object, or a permanent artificial monument or mound set for the purpose, or in such other manner as to admit of its being readily identified when the lines of the official survey come to be extended.

"When the applications shall have been made, you will deliver the same to the local land officers of the district wherein the lands are situated for certification by the Register, to the effect that there is no prior valid adverse claim to the lands applied for and described in each application, and to be forwarded by them to the General Land Office for Consideration and action."

In accordance with foregoing instructions, on the 18th day of September, 1891, I proceeded to the Kootenai village, on Dayton Creek, on this reservation, where I held council with Chief Eneas of the Kootenai Indians, and his band. After listening to the interpretation of my instructions from your office in regard to allotments of lands outside of the Northern boundary of their reservation, as surveyed by Deputy Surveyor Harrison, the Chief expressed for himself and his Indians, their gratitude to the Government and the Indian Office, for being allowed to get title, and to occupy the lands which they always believed to belong to them in accordance with the provisions of the treaty of 1855, but cut off on account of misunderstanding as to the exact point half way in latitude between the Northern and Southern extremities of the Flathead Lake. The Indians, always claiming the point, to be some six miles further North, until an actual survey decided the line as running very near to the Kootenai village, on Dayton Creek, and cutting off from them land which they and their fathers always claimed to be inside of the Northern Boundary of the Flathead reservation.

On the 23d of September, I commenced making the allotments, as designated by the Indians, to the following list of claimants, all being over twenty-one years of age and the head of a family.

No. 1. Antoine Dominic, 160 acres for Grazing purposes.
No. 2. Philip Kunikuka 80 acres for Farming purposes.
No. 3. Abraham Kanmekolla, 160 acres for Grazing purposes.
No. 4. Mat Kowiltawaam 160 acres for Grazing purposes.
No. 5. John Kallawat 160 acres for Grazing purposes.
No. 6. Patrick Kitcowholakoo, 80 acres for Agricultural purposes.
No. 7. William Kanklutepleta, 160 acres for Grazing purposes.
No. 8. Joseph Chuakenmum 80 acres for Agricultural purposes.
No. 9. Custa Smoketmalsukes 160 acres for Grazing purposes.
No. 10. Patrick Koskolt, 160 acres for Grazing purposes.
No. 11. George Kolkonee, 160 acres for Grazing purposes.
No. 12. Paul Chatchadoman 160 acres for Grazing purposes.
No. 13. Joseph Jean Jan Graw 160 acres for Grazing purposes.
No. 14. Bazile Tatscum 160 acres for Grazing purposes.
No. 15. Francis Nacksaw 160 acres for Grazing purposes.
No. 16. Malta Sechkolke 160 acres for Grazing purposes.
No. 17. Isaac Paul 160 acres for Grazing purposes.
No. 18. Lemo Wahomne, 160 acres for Grazing purposes.

No. 19. Jena Jan Graw, 160 acres for Grazing purposes.

This number of allotments to heads of families, being all the lands which Kootenai Indians claimed, or asked for, outside of the point half way in latitude between the Northern and Southern extremities of the Flathead Lake, as established by Deputy Surveyor Harrison, who ran the line due West therefrom. I trust, as the lands in question were unsurveyed at the time I made the allotments, that no prior valid adverse claim to the lands applied for and described in each application, will be made or substantiated. This allotment will have the effect to satisfy the Indians that no attempt has been made by the Government, in making the survey, to take from them any land that they have heretofore claimed or occupied in the honest belief that such land was inside of the boundary of the Flathead reservation.

Being advised that Non Mineral Affidavits required to be made before either the Rigister or Receiver of the Land District in which the land is situated, or before the Judge or Clerk of any Court of Record having a seal, I proceeded to Missoula, and applied to Judge Marshall, of the Circuit Court of Montana for the appointment of Eugene Humbert, as Deputy Clerk of said Court, with power to take Indian depositions, in order that the seal of the Court might be attached, without bringing the Indians, applying for allotments, either before the Register and Receiver of the local Land Office or a Clerk of a Court having a seal. This was done in the interest of economy as the Indians making applications, according to my information would be required to appear in person to make affidavit "either before the Register or Receiver of the Land District in which the land is situated, or before the Judge, or Clerk of any Court of record having a seal." Transportation would involve a distance by horseback or wagon, and by rail, of about one hundred miles, while subsistence etc., etc. for the Indian applicants would make the bill of expense a large one.

In the Second place the Chief especially requested that the Allotment papers be made legal without bringing the applicants to the town of Missoula, and thus avoid the annoyance which the temptations of the place and its surroundings might produce among the Indian applicants for title to their lands. The appointed Deputy Clerk of the Court accompanied me to the Indian village and witnessed their marks. I have the honor herewith to enclose receipt from the Register of the local Land Office for said applications and also vouchers covering expenses in the execution and completion of this work, and have the honor to be

Very respectfully
Your obedient Servant
Peter Ronan
United States Indian Agent.

First Enclosure:

Copy of notice

To whom it may concern

   I claim this land as an Indian homestead, from this post or tree North one mile and east and west one Quarter of a mile. taken under instruction of the Commissioner of Indian Affairs to Peter Ronan, U.S. Indian Agent dated Sept 7th, 1891.

Antice Dominick
his X mark

witness
Peter Ronan, U S Indian Agent
Robert Irvine.

Document 34

White Trespassers Force Kootenai Farmers Off Their Allotments December 1891

Source: "Drove the Indians Off," *The Helena Independent*, December 13, 1891, page 1, col. 7; "The Flathead Trouble," *The Helena Independent* (daily), December 22, 1891, page 1, col. 6.

Editors' note: Agent Peter Ronan spent considerable time in the last three years of his life trying to get the United States Government to protect the rights of the Kootenai Indian allottees north of the Flathead Reservation boundary. At one point he was able to get the United States Marshal to remove whites who had trespassed on the allotments, but unfortunately the white men just returned after the marshal left. See the numerous Ronan letters to the Commissioner of Indian Affairs about the trespassers in Peter Ronan, *Justice To Be Accorded To the Indians: Agent Peter Ronan Reports on the Flathead Indian Reservation, Montana, 1888-1893*, ed. Robert J. Bigart (Pablo, Mont.: Salish Kootenai College Press, 2014), pages 225 through 367. After Ronan's death in 1893, the Flathead Indian agents paid little attention to the rights of the Kootenai allottees and the government left the white trespassers in possession of the lands until the early twentieth century when the trespassers were allowed to pay small sums to the Kootenai to relinquish their rights. See also the August 10, 1892, article below.

Drove the Indians Off.
Armed White Men Jump Lands Alloted to the Kootenai Indians.
Major Ronan Averts Trouble Until the Authorities at Washington Can Act.
The Attorney General Instructs the United States Marshal to Drive the Jumpers Off.

Arlee, Mont. Dec. 12. — [Special.] — Trouble is brewing in the northern part of the Flathead reservation between some claim jumpers and several Indian families who were placed on allotment lands on Dayton creek a short time ago. Under orders from the authorities at Washington Major [Peter] Ronan, agent of the Flatheads, located nineteen Kootenai families on choice land bordering on Dayton creek which had been set apart for them. To-day a force of twenty-five men, fully armed with Winchesters, drove to the section occupied by the Kootenai and jumped the lands, driving the Indians off with hostile demonstrations. The young bucks among the Kootenais wanted to make a fight when the order was given by the leader of the jumpers for the Indians to move, but the old men of the families prevailed upon them to make no resistance. It has been difficult for the old men to hold the bucks in restraint as long as they have, and it is only to the assurances of Major Ronan to see that they are righted have the Kootenais preserved a non-hostile stillness. They have agreed with the agent to remain quiet until he can arrange with the federal authorities to have the claim jumpers driven off and the families put in possession of their lands. Major Ronan has been in communication with the commissioner of Indian affairs by wire this afternoon. The commissioner telegraphs him that the attorney general has instructed the United States Marshal at Helena to render Major Ronan any assistance necessary. The commissioner does not think that it will be necessary to call for troops unless the jumpers should defy the authority of the marshal and his deputies.

* * * * * * * *

The Flathead Trouble.
Five of the Jumpers Still Hold the Land on Dayton Creek.
They Send a Message to the United States Marshal at Helena.
The Dispossessed Nineteen Kootenai Families Patiently Waiting for the Government to Act.

United States Marshall Furay received a letter yesterday from his deputy on the Flathead reservation, who started a week ago last Saturday to order off the white men who jumped lands on Dayton creek, allotted to nineteen Kootenai families, in the northern part of the reservation. The deputy found the twenty-five jumpers on the land when he reached there. All but five said they would obey the marshal's orders. The five who would not leave sent word by the deputy to the marshal that he would have to come and put them off. Yesterday afternoon the marshal telegraphed to Attorney General Miller for further instructions, which he expects to receive to-day. Meanwhile the Kootenais who were driven off are patiently waiting until the complications of red tape are overcome, replying upon the assurances of Major Ronan, of the Flathead agency, that the Great Father will see justice is done them.

The real origin of most of the disturbances in this region is perhaps the possession by the Indians of coveted lands. The valleys they occupy are well watered; there is good timber on the reservation, and it is thought also to possess mineral wealth. Its advantages are not wholly thrown away on the

Indians, as some of them are good farmers, and not only raise their own wheat, but have it ground into flour at their own mill. The Flatheads have always had the reputation of being friendly to the government, especially those in the lake region, although the Kootenais, of Tobacco Plains, further north, are said to be less placable [sic], and have been accused of various murders. The Flatheads have for more than thirty years had the advantage of the Catholic mission, which has labored faithfully among them. As an offset, the Indians are sometimes supplied with whisky, and troubles come from that source. Still, the constant desire to encroach upon these fertile lands is doubtless at the bottom of the race feuds. When a brawl occurs in which a white man is concerned, if he proves the victim there is a great outcry, and the sheriff and perhaps the militia are called in, but the regulars from the nearest post generally quiet the disturbance.

In the summer of 1889 there was serious fear of a conflict, arising from the fact that the sheriff of Missoula county was upon the reservation to arrest three Indians accused of murder. He took a posse of citizens with him and killed one Indian on the reservation; but fortunately three companies of the Twenty-fifth infantry were despatched [sic] from Fort Missoula, and no outbreak occurred. The following years there was more trouble, arising from the killing of an Indian and a white, and again troops went up from Fort Missoula. Now for a third successive year come disturbances.

That the authorities will protect the rights of the Kootenai families whom they established on the reservation may be taken for granted. The government and the people of that region have profited of late by the willingness of various bands of Indians to remove from lands in Idaho, Washington, and elsewhere, and settle on the Jocko reservation. An important agreement was made for that purpose not long ago. And since the existing troubles may call the attention of congress to that region it would do well to supply some legislation needed to maintain the good faith of the government. Under the provisions of the act of March 2, 1889, the band of Flatheads living in Bitter Root valley agreed to give up a tract including 7,871 acres, and to go upon the Jocko reservation. The reason for this removal was the desire of the neighboring people to purchase the lands. The Bitter Root valley, according to a description furnished by the interior department, "is one of the most attractive and lovely in our country. The high mountains on either hand supply it with the clearest and coolest streams, and the soil under ordinary irrigation bears grain, grasses and fruits in abundance and perfection. The climate is most healthful, and here this tribe for many years lived in peace and comparative comfort. The Jocko reservation is, however, also good land, and well watered, and as the new state, Montana, demands as much fertile soil as can be found available in its borders the retirement of the Indian seemed desirable." Congress at its last session made the necessary appropriation to remove them, and their old lands were offered for sale, under the law requiring that the amount so received should be paid to them in their new home or be expended for their support.

Unfortunately, at the sale last October only a very small portion of the land could be disposed of at the appraised value and the prospect was of no further sales for a long time. Nevertheless, the Indians consented to leave their home and trust to the government to take care of them. The band was that of Charlos, "a man of great intelligence and elevated character," who had suffered wrongs, as he thought, in previous dealings with the whites, but did not allow this sentiment to influence him. His people marched to the church carrying the Stars and Stripes and held a service there. Then the removal was carried out. Congress has accordingly been asked to make an appropriation for their support during the present winter, and this subject should receive due attention. That those Indians, also, who removed from other homes at the wish of the government and were placed by authority on lands of the Flathead reservation should be protected from the attacks of armed men cannot be doubted.

Document 35

Indian Police Arrest Tribal Members in Missoula

February–March 1892

Source: "The Bad Women," *The Weekly Missoulian*, February 17, 1892, page 3, col. 3; Peter Ronan, *Justice to Be Accorded to the Indians: Agent Peter Ronan Reports on the Flathead Indian Reservation, Montana, 1888-1893*, ed. Robert J. Bigart (Pablo, Mont.: Salish Kootenai College Press, 2014), pages 283-284.

Editors' note: In 1892 efforts by Flathead Reservation tribal police to arrest tribal members in Missoula brought up questions of jurisdiction.

The Bad Women.
How the Indians Punish Those Guilty of Violating the Regulations.

Elsewhere is a paragraph stating some fifteen Indian police are in the city from the reservation to arrest a number of the recalcitrant members of the Flathead tribe. The reasons for arrest are various. Some were charged with a general violation of the Indian laws, others with gambling, horse stealing, running away with other men's wives, etc.

It is known the Indians have their own laws and courts of justice, which they aim to enforce; but as a rule it appears the punishment is made to fit the case; that is, the guilty Indian is "sized up" beforehand.

This afternoon a representative of the *Missoulian* asked Agent [Peter] Ronan a few questions about these Indian regulations. He said those charged with any of the offenses are arrested by the Indian police and taken before the four judges. Their laws are printed, but it is not presumed the Indian judges, in handing down decisions, stop to read the laws, though Agent Ronan did not say so.

In the cases of gambling, stealing ponies, etc., the most frequent punishment is confinement in the jail for a short time. If an offender is known to have money, he is usually fined so many dollars, and if he has a good deal of money, horses and cattle to spare, his fine is apt to be heavy. If an Indian steals a horse from a neighbor he is usually required to return the cayuse and make suitable restitution in silver dollars.

This forenoon three Indians were arrested here to be taken back, and other arrests were expected. Two of them were women. It seems the Indian ladies are very precise in their demands upon their husbands in this enlightened age. If their bucks don't come up to the stratch in providing for them in every particular, they are apt to kick, perhaps elope with some other fellow.

Agent Ronan says that in case of desertion or elopement, an effort is usually made to get the couple together. If a married woman runs off with some handsomer fellow, she is induced to go back to her home if possible. If the Indian running away with her can pay as damages a medium cayuse, it may be satisfactory, but if he can put up a couple of fine young ponies, the offended husband is apt to consider the affair greatly to his advantage, and the pipe of peace is smoked around the camp fire in the evening, all the neighbors being invited.

* * * * * * *

United States Indian Service,
Flathead Agency,
March 8th, 1892.

Hon. Commissioner Indian Affairs,
Washington, D.C.
Sir:

I have to report that occasionally young Indians of bad habits lure to the towns young s....s, and sometimes the wives of Indians of good character, where they establish camps, and use the women for immoral purposes to obtain whisky, or money upon which to gamble. The better class of Indians on the reservation feel the disgrace of such conduct, and the Indian police receive orders from the Indian Judges to arrest such class, bring them back to the reservation, give them a trial before the Court of Indian Offences and sentence them to fines, imprisonment, or hard labor for transgression of Indian laws governing the reservation. When the transgressor is a married woman who deserts her husband she and her paramour are held in jail and an effort is made by the judges to conciliate the husband and wife, who generally live together again.

On the 11th of February the captain of the Indian police, with fourteen of his men, proceeded to Missoula to arrest a number of women and men of the class described. I gave the police Captain a letter to the Sheriff of Missoula County, Montana, explaining the business and asking as a matter of courtesy and in the interest of the people of the town of Missoula, as well a comon decency toward the Indians of the reservation, to give the police moral support in ridding the community of such a class. The Indian police succeeded in making the arrests and the County sheriff kindly allowed eight of the worst characters to be placed in the County jail for a few hours, or until the Western bound Northern Pacific railroad train arrived at the depot at Missoula, when the Indian prisoners would be transferred by the Indian police to the cars and brought to this reservation. I was notified that a citizen of Missoula employed an attorney and that a writ had been served upon the Sheriff requiring that the Indians be released from arrest. At the hour set for the hearing of the case before District Judge [Charles S.] Marshall, — deeming it for the best interest of the Indian service — with an employed Attorney, met the case. An afternoon was passed in court in the argument of legal points before the Judge. The Captain of the Indian police was made to testify and I was also called upon to testify before the Court in regard to the status of the Indian Court of offences. The Judge finally decided to place the prisoners in custody of the Indian police, and they were taken back to the reservation. There were four Indian women among the prisoners who were married and who had deserted their husbands to live a life of shame with the four Indian men who were arrested at the same time. The Indian Court of offence will hear the cases and all will be settled according to the regulations, sense of justice and regard for suppression of such disgraceful conduct. I herewith enclose bills that were necessary for me to make in order to enforce right and justice to the Indians in accordance with the law of the State and I trust my action will receive your endorsement and approval. I herewith enclose newspaper clippings regarding the affair.

I was compelled to employ council as the United States Attorney resides at Helena, the Capital of this State, and before he could be summoned in the case, the arrested Indians would probably be discharged under the writ of habeas corpus, a procedure that would have, in my opinion, a very bad effect upon the future effectiveness of the Indian police, when called upon to do duty outside of the boundary line of the reservation. Trusting that my action in the case will receive the approval of the Hon. Commissioner of Indian Affairs,

I have the honor to be

Very respectfully,
Your obedient Servant,
Peter Ronan,
U.S. Indian Agent.

Document 36

Alcohol Fueled Party Brings Assault Verdict

May 19, 1892

Source: "Drunken Dance," *Helena Journal* (daily), May 19, 1892, page 5, col. 3.

Editors' note: Much of the newspaper reporting from the Flathead Reservation in the 1890s emphasized crime and law and order.

Drunken Dance.
It Resulted in an Assault for Which Barnaby is Found Guilty.

The story of a drunken Indian dance was told in the United States circuit court yesterday by copper-colored narrators.

Its sequel took the form of a verdict, returned about half past four in the afternoon, declaring Adolph Barnaby guilty of murderous assault upon Alex Ashley on the Flathead reservation.

It was on the night of February 19th last that the melee occurred which resulted in the crime for which Barnaby is to be punished. It was a sort of aboriginal accompaniment to the tripping of the feathery moccasin.

But it proved an expensive accompaniment. The Indians themselves have come to that conclusion. Yesterday afternoon, after the trial, a dozen of them stood bunched before the window to Clerk Geo. Sproule's office drawing their orders for witness fees.

"And you are the fellow that gave this dance," said the clerk to John Lumphreys, when his turn came to tell how far he had had to come so that his mileage could be recorded.

"Uh huh," was the gutteral affirmative from the dusky Blackfoot [sic].

"Purty big cost that dance was," suggested another Indian as he eyed the large pile of orders accumulating before the clerk.

"Yes, heap cost," admitted John as he reached over for his order of $27 for mileage.

"Better not have no more dances like that, John," admonished a half-breed.

"No, me no have dance that kind some more," responded John, and he pushed the order down in his pocket in a satisfied sort of way as if he were applying balm to his penitent spirit.

The trial of the case against Barnaby took up the greater part of the day before Judge Knowles. It was a little after 4 o'clock when the case was given to the jury. A verdict of guilty was returned in about twenty minutes.

After the reading of the verdict District Attorney Weed entered a nolle pros in the case of the government against Felix Barnaby. The indictment, it appeared, had been made exactly the same as in the case of Adolph Barnaby, while the nature of the assault was different. Adolph had used used [sic] a knife as a weapon while Felix had used a stone.

Document 37

Michel Rivais Tells About His Life

May 25, 1892

Source: "An Intellectual Indian," *The Kalispell Graphic*, May 25, 1892, page 6, col. 2.

Editors' note: This article included some interesting biographical information about Michel Rivais the blind longtime government interpreter at the Flathead Agency.

An Intellectual Indian.

Michel Rivais is the name of the interpreter in several cases of the government against Indians now occupying the attention of the United States court. He looks to be a full blood Indian. His grandfather was a Frenchman and his father a half-breed, but his mother was a full blood Flathead. The nationality of his grandfather explains why such a name as Rivais should be attached to an Indian.

He was born in Oregon fifty-seven years ago. Michel Rivais is an intellectual Indian. He speaks English, French and three Indian languages.

Rivais got his education at Vancouver after which he returned to his tribe the Pend d'Oreilles. He married a full blood Flathead s.... and has two children neither of whom can speak English.

"I was never engaged in any of the regular battles between the whites and Indians, he said to a Journal reporter. "But we used to have some hard fights between ourselves. Along about eighteen or twenty years ago we, the Flatheads, were frequently encountering the Blackfeet and they in turn would attack us. Up and above Fort Benton was our fighting ground and some bloody wars we have fought."

"What was the object of this continual fighting?"

"Oh, we fought for fun. We liked it. They would steal our horses and get us to fight and we would reciprocate. You remember our brave old chief, Alexander. He lived to be an old Indian. Between wars we would hunt buffalo. We also chased deer, elk and antelope."

"What are the causes of the decimation of your race?"

"Well, they die off. In the first place only a few have children. Most of them marry but few have offspring. Then they die of consumption and scrofula. Consumption is brought on by exposure. The Indians are not adapted physically to indoor life. In the winter they lie and sweat in a warm house and then go out in the snow in moccasins and blankets. They take no care of their bodies and the race is fast becoming extinct. There are only 200 Flatheads. An Indian rarely lived to be over 50, though we have to or three who are nearly a hundred. The most deaths occur between twenty-five and fifty. It seems impossible to adapt ourselves to civilization."

— Helena Journal.

Michel Revais
Source: Missoula Publishing Co., *Flathead Facts: Descriptive of the Resources of Missoula County* (Missoula, Mont.: Missoula Publishing Co., 1890),
page 22.

Document 38

White Trespassers on
Kootenai Indian Allotments
August 10, 1892

Source: "The Indian Trouble," *Missoula Weekly Gazette*, August 10, 1892, page 1, col. 1-2.

Editors' note: The long running troubles over the Kootenai Indian allotments north of the Flathead Reservation boundary were outlined in the October 7, 1891, and December 13, 1891, articles and annotations above. Despite Agent Peter Ronan's efforts, in the end the United States Government failed to protect the rights of the Kootenai allottees.

The Indian Trouble
Concerning the Hay Cutting on Allotment Lands.
The Story of How the Trouble First Started
and What Its Present Status Is.

The story of the trouble between the Indians and whites at Dayton creek, which began last month and is not yet settled, concerning the cutting of hay on Indian allotment lands, is about as follows:

On the 25th of July Major [Peter] Ronan received word from James Kerr, captain of the steamboat, State of Montana, that a warrant had been issued for the arrest of Chief Eneas on the charge that the chief had ordered Eugene McCarthy off his own ranch, saying that if he did not vacate he (the chief) would kill him.

Major Ronan at once wired United Jtates [sic] Marshal Furay to instruct his deputies to make no arrest of Chief Eneas for threatening violence to a jumper of the Indian allotment lands until he could arrive on the scene and make investigation. The Major left the agency at once, and reached Dayton creek on the morning of July 27th, after having also wired what he had done to the commissioner of Indian affairs at Washington. When the Major reached Dayton creek he learned from Chief Eneas that allotment No. 19, made to Jean Jan Graw, September 26, 1891, and allotment No. 13, made the same time to the same person, were occupied by white men who were cutting hay, despite the fact that on allotment No. 19 the Indian or half-breed occupant had a house, barn, a cultivated field enclosed with a stack of hay of at least fifty tons, cut last year. The Indian family claim that the hay on this allotment has been cut and stacked by them for the last twelve years. Allotment No. 13 has a log cabin, a small enclosure for a garden, and the hay has been cut by the family for several years. The chief being a suf[f]erer from rheumatism was carried to a wagon and taken to allotment No. 19. Not having an interpreter, he claims he made the white men working in the hay field understand as best he could that the ground belonged to his people by years of occupancy as well as by allotment from the government of the United States, and asked them to vacate. The whites did this but swore out a warrant against the chief in the town of Demersville, before a justice of the peace, who sent a constable on the reservation to make the arrest. The chief resisted the arrest by stating that he was too ill to leave his home. The chief then sent a messenger to the agency to apprise the major of the circumstances. The trip from the agency to Dayton Creek involves a distance of about seventy miles. The day after the major's arrival at that place the constable from Demersville made his appearance, and demanded the arrest of the chief, stating that if he refused to accompany him a posse of citizens were likely to march to the reserve and make the arrest by force of arms. The major sent for the chief, who was hauled to his camp by his Indians in a wagon. He was willing to go before the court, but felt in his condition the trip would be death to him. Therefore, in order to preserve peace and to prevent the coming of an armed posse of excited people to the Kootenai Indian village to arrest their chief, the major volunteered to accompany the constable to Demersville, where he went before the justice of the peace who issued the warrant and signed a bond in the sum of $500 to bring Chief Eneas before his court on the 2nd day of October, 1892, to answer the charge preferred against him if he were alive and able to come. The major then returned to his camp and sent word to the trespassers on allotments 19 and 13 to appear before him at his camp where he would try to explain to their satisfaction that they were trespassers upon Indian allotments, and that time, trouble and expense would be saved if his advice was listened to. A curt reply was received that they intended to cut hay and hold the ground unless arrested by the United States marshal, and that if the Indians attempted to cut the hay they would have them arrested by state authorities. Before appearing before the justice of the peace at Demersville the major sent word to the United States District Attorney Weed at Helena about as follows:

"Trespassers on Indian allotments refuse to vacate unless arrested by United States authority. The best interests of Indian service and justice to settlers demand that a test case be made by arrest of one or two trespassers. Send Marshal Furay in person. I shall remain on the ground until he arrives. No posse will be necessary. Allotments were made to Indians according to law and department instructions. An avoidance of bloodshed demands immediate action."

To this the major received reply that Marshal Furay was not in Helena and that his whereabouts were unknown, but that as soon as he could be found he would be notified. The major then ordered the Indians back on the ground and set them to work cutting hay. He asked the justice of the peace at Demersville to notify the trespassers not to come again on allotments Nos. 19 and 13 under penalty of arrest, and having put the Indians in possession without the aid of the United States marshal, he returned to his camp only to find there a dispatch, under date of August 6, to the effect that the whites in the vicinity of Bonner's Ferry were cutting hay off of Indian locations. The major wired the commissioner of Indian affairs that he would leave the agency August 10 to go to Bonner's Ferry to carry out the commissioner's instructions with regard to certain allotment of lands to Indians in that section. "Land 23,602, authority 31,323," under date of Washington, July 7, 1892.

The major has accordingly left for Bonner's Ferry. In his report to the commissioner of Indian affairs he says:

"I expect to find locations and lands of the Indians occupied by white men, who will persist in cutting hay and otherwise trespassing. I therefore desire that full instructions be forwarded to me at Bonner's Ferry, Idaho, as to what authorities I shall call upon, and what steps I shall take to give Indians that occupy their lands in Idaho, full, free and uninterrupted occupancy of the same and the right to cut their hay without molestation. Unless I have some authoritative instructions to act or call upon state or United States authorities to aid me in this work my presence there will be a useless failure, and I trust that I shall be sustained by the Indian office in doing justice to Indians as well as white occupants of public land, in my humble capacity as Indian agent acting under orders from the honorable commissioner of Indian affairs."

Document 39

John Aneas Visits Western Montana

October 7, 1892

Source: "A Returned Wanderer," *Morning Missoulian*, October 7, 1892, page 5, col. 1.

Editors' note: Biographical information about John Aneas, a Salish mixed-blood.

A Returned Wanderer.
John Aeneas Visits Missoula After 28 Years' Absence.

John Aneas, a halfbreed Flathead Indian, arrived in town this morning riding a horse on which he has travelled 600 miles. This is his first visit here after an absence of twenty-eight years at which time he knew everybody in this vicinity and the Bitter Root valley. He was the intimate friend of most of the pioneers of this section of the country, many of whom have passed away during his absence, and he has the earlier history of the county at his tongue's end. He speaks English, French and Spanish fluently and is a man of very great intelligence. He has the appearance of being about 60 years of age but says he is 83. He is the owner of a fine ranch in Wyoming where he has a large family and where he raises cattle and crops. He naturally is lost in the new Missoula so different from the little settlement of long ago and can hardly be made to believe that the Bitter Root valley lies beyond the little colony of beautiful homes he sees in South Missoula. He is a very well dressed man, and while he would be recognized anywhere for what he is he has a well-to-do appearance in striking contrast to the average half-breed of this section of country. He wears a sombrero, a woolen shirt, blanket-lined overalls and moccasins. His hair is long and thick and has hardly a gray strand in it. Since leaving here he has been all over the United States and as far south as Mexico. He says he is here on business.

Document 40

Reporter Described Indian Workers on Irrigation Ditch December 12, 1892

Source: "How the Indians Work," *The Anaconda Standard*, December 12, 1892, page 8, col. 1-2.

Editors' note: The reporter described the scene as Indians workers dug the new irrigation ditch in the Jocko Valley. Some misspellings and typographical errors have been left in the text.

How the Indians Work
Present Busy Scenes on the Flathead Reservation.
Excavating Big Ditches
Major Ronan's Charges Handling Picks and Shovels —
A True Solution of a Problematic Question.

Special Correspondence of the Standard.

Missoula, Dec. 10. — This week the *Standard* reporter visited the Flathead agency and was surprised to note the busy scenes around its immediate vicinity. United States Indian Agent [Peter] Ronan last month was notified by the commissioner of Indian affairs that authority was granted him to construct an irrigation ditch for the use of the Bitter Root Flathead Indians, settled near the agency. A survey has already been made of the ditch converting the waters of a never-failing stream that flows from a mountain lake in the rear of the agency, which is a natural reservoir, it and will cover a vast area of rich agricultural land selected by Chief Charlot and his band of Flatheads, removed from the Bitter Root valley to the Jocko reservation.

The ditch is of the following dimensions: 2 feet deep, 3 feet wide on the bottom and 4 feet wide on the top, with a fall of one-fourth of an inch to the rod and a water capacity of 1,000 inches, miner's measurement. The work of excavation is being entirely done by Indian labor. The Indians take contracts by the rod — in hard, rocky diggings they are allowed $3 a rod and upwards. In less difficult places they get from $2 to $2.50 a rod. It is an amusing sight to watch the Indians engaged in their work of excavation. They are all anxious to complete their contracts and collect their wages. Nearly all of them own farm wagons, harness and horses, and at early morning every member of the family having a contract are hauling upon the ground, and work commences by some of the party seizing the picks and swinging them until tired out, when perhaps the s....s and children or others interested in the completion of the work seize upon the shovels and throw out the dirt, while the first toilers sit upon the bank by a blazing fire and leasurely roll up thier [sic] cigarettes and smoke until their turns come to swing the impliments of labor and give the other toilers a smoke and a rest. Others have their lodges and families at the work and make themselves comfortable and happy in their toil. They suffer no inconvenience, as a lodge is the natural home of an Indian and his family.

Authority has also been granted for the enlargement and construction of a new flume on the old irrigating ditch constructed by the present agent several years ago, on the north side of the Jocko river, which will double its former supply of water for irrigation purposes. Two hundred and seventy-five joints of flume will be used for this work, requiring the delivery of 80,000 feet of sawlogs at the mill. The logs are delivered by Indians who haul them upon trucks furnished to them by the agent. An Indian mill crew is also employed to assist the agency sawyer and engineer, packing lumber, slabs, etc., from the saw and placing them in piles for future use.

Labor is the true solution of the Indian question. Instead of furnishing supplies, blankets and clothing to them if the Indian department would inaugurate a plan to supply and pay for labor by Indians on their own reservations, by constructing water ditches, cutting the magnificent timber that grow upon their reservation, and delivering it at the different railroad stations for shipment to lumbermen in the state, willing to pay a regulated price for stumping and Indian labor. In short, to inaugurate a system of labor that will furnish employment to Indians at living wages, upon their own reservation, where the natural resource will enrich the tribes from their own efforts, relieve the people from taxation, and place the Indian in a position of independence and self-reliance, which will result in civilization, an abandonment of the chase, and eventually, to the settling down of these people to the comforts and refinements of homes won by their own industry, stimulated by a sense of well paid for and independent toil.

Document 41

A Kootenai Indian and Kalispell Police

1892

Source: Harry Stanford, "Jousting with Lame Louis," *Twelfth Annual Report of the Water Department, City of Kalispell, Montana*, Dec. 31, 1925, pages 49-51.

Editors' note: Stanford gave the Kalispell police version of their 1892 arrest of Lame Louis, a Kootenai Indian. Louis' side of the story was not preserved in the historical documents.

Jousting with Lame Louis

Thirty-three years ago Kalispell, just incorporated as a city, was a lusty infant in swaddling clothes. Benton D. Hatcher of the Globe National Bank, was mayor; George Grubb was was city clerk and attorney; Hawes, partner of the late J. B. Gibson (these two men being civil engineers who platted the townsite), was I think, city engineer; Fred Merigold, then with the Globe National, was, if I mistake not, city treasurer; Frank Exline was police magistrate. The six original councilmen were Paul Handley, M. Brandenberg, Jim Ford, J. H. Edwards, H. S. Cannon and Joe Cox. These men, I think, are all living except Paul Handley, J. B. Gibson, Hawes and Brandenburg. Jim Shelton, who died in Lewistown, was city marshal. The police force of the new town being (as the Mexican army was then said to be) all officers, the night man was officially designated chief of police, doubtless in anticipation of a heavy increase in numbers, which increase did not materialize for some years. To further enhance the dignity of the city, the chief was all dolled up in a full uniform — double-breasted coat, helmet, brass buttons and all. As Charlie Griffith relates, "An envious stranger from the neighboring metropolis of Sccoptown (Demersville) gazed upon him and made oration thusly — 'By G-d, sir, it will take Kalispell a long time to grow up to that feller!'" And it was even so. The writer did not think it particularly funny at that time, but he enjoys that remark hugely now.

Our fellow citizens, the Kootenais, from whom we had filched the valley, were much about. The bootlegger of that day had not sunk so low as to sell liquor to kids, and his only customer was "Lo." Thus it was that an intoxicated buck was anything but a rarity.

And after we had become civilized by the incoming waves of culture from the east, and we could no longer hear the all night chanting of the Kootenais as they beat r[h]ythmically with sticks upon a dry cottonwood log, and gambled their shirts on their "odd and even" game (quite similar to the finger game of the Chinese), the nights, somehow, had lost something, never to return.

It was only natural that women living on the outskirts of town, and at Ashley just to the west, should be just a little bit timid, and strongly object to a drunken buck, stripped to shirt and breech-clout, riding hell bent through a clothes line hung with a hard day's washing. And so it come about that the police force was frequently called upon to abate the nuisance.

 On the occasion I am about to tell of two stripped Indians chockfull of forty-rod, had been riding around in the dark for an hour, and yelling like — well, Indians, whenever they got separated.

The police force at that time habitually carried a heavy loaded bitter-root cane, and ambushing himself at a house corner (just where George Roper lives on the west side), as one of those Indians came past at full speed and in full cry, he got that rider square between the eyes. My, what a fall that fellow took.

This Indian had, when the bitter-root stick caught him, a Three Star Hennessy bottle raised high in his right hand, and when he hit the ground senseless, so tightly was his thumb corking that bottle that no drop of the "red eye" contained therein was spilled.

Ablum thus disposed of and promptly incarcerated in the bowels of the "city cooler," it was highly necessary to get his pal, Lame Louis, who was a big bad hombre, with a reputation of devilment.

Louis was flushed out of the night near the Pioneer Hotel, at the time conducted by Kauffman & Benkendorf, now Jim Broderick's furniture store. Now Louis was not the man who would stop from the white man orders, and so it was thought a shot or two might cool his ardor, and three were sent in his general direction, two being kept in case of later need.

Louis took no immediate harm from all that shooting, which had the sole effect of further accelerating the going of his already running cayuse That scared horse ran abreast on to a high wooden sidewalk about where the archway is in the Buffalo Block, and threw Louis clear over the walk into the middle of the street, almost stunning him.

Before he could gather himself we hopped him, and sticking the muzzle of the big Colt in his ear, started for the "calaboose," which may still exist in the rear of Jack Frohlicher's building, then the newly purchased city hall.

Did that gun bluff Louis? It did not! He slapped his bare breast until it sounded like a toy drum, and made heated remarks in both Kootenai and English, rudely criticising [sic] the police force — the police force's ancestry particularly upon the female side — and called upon his dusky gods to bear witness that he was a "Heap good Injun," and not afraid of any gun or any white man. Later in the night, singing over his troubles in his dungeon cell, as one would sing his death song, upon urgent request of awakened citizens it became necessary to silence Louis, and a pail of ciy water thrown against his bare midriff as he stood shaking the grated door of the little jail, did what a gun could not. That subdued Louis.

And when Louis came out of this jag he had it in his head that the police force had man-handled him in combat, and knowing his own prowess, he greeted the police force upon meeting, as long as he lived, by the emphatic ejaculation in Piegan [sic], "Squin-a-taps napeequoni!" In English, "strong man!"

And the police force never did tell Louis that it was the cayuse that threw him half way across Main Street.

— Harry Stanford.

Document 42

Vanderberg Described Charlo's Years in the Jocko Valley 1892 plus

Source: J. Verne Dusenberry, "Samples of Pend d'Oreille Oral Literature and Salish Narratives," in Leslie B. Davis, ed., *Lifeways of Intermontane and Plains Montana Indians*, Occasional Papers of the Museum of the Rockies No. 1 (Bozeman, Mont.: Montana State University, 1979), pages 116-118.

Editors' note: Vanderberg described the arrival of the Bitterroot Salish at Jocko in 1891 and Charlo's devout Catholic faith.

Charlot's Later Years
by Victor Vanderberg

By 1893 [sic], the people were unhappy in the Bitterroot Valley. Whites had moved in and fenced the place so that wild game was no longer plentiful enough to provide anything to eat. Several of the Indians made offers to my father, Louis Vanderberg, to lead the people over to the Jocko. He turned them all down and said that Charlot was the chief of the Bitterroot Salish and that he would not go until Charlot went. Finally, Charlot changed his mind and agreed to move because so many of the Indians wanted to go.

Charlot ordered the people to pack up. He made no speech when he left. He felt very bad in having to leave the Bitterroot, as did all of the old people. Many of them cried. The young people, though, were glad. The trip over took three days. The first night we camped at Lolo, the second night near DeSmet, and the third night at a place about five miles from the agency — Schley. The next morning, we got up late and stayed around there until almost noon. Charlot made his only speech that morning. He told us to get on our best horses, put on our finest clothes, and paint our faces. That way, we would come to the Agency just like the way people used to return to the tribe after they had been out on a successful buffalo hunt or war expedition.

We did as Charlot told us and rode to the Agency. It was Sunday morning, and we rode into the Agency yard singing and yelling. Someone rang the church bell. The priest came out and made a speech and shed tears. Many of us cried. Then we all went to Mass. After Church, we wondered where we would camp. Most of us looked around and found places just east of the Agency and there we set up our camps. There were a few among us who had brought their things in wagons, but the most of us came by horseback.

At last we got settled and built our cabins. Charlot became kind of a lazy chief over here. He never called meetings to plan anything. He never took much interest in what was going on. He owned both cattle and horses, but he did not do any farming. Nor did he encourage people to do any farming either as he had done years before in the Bitterroot. After the reservation was opened to the White settlers, he objected but did not show much of his feelings to the Salish people.

In the Bitterroot, he had many White friends and used to go visit them, going from farm to farm and talking with the settlers. He even got so that he could get along without an interpreter. Here he was so hurt that he never visited any of the White people and had no friends among them. He always refused to speak any English or to understand it. Whenever he did have to talk, he had an interpreter. Although he had some good White friends in Missoula, he refused to go there after he moved here. Another thing about him over here was the fact that he always wore old Indian clothes all the time — just a shirt and leggings and a breech cloth. He didn't even have a fancy outfit for the celebrations.

Charlot was a very good Catholic. He didn't like anything else about the White man but the religion. Before we moved over here and before the buffalo were gone, Charlot went on hunting trips. Each morning and evening, he had a little bell that he rang in the camp. That meant prayer time. After he moved over here and on Sunday mornings when the priests couldn't be here, Charlot rang that bell and summoned the people to his house where he led prayers. Then he would preach. After each prayer, he made a speech. Several hours each day, he always spent alone in prayer. Then, too, when anything turned up among the people such as sickness or death, he would lead the prayers.

Oftentimes on Sunday when he finished the prayers, Charlot asked some of the old people to stay with him. He lit his pipe, and, after everyone had smoked, he would tell the people to go out and do something that pleased them. The old people went outside and got some of the young people to join them and they played ball games. Charlot was always pleased with ball games. He said he wanted everyone to enjoy clean pastimes, and he considered ball playing as being clean. After everyone had played and it got dark, the people went home in the late evening.

Several years after we came over here to the Jocko, Charlot saw the Indians leaving the reservations and going to visit other tribes to take in their celebrations. Charlot did not like that, so he started a Fourth of July celebration to keep his people at home. Even at the celebration, Charlot was boss. Whatever the people wanted to dance or to do, they always asked him about it first. He did not dance himself, but he always stayed right there watching the others. After about a week of this celebration, he would tell the people to go home.

Charlot did not like to see the people following Indian ways. He was very much against our taking sweat baths and praying while we were sweating, because he said it was against the teachings of the real religion. By that, he meant it was against what the priests taught us. Most of us kept on taking sweat baths, though. He didn't even like us to tell our stories or legends. Our old people kept on doing that, too, but Charlot would never join in. He said it was against the teachings of the priests.

Whenever there was feast, usually a death feast, Charlot always attended and talked to the people and informed them about the Catholic religion. He advised people not to gamble and drink, but instead to obey the instructions of the priests. He told people not to separate. Also, he warned people not to go to the Medicine Dances in the winter because they were Christians and Christians did not believe in such things as the Blue-Jay Dance and other Mid-Winter Dances.

The Salish have always liked to dance just for good times' sake in the winter before Lent starts. You know, we still do that. In the Bitterroot, Charlot used to go to these dances and sometimes dress up and dance. Over here, he never gave a dance and hardly ever went to one of them. At the dances in the Bitterroot, he always took a drink with the other people; here, he might take a drink or two and then go off someplace and go to sleep. The next time he had the chance, he lectured his people about drinking.

Most of the people in the tribe respected him and usually tried to follow his advice. He could not control the gamblers, though. In his time, like now, there were always many stick games being played. Charlot tried to forbid these games, but he had no luck. The gamblers just laughed at him.

During his life, Charlot was a very healthy man, but he was sick quite awhile before he died. Just before his death, the older people visited him, and when he got weak more and more people came to see him. One night at a Jumping Dance, shortly after midnight, the word came that Charlot was dead. The crowd broke up and went to Charlot's home. They held a wake for one night and one day. Several days after the funeral, they had a feast. All of the Salish people were there.

Document 43

A Mixed Blood Family in the
1890s Flathead Valley
1892 plus

Source: "Mrs. Clara Cramer," in Tom Stout, *Montana: Its Story and Biography* (Chicago: The American Historical Society, 1921), volume 3, pages 856-857.

Editors' note: This biographical sketch gives sanitized information about a member of the Ducharme family, a prominent mixed-blood family on the Flathead Reservation. In 1921 the Cramers had lived in the Polson area for 29 years, so they moved there about 1892.

Mrs. Clara Cramer is the wife of Ben Cramer, and both of them deserve record as among the pioneers of the Polson district of Flathead County.

Ben Cramer was born in Gratiot County, Michigan, August 21, 1865, son of Martin W. and Delinda (Sias) Cramer. Martin W. Cramer was a Civil war veteran, a member of the Fourth Michigan Cavalry, and was for four years in the service of his country, a volunteer. He took part in many of the notable engagements, and was wounded seven times. Martin Cramer's father was a minister of the Disciple Church. Ben Cramer has frequently been a delegate to the republican state conventions, and was a delegate to the Chicago National Convention in 1916. At present he is marshal of Polson. He has always been friendly to the Indians. At one time Chief Antone was sever[e]ly wounded in a fight, and as there was no physician in the country Mr. Cramer had him carried home on a stretcher and sewed up the gash with silk thread. The chief was always afterward grateful to him.

Mrs. Cramer belongs to the real pioneer stock of Montana and was born at Frenchtown in Missoula County, a daughter of J. B. and Catherine (Wood) Ducharme. Her father was of French ancestry. Clara Ducharme was the youngest in a family of twelve children. When she was eight years of age her parents moved to western Canada, to what is now the province of Alberta, and while there her mother died when the daughter was thirteen and two years afterward the father followed. After the loss of her parents she returned to Great Falls, and while there met and married Ben Cramer.

Soon afterward they moved to the Flathead country south of the lake, where Polson now stands. They were the first to locate in that Indian country, and subsequently filed on a homestead. They were established and in readiness with their hospitable hearts to help the first comers to Polson. Mr. Cramer developed an extensive business as a rancher and stockman and enjoyed unusual success in that industry. Several years ago he sold his homestead and removed to Polson, where he erected a modern bungalow, one of the best homes in Polson.

Mr. Cramer in former years was one of the great nimrods of this country. The district is still noted for its big game, and only recently a mountain lion and a cougar were killed in what is known as the Cramer Addition to Polson. During one hunt Mr. Cramer killed two elk, a mountain goat, a cinnamon, black and grizzly bear and several deer. His home is adorned with the trophies of the chase, including the mounted heads of two elks, perhaps the finest specimens of the kind in the state, and for one of which Mr. Cramer was offered, but refused, a thousand dollars.

While living on the ranch Father [Anthony] Ravelli, a pioneer priest, was a frequent visitor at the Ducharme home and often enjoyed its hospitality. Mrs. Cramer's father, J. B. Ducharme, was a prominent pioneer Catholic of Montana, and lived to the extreme age of 105, dying on his birthday. His home ranch was at Frenchtown.

Mr. and Mrs. Cramer never had any children of their own but reared two girls from childhood. One was Mary Beauvais, who became the wife of Harry McKenzie of Polson. The other is Miss Nettie Moss, now a student at Chemawa, Oregon, and a vivacious young woman with an interesting outlook on life. Both these adopted daughters have been a great comfort to Mr. and Mrs. Cramer. Mrs. Cramer attends the Presbyterian Church at Polson, both are stanch republicans, and their political sympathies are indicated by a fine portrait of the late Theodore Roosevelt that hangs in their home.

In the early days Mr. and Mrs. Cramer had some exciting experiences when they first came to the reservation. They were regarded by the native Indians as intruders, and the mounted policemen of the Indians never omitted an occasion or opportunity to do what they could to frighten and intimidate the white settlers. Mr. and Mrs. Cramer were proof against their wiles and threats. One day during the absence of Mr. Cramer some Indians came riding up on their horses, and seeing Mrs. Cramer at a distance gave chase. She was mounted on a swift horse and easily kept ahead of her pursuers until the horses of the Indians were tired out, and instead of being frightened she confesses that she really enjoyed the chase as good sport. Mr. and Mrs. Cramer have seen many changes in this district, having lived here for twenty-nine years, during which time Polson has been developed from nothing into one of the thriving and pretentious commercial centers of the Flathead district.

Document 44

Strange Murder Trial in 1893 Missoula

June–July 1893

Source: "The Story of a Crime," *The Anaconda Standard*, June 3, 1893, page 1, col. 6; "Angus M'Donald's Tale," *The Anaconda Standard*, July 2, 1893, page 1, col. 4-5; "Angus M'Donald Free," *The Anaconda Standard*, July 3, 1893, page 8, col. 3.

Editors' note: The murder of Curley Stevens left many questions unanswered, but adopted tribal member Angus P. McDonald was found not guilty of murder by a white jury.

The Story of a Crime
No Clue to the Murderers of Stevens at Horse Plains.
M'Donald Is Innocent
He Was in Stevens' Company at the Time, but Was Too Much Under the Influence of Liquor to Have Done It.

Special Dispatch to the Standard.

Missoula, June 2. — On Tuesday, May 23, nearly two weeks ago, a stranger known as "Curly" Stevens was brutally murdered on the main road leading from Horse Plains in this county, an account of which appeared at the time in the *Standard*. Up to the present time there is no clue to the actual perpetrator of the dastardly crime. True, a half-breed, Angus P. McDonald, is confined in the county jail charged with this particular murder, but from the evidence now on hand, there can be no doubt of McDonald's innocence and the officers must look elsewhere for the culprit. The circumstances attending the commission of the crime are as follows:

On Tuesday morning, May 23, Angus P. McDonald, bound for his sister's ranch, Jack Curry on his way to his home at Pleasant Valley, and the stranger, Stevens, who was going out to Arthur Laravie's ranch in search of work, all well loaded with Horse Plains' best snake bite lotion and supplied with several doses of the same medicine stored about their persons, left Horse Plains in the saddle via the main traveled road leading north. When out about a mile and a half the little party met a couple of Indian policemen. McDonald stopped and shot at a mark with these men for whiskey, Curry and the stranger continuing on. McDonald was unsteady and the Indians won his supply of liquor. When McDonald caught up with Curry and Stevens, near Dog Lake, about eight miles out from Horse Plains, it was noticed that he had lost his mail package that had been strapped to his saddle and he and the stranger turned back to look for it, while Curry bade them good-bye and continued his journey to Pleasant Valley. After traversing half the distance on the return trip, the two men dismounted and fastening their horses to a fence, commenced to put themselves outside of what whisky the stranger had brought with him. During the performance, a man named Duncan, a farm laborer in the employ of Peter Demer, came along and joined them in a drink and then proceeded to his work a short distance off the road. Duncan says that McDonald was the drunkest man he ever saw, while Stevens was so far gone as to be unable to maintain himself in a sitting posture. After reaching his destination some 25 minutes later, Duncan said two men galloped up the road, followed short after by a single rider going in the same direction. Duncan, thinking that the first two men were McDonald and Stevens, paid no further attention to the matter, although he now admits that it would have been impossible for the men to have mounted their horses in their then condition. The rest of the story told by McDonald is to the effect that he roused himself about 5 o'clock in the afternoon and attempted to awaken his companion and continue their journey, when he was horrified at finding Stevens covered with blood and his skull completely crushed in. McDonald immediately returned to town and reported the circumstance to Colonel McGowan and Constable Joe Thomas. An investigation elicited the fact that the stranger's revolver and whisky bottles were missing, as well as $70 that McDonald had received from Colonel McGowan that morning. McDonald's revolver was found by the side of the murdered man, but bore no evidence of having been used in the deadly work. A thorough search has been made of the adjoining country but no trace of revolver, bottles or money has been found and it is this fact that points strongly to McDonald's innocence. It is extremely probable that the horsemen seen by the man Duncan, galloping up the road, were the murderers of the unfortunate Stevens, and that the robbery of McDonald, who was known to have money, was their motive, an interference with their plans on the part of Stevens, bringing about the terrible beating that caused his death.

* * * * * * * *

Angus M'Donald's Tale
He Narrates the Events of the Day on Which Stevens Was Killed.
A Horrible Awakening
He and Stevens Fell Asleep and When He Was Aroused His Arm Encircled the Dead Body of His Friend.

Special Dispatch to the Standard.

Missoula, July 1. — In the presence of a well filled courtroom, and the interest almost at fever heat in Missoula's now celebrated murder case, Angus P. McDonald took the witness stand this morning to explain what he knew of the circumstances surrounding the murder of his companion, John Stevens, on the 23d of last May, and for which offense he, himself, is at present on trial. McDonald proved to be an excellent witness. He was far more composed that many of those who had preceded him, testifying to matters of but little importance. His answers to the interrogations put to him by the court and counsel were free and distinct and at the conclusion of his testimony, many in the court room were deeply impressed in his favor.

McDonald testified that he had first met Stevens about seven or eight days prior to the day upon which the crime was committed, and that he next saw him at a saloon in Horse Plains on the morning of May 23, when Stevens informed him that he was going out to Arthur Laravie's ranch, where he had been promised employment, and requested permission to accompany the witness and Jack Curry, who were about to proceed in the same direction.

"When out from Horse Plains something more than a mile, we met two Indian policemen and stopped to talk with them. The Indians asked me for some whisky but I was skeptical about giving it to them, and asked Curry and Stevens to ride on and I would overtake them. After they had gone on the Indians again requested some whisky and I finally agreed to shoot with them at a mark, for the bottle that I had, and they won it from me. After taking two or three more drinks, I proceeded on my way and overtook Curry and Stevens, when they were about four and a half miles from Horse Plains. Curry then noticed that I had lost a package that had been strapped on behind my saddle and I concluded to turn back and pick it up. Stevens wanted to accompany me, but I told him he had better go on with Curry, as my horse was better than his and we would not lose so much time if I went back alone. Stevens, however, insisted on returning with me and we turned back, Curry continuing on. I was pretty drunk at this time, and can only remember that we dismounted, at some spot in the road, and took three or four more drinks out of a bottle we had with us. From that time on, my mind is a perfect blank until I was awakened, I think, by something rubbing against my head. At this time, Stevens was lying by my side, with my right arm around his shoulders and neck. I shook him and told him to get up, as it was getting late and we had to continue our journey. Not receiving any response from him, I raised his head and then noticed that he was dead. I immediately stood up and noticed that I had befouled myself.

"After arranging my toilet as best I could under the circumstances, I lighted a cigarette, got on my horse and went back to Horse Plains as fast as my horse could travel. I immediately hunted up Joe Thomas, the constable, and in the presence of Colonel McGowan explained to them that my companion of the morning was lying dead by the roadside about three miles from town. We three went back to where the body was found, and then returned to Horse Plains, when I was placed under arrest. After my arrest, and until I went to bed, about 30 minutes later, I conversed with a number of people in McGowan's store, but never in any way, shape or form admitted that I had killed Stevens or knew anything concerning his death. On the contrary, I steadfastly denied any knowledge of the affair. The statements made by Witness Sears, yesterday are all false and were actuated by a personal enemity [sic] existing between us. I never told Cummings that I had had trouble with Stevens on the hill, and that I might have struck him over the head with my revolver. Stevens and I were very friendly for short acquaintances. I had taken a great fancy to him and am positive that I never struck him."

McDonald in his cross examination, was handled in an able manner by County Attorney Denny, but he stuck steadfastly to his story in all its particulars.

The first witness called this morning by the defense, Elemehum, a Pend d'Oreille Indian, togged out in a new suit of clothes of a decidedly "ice cream" character, testified that he was on his way to his camp at Camas prairie, late on the afternoon of the murder, and when near the spot where the body was subsequently found, saw three horses, saddled and bridled, grazing near the side of the road, one a black horse, one cream and the other a bay. He also saw two men working at a fence some distance up the hill for where the horses were seen.

Eugene McCarty had known Stevens in his life time, and had heard him say that he had had trouble with the Kootenais over some land and a horse race during the summer of 1891, and that the Indians had then threatened his life, and he feared that if he went back on the reservation, they would attack him.

William Moser, a mild mannered young gentleman from Horse Plains, appeared in court on crutches, the result of being too frisky on the court house lawn, yesterday evening, and testified that he had been present during the entire time that McDonald was confined in McGowan's store, on the night of the murder, and had heard everything that the prisoner said in regard to the crime. Moser was positive that McDonald had on every occasion denied any knowledge of it. The witness flatly contradicted the witnesses for the prosecution who claimed to have heard McDonald admit that he had killed Stevens.

The defense then called Pierre, a Kootenai, by whom they intended to show that an Indian had gone to the witness' camp the day following the murder and confessed to him that he had committed the crime, but Judge Woody flatly declined to admit any testimony of this nature, and with the evidence of McDonald, which followed, the defense rested. Some unimportant testimony in rebuttal, was offered by the prosecution, and Attorney Dixon began his opening address to the jury. Mr. Dixon was followed by Attorneys Wood and Judge Reeves for the defense and County Attorney Denny, in closing, for the state. At 8 o'clock the case went to the jury, but at a late hour to-night a verdict had not been reached.

* * * * * * * *

Angus M'Donald Free
The Missoula Jury Brings in a Verdict of Acquittal.
Special Dispatch to the Standard.

Missoula, July 2. — After being cooped up for 24 hours in the dingy little jury room at the court house, the jury in the case of Angus P. McDonald to-night returned a verdict of acquittal. The *Standard* has all along maintained that McDonald had not murdered his companion on that memorable trip from Horse Plains to the reservation, and the verdict of the jury, composed of a dozen of Missoula county's representative citizens, has sustained this paper in its belief. It might truly be said that the strongest evidence against McDonald was the inability of the county officials to locate the actual perpetrator of this mysterious crime.

Document 45

Indian Relatives Look for Hidden Gold

July 24, 1893

Source: "Allee Samee White Man," *The Evening Missoulian*, July 24, 1893, page 1, col. 5.

Editors' note: This is an interesting case of hidden treasure.

Allee Samee White Man.
Relatives of a Dead Injun Looking for Concealed Wealth.

Jocko, Flathead Indian Agency, Mont., July 24. — [Special correspondence to the Missoulian.] — On Thursday last the body of the widow of George Red Crow, a rich Nez Perces Indian who formerly lived in the Bitter Root valley, but some time ago removed to the Flathead reservation, was buried at the agency graveyard. Red Crow had at his death about $18,000 in gold coin, which he realized from the sale of a large band of horses, and also from the sale of a ranch in the Bitter Root valley. Realizing that death was approaching, Red Crow called his wife and relatives about him and stated that he had $4000 in the hands of his wife, and that the rest of the gold was concealed, but that he had revealed the hiding place to her, and to her he gave the money, his ranch and crop on the Jocko, and his gentle horses, and bade her take care of his blind aunt as long as she lived. Having no children he gave to his relatives his band of wild horses and some cattle. Soon after his burial the rapacious relatives of Red Crow made the widow's life almost unendurable, demanding a division of her husband's hidden wealth and the blind aunt compelled her to give up every cent of the money left in the house. Thoroughly disgusted, the widow started with some Indian women to Butte, where they camped for a short time. There she stated she never would reveal to her husband's relatives the hiding place of his gold. One day she was stricken by a fit of paralysis, from which she never recovered nor ever spoke a word. Subsequently she was brought back to the agency, where she died and was buried as above stated and the Indians are now wondering where to look for the hidden treasure.

Document 46

Allard Wild West Show

October 1893

Source: "Looked Like Old Times," *The Anaconda Standard*, October 9, 1893, page 5, col. 1-2; "Old-Time Cow Puncher Rides Modern Stages," *The Daily Missoulian*, November 26, 1936, page 12, col. 1.

Editors' note: Charles Allard tried a wild west show to exhibit and profit from his buffalo herd in 1893. Unfortunately, after a few presentations in different Montana cities, the show was disbanded later the same year.

Looked Like Old Times
Allard's Herd of Buffalo Disport Themselves at the Race Track
Experts with the Lariat
Clever Exhibition of Riding 2-Year-Old Bulls —
The Herd Soon to Be Reinforced by Additions.

Butte, Oct. 8. — Charles Allard exhibited his famous herd of buffalo at the race track this afternoon to a crowd that was remarkably large considering the state of the weather, with rain and snow overhead and wind and mud underneath. Had the weather been fine 2,000 or 3,000 people would have been present. The exhibition was a decided novelty and gave the best of satisfaction. Although the herd of buffalo was not as large as Mr. Allard expected it to be, there were enough of them to surprise people who have become accustomed to the broncho-bucking exhibitions that have been given in Butte the past few years. The buffalo are all big fellows and in good condition, and the way they tore around the track and kicked up the mud reminded the old timers present of the early days when the hills and valleys were covered with the noble beasts.

The horses were all well trained animals that understood their business, and their riders were experts in the art of throwing the rope. There was no promiscuous throwing of ropes by unskilled hands, but every time a lariat went sailing through the air it counted. The best feat of the afternoon was the riding of a vicious young 2-year-old bull by one of the cow boys. The bull was first roped and thrown by Mr. Allard and two of his assistants, after which the saddle was put on him, the ropes were loosened and the maddened beast started off with the boy clinging to the saddle with one hand and waving his hat in the air with the other. The buffalo did not do much bucking, but tore around the track like a race horse. As the big herd went tearing around the track with their shaggy heads lowered, they did not seem to be going very fast until one looked at the horses which were running alongside and straining every nerve to keep up with them.

The herd which is now here numbers 53 full-blooded buffaloes. By tomorrow, however, they will be reinforced by 51 full-bloods and 15 half and quarter breeds, which Mr. Allard bought from Buffalo Jones at Omaha. These buffalo were shipped last month and the officials of the road guaranteed that they would be here Friday or Saturday. They did not arrive, but rather than disappoint the crowd Mr. Allard went on with the exhibition as advertised. Another exhibition will be given at Anaconda next Wednesday or Thursday, when the new buffalo have completely recovered from their long ride. There will certainly be a lively fight when the two herds are put together, as the leaders of each herd will get together and decide the question of supremacy at the first opportunity. The herds will not be thrown together until the next exhibition is given, and the fight will take place in front of the grand stand. With the cows and calves which he now has at his ranch in the Flathead reservation, Mr. Allard has about 120 head of buffalo, which is undoubtedly the biggest herd in the world. They range in age from 17 or 18 years down to young calves. Mr. Allard values them at $75,000, but that amount of money would not buy them as none of them are for sale at the present time. Just before he left Chicago he was offered $1,000 a head for seven cows and one bull, but he refused the offer. He paid $18,000 in cash for the herd which he bought of Buffalo Jones, and the others he bought from the Indians on the reservation. Mr. Allard has a ranch two miles square in the Flathead country and he will take the buffalo directly to his ranch after leaving here and breed them, and none of them will be for sale for at least a year. A few of them will probably be taken to the midwinter fair at San Francisco.

Mr. Allard, or "Montana Charlie" as he was known in the early days, has had a decidedly adventurous career. He was in Montana long before most of the so-called old timbers. Twenty years ago he carried the mail from Horse Plains to Missoula. In 1868, when he was boy of about 18 years, Charley walked all the way from Oregon to Montana, and went directly to Bear Gulch, in those days of the gold excitement the greatest camp in the state. While there he rode race horses for James A. Talbott and managed to save up considerable money. He then went up into the Kootenai country and bought a horse ranch, in which he soon lost all of his money through being too easy with men who owed him. He then went to Cedar Creek and from there he went down into Texas for cattle for T. J. Demars. On his way up from Texas in the summer of 1871, he ran across his first buffalo on the plains of Kansas and succeeded in getting away with him after a hard fight. The buffalo was a big bull who had wandered away from his herd, and Charley and his partner, Bill Demars, caught him alone. The only rope that he had was a long one, one end of which was in his horse's mouth in lieu of a bridle. He quickly made a noose in the other end and got it over the buffalo's horns at the first throw. After a hard fight in which he came very near being killed, Charley got the big beast down and his partner then ran up and hamstrung him, after which they killed him. This was the first full grown bull that Charley ever threw a rope over, and he has never tried to rope one since. He says that his first experience was sufficient, and he did not care to take any more chances on being killed where the odds were so much against him.

During the summer of 1871, Charley and his partner caught eight buffalo which they kept during the winter on a ranch on the Big Sandy creek on the Arkansas river, just south of Fort Lyons. They brought them up to Montana in the spring of 1872. Their's was the first ranch ever on the Arkansas river.

The closest call which Mr. Allard ever had was in the winter of 1874, and he says that he will remember that experience with horror to his dying day. He had bought a lot of horses in Lewistown and in company with John Hammer started across to Missoula with them over the old Lo Lo trail. This trail was always known as being the worst in the mountains, and Charley trusted Hammer to take him through, as he had never been over it before. After they had been out two or three days, a heavy snow storm came up, and Allard wanted to turn and go back, but Hammer prevailed on him to keep on. On the seventh day the snow got so deep that they were compelled to leave the horses, after killing one of them to get a supply of meat. For 11 days they tramped on through the snow going down, up to their waists at every step. Then their supply of meat gave out and they lost the trail at the same time. They gave up all hope, but with grim determination they tramped on, and at the end of the 22nd day, after having been without a mouthful to eat for days, they came in sight of Missoula from the top of a high mountain. They had fortunately walked in the right direction and their lives were saved. When they reached Missoula they were in rags and so emaciated that their friends did not recognize them. Charley lost 23 pounds during the trip, and was frost-bitten all over.

In 1876 he drove the first cattle across the plains from Montana to Winnipeg, and while there he gave a private exhibition of his skill with the lariat before Lord Dufferin, who was then governor general of Canada. When he returned in the fall of 1876 he came right through the Sioux Indians who had participated in the Custer massacre. He repeated his trip to Winnipeg in 1877 and 1878. In 1880 he went into the Black Hills with a herd of cattle. In

1883 he started out on his own hook and butchered for the Northern Pacific when that road was built through. After that he ran a stage line from Ravalli up to Flathead lake and made a barrel of money notwithstanding the fact that he carried passengers free for two months and threw in their meals in order to beat an opposition line. Since then he has been raising cattle and buying buffalo, which he always thought would be valuable some day.

* * * * * * * *

Old-Time Cow Puncher Rides Modern Stages
Malcolm McLeod of Hot Springs Takes Up-to-Date Travel Facilities.

"I rode the first wild buffalo in Montana."

That was the assertion in Missoula Wednesday of Malcolm McLeod of Hot Springs, visitor in the city for the day.

"I rode the buffalo at the first wild west show ever put over in the state," Mr. McLeod said. "That was long before they started calling them rodeos.

"I was a cowboy working for Charlie Allard, who had the big buffalo herd in the Flathead valley. Mr. Allard took a big outfit to Butte to put on a real wild west show at the old Marcus Daly race track.

"A miner from Butte bet me five dollars that I could not ride a buffalo. I took the bet and won, for I rode the big bull right down the race track. It was on October 8, 1893, just 43 years ago.

"I will admit now when I am in my sixties that I had a tough ride, but I never admitted it then. When I had ridden one animal, I told them to trot in another. Today I will admit that I am glad they did not, for that was the toughest ride that I have ever had on the back of a wild critter.

"I have been able to ride all kinds of horses and steers, but that buffalo that I rode in Butte gave me the toughest job that I ever had with chaps and spurs."

However, the 66-year, old-time cow puncher, who knew only one means of travel — that of the bronc and the saddle, took the modern automobile stage from Missoula Wednesday afternoon on his return home to be there in time for his Thanksgiving turkey.

Charlie Allard was a former resident of the Flathead valley and owned the Allard herd of buffalo, which was later purchased by the Canadian government. The present herd of buffalo in Canada came from the Allard band on the Flathead. Mr. McLeod helped to round up the band in the Flathead, when they were shipped to the dominion.

Document 47

Reporter Described Jocko Agency and Visits to Indian Homes November 1, 1893

Source: "At the Reservation," *The Anaconda Standard*, November 1, 1893, page 6, col. 1-2.

Editors' note: This feature newspaper article described life at the Jocko Agency and visits to Alex Matt's and Chief Charlo's homes in 1893.

At the Reservation
Habits and Traits of Character of the Flathead Indians.

Missoula, Oct. 30. — He who alights from the Northern Pacific train at the little station of Arlee expecting to see crowds of Indians loafing around in gay blankets, is destined to be disappointed. If he is seeking the picturesque he will be unhappily disappointed, but if he views the existing conditions in the light in which they appear to those who are working for the welfare of the red man, he will rejoice that the agency Indian of romance has so nearly disappeared from the Jocko reservation. In all the four mile drive from Arlee station to the agency — and they are extremely long miles — the visitor will probably not see more than four Indians, and if he sees that many they will not be posing in picturesque attitudes, but will be busy at work on their ranches and will not present any of the appearance of the Indian of Eastern literature. The Indians on the Flathead reservation have, as a rule, taken kindly to the new habits and conditions and many of them have fine ranches, which produce a good crop of grain and besides this they have accumulated small herds of stock which range the open parts of the reservation and the foot hills.

* * * * * * * * *

The agency buildings are pleasantly situated near the base of a lofty spur of mountains, with a clear creek rushing merrily along in front of them, from which ditches are run to supply the ranches in the vicinity. In the area enclosed by the high picket fence are the agent's residence, occupied by the family of the late agent, Major [Peter] Ronan, the agency office and store room, the "quarters," large stables, a blacksmith shop and a saw mill. Just outside the enclosure is the mission church, presided over by Father [Jerome] D'Aste. In the rear of this little church is the agency burial ground in which lie the remains of the last of the great war chiefs of the Flatheads, Arlee. His funeral was held at the agency four years ago, but the Indians still recount to the visitor the splendor of the funeral pageant and the large number of whites and Indians who attended the obsequies. About 100 yards from the church is a neat two-story frame building where the Ursuline nuns conduct a kindergarten school for the little Indians and half breeds whose parents can be induced to permit them to attend. But they are not many, for the Indians do not like to see their boys' long hair cut off, and prefer to have them grow up on horseback, in blanket and leggings. Consequently the larger part of the pupils are half breeds.

* * * * * * * * *

Some idea of the feeling which is entertained by the Indians regarding the school can be gained from the narration of a little incident which was witnessed Sunday morning after the close of mass. The school children had returned to their building in charge of the sisters and were playing in the yard when three little lads in long hair, braided on the sides, wearing bright blankets and beaded moccasins, crawled upon a huge boulder that is about 50 feet from the school fence. Here they established themselves and peered over the top of their barricade, calling to the little fellows in the yard and cracking jokes at their expense. Finally when a party of girls came out through the gate and started toward the agency buildings, the little rascals pursued them with a volley of stones. Two of these boys were full blooded Indians, but the third had hardly a tinge of bronze on his cheeks, while his hair was soft and brown.

* * * * * * * * *

The school at the agency is small when compared with those at St. Ignatius mission, where 300 children, mostly of mixed blood, are under the tutelage of the fathers and sisters. But even at the mission the instructors have to contend against the same opposition from the Indians that is experienced at the agency. Considering the tremendous difficulties which confront them on every hand, the work accomplished in these schools is remarkable. The young men and women are instructed in trades and some of them have become accomplished artisans.

* * * * * * * * *

There are in all 2,000 Indians on the reservation scattered over many miles of territory. They are in four tribes, the Pen d'Oreilles, Kalispels, Kootenais and Flatheads, each with its own chief and tribal divisions. The larger part of these Indians are located in the Mission valley, the only ones in the immediate vicinity of the [agency are the] Flatheads, under Chief Charlot and Chief Antoine. These came to the reservation later than the others and are not so well situated as the others, although Antoine's band have good ranches. Charlot's Indians have been on the reservation but three years and have not yet received the fence material and agricultural implements promised them by General [Henry] Carrington when they were removed from the Bitter Root valley. This tends to make them dissatisfied and renders the task of the agent a difficult one, for he represents to them the government; and it is the government, they say, that has deceived them.

* * * * * * * * *

It was with no little curiosity that the *Standard* correspondent visited some of the houses which the government has built for the Indians and in which they live. The curiosity was changed to surprise when the first one — that of Alex Matt, a Piegan halfbreed — had been inspected. Matt is the blacksmith at the agency, and his Indian wife keeps his home in better order than do the wives of many of the laborers in smelting and mining towns. In the center of one of the two rooms stood a cook stove, upon which was simmering the dinner for the family, a stew of beef, carrots, turnips and potatoes. In the other room were the beds, neatly covered with blankets. The floors were tolerably clean and the whole house had an unexpected air of tidiness.

The next house visited was that of Chief Charlot. Here the floor was covered with skins and rugs, and three beds were neatly ranged about the room. In the kitchen the same sight was presented that had been witnessed in Matt's house. The old chief, who is losing his eyesight, sat on the floor of the living room and from there returned the greeting of the correspondent rather gruffly. Matt acted as interpreter, and through him the grim old chief recited his wrongs, real and fancied. He told how he had been induced by false promises to move his people from the Bitter Root valley and how his tribe was suffering from the failure of the government to supply them with materials for starting ranches. He neglected to state that the government offered 10 years ago to establish his tribe upon ranches, to pay them for thair [sic] Bitter Root land and to settle an annuity upon the chief himself, if they would at that time leave their old home on the Bitter Root, and that he had refused and had only come to the reservation when crowded out by the whites. These facts were supplied by blind Michel, the interpreter at the agency, who has a poor opinion of Charlot and who thinks that the old man has no one to blame but himself for his present predicament. However, the old chief's feelings might be greatly assuaged if the department would fulfill the promises made by General Carrington at the time of the removal of the tribe.

* * * * * * * * *

The success of the Indians at ranching is remarkable. Some of them have raised excellent crops of grain this year and they have some fine horses. Just across Mill creek from the agency is a ranch which is owned and operated by two Indian women, an old woman and her daughter. No man has ever done any work on the place since the government work was completed, and the women have a very productive ranch.

Another surprise is the presence of sewing machines in the houses of many of the Indians and the fact that the women use them and make neat garments for themselves and their children. These machines are furnished by the government and the one in Charlote's house gave evidence of constant use.

Taken in all, the condition of the Indians on the reservation is as satisfactory as could be expected and affords abundant evidence of the excellence of Major Ronan's administration as agent. True, as one of the ladies at the agency expressed it, "our Indians are too civilized to be interesting," but there is demonstrated the fact that the Indian can be made self-supporting, and those parts of the reservation near the agency afford good illustrations of what can be done with the Indian.

Document 48

Mixed Blood Arrested and Tried for Murder

January–June 1894

Source: "Much Bad Whisky," *The Evening Missoulian*, January 9, 1894, page 1, col. 7; "La Rose a Free Man," *The Helena Independent*, June 17, 1894, page 8, col. 2.

Editors' note: An example of the white court system and justice for an accused murderer on the Flathead Reservation in 1894.

Much Bad Whisky
Provokes a Murder on the Reservation.
Killed with a Neck-Yoke
Daniel Larose and Wm. King Loved Each Other's Wives
— The Latter Killed.

United States Marshal Furay returned from a hurried trip to St. Ignatius Mission this morning, having in custody a half-breed named Daniel Larose, who is charged with the murder of a fellow half breed on the reservation, known as William King, on the night of January 2d last. Larose waived his preliminary examination before Judge Logan this afternoon and was committed to the county jail at Helena to await the action of the federal grand jury, which meets at that city in April next.

From Marshal Furay the following facts in the case were learned. Larose and King, accompanied by their wives, attended a dance given on the evening of January 2d, by Joe Pion, a rancher on Post creek about five miles northwest of the Mission. During the evening some one introduced a two-gallon demijohn of Indian whisky into the festivities, and in a short time nearly all hands were as drunk as lords. About this time Larose began to exhibit an undue affection for the spouse of King and the latter retaliated by showering loving glances and tender speeches on the buxom bride of the gay Larose. These inter-familiar disagreements, together with the whisky, soon caused bad blood to spring up between the men and a general fight resulted. Larose says he was roughly handled, and a pair of black eyes, a dislocated nose and other marks about the head would tend to bear him out in this assertion. During the melee Larose went over to a farm wagon that was standing close by and picked up the heavy neck-yoke from the end of the tongue, and, returning to the crowd, struck King a heavy blow on the back of the head, completely crushing in the skull. An iron ring in the end of the neck-yoke also struck a bystander, whose name is not learned, and cut his head in a terrible manner. King was promptly removed to his cabin and lingered until yesterday morning at 5 o'clock, when death came to his relief. Larose was taken in charge by Partee, the chief of the Flatheads and formally placed under arrest by Marshal Furay yesterday evening. Larose, the murderer, is a young man about 27 years of age, talks English fluently and has always been regarded as a peaceful man. He has two children, one a boy of 3 years of age. Larose claims that he struck King in self-defense, as he was being badly used up in the general row that prevailed just previous to his using the neck-yoke.

It is understood that several more arrests will shortly follow.

* * * * * * * *

La Rose a Free Man.
After Deliberating for Twenty-Four Hours the Jury Brings in a Verdict of Acquittal.

Yesterday afternoon the jury in the case of Daniel LaRose, charged with the murder of Wm. King, on the Flathead reservation last winter, brought in a verdict of not guilty. The case was given to the jury at 4:30 Friday afternoon, and the verdict was brought into court at 4:15 yesterday. While they were out the jury took eleven ballots. The first two were on the question as to whether LaRose was guilty of murder in the first degree. It did not take long for the jury to agree that he was not. Then the balloting on the question as to whether he was guilty of manslaughter or was innocent of any crime began. On the first ballot on this question the vote stood seven for acquittal and five for manslaughter. It took a long while for the jury to get together on one of these propositions. At noon yesterday they came into court and told the court they could not agree. They were sent back again, and another ballot was taken. Pretty soon the vote stood ten for acquittal and two for conviction of the crime of manslaughter. The ninth and tenth ballots stood that way, but when the eleventh was taken they all agreed, and then they came into court. The defendant kept his composure very well until the result had been announced, and then when it was all over he showed the strain he had been under by quietly crying. LaRose, who is a half-breed, after his release, went to the camp established by his friends beyond the Broadwater. Going out in the car he seemed almost unable to realize that he was a free man, and he would every once in a while break into a little laugh. He feels very grateful to his attorney, T. J. Walsh, who defended him, and lost no opportunity to express his appreciation of his efforts, when talking to others of his case.

Document 49

Indian Complaints Relative to Reservation Boundary Survey February 1894

Source: Joseph T. Carter to Commissioner of Indian Affairs, February 6, 1894, letter received 6591/1894, Records of the Commissioner of Indian Affairs, RG 75, National Archives, Washington, D.C.

Editors' note: These petitions represent another attempt by tribal members to have their complaints heard by the Office of Indian Affairs. The erroneous survey of the southwest corner of the Flathead Reservation continued to be a problem until well into the twentieth century. Eventually, the land was not returned, but the tribes did receive a cash payment.

United States Indian Service,
Flathead Agency
Feb'y 6th, 1894

Hon. Commissioner Indian Affairs,
Washington
D.C.
Sir

I herewith forward two communications addressed to the Hon. Commissioner, which purports to be the wishes of a council held at St. Ignatius about Feb'y 1st 1894.

I have only to say that I consider the matter worthy of little attention. The council was called ie: — (beef furnished), by a meddlesome half breed [Duncan McDonald], an "ex-trader" who desires to shine as a man of influence and who properly belongs upon the Nez Perces reservation. In past years he has caused considerable trouble to the former Agent. The objection to the trader Alex Dow is very vague, at present I would not recommend his removal.

As to the survey I would scarcely recommend reopening the matter. The Indians while claiming more, had acquiesced to the line as surveyed until the matter was agitated by this halfbreed. Allotments to all Indians claiming land outside of the boundary survey, had been under way and the Indians apparently satisfied, but now persuaded that their petition will cause a new survey to be made and give to them the lands they claim, the Indians now refuse to take allotments. Were it not for this effect I would not consider the matter of much moment. The land in question is on the West boundary and is of little value excepting possibly the ranches of Josephus and Big Head, whose land I will allot to them pursuant to the instructions of the Hon. Commissioner in letter dated November 22, 1893 Land 36376-1893 as soon as they will consent to take them. The balance of the strip claimed by the Indians is mountain land and a narrow flat in the canon of the Clarks Fork river. The description of the boundary in the Flathead Treaty, — page 385 Revised Indian Treaties is very indefinate and naturally there is a difference of opinion as to where the line should cross Clarks Fork river.

I am of the opinion that any decision or instructions the Honorable Commissioner may see fit to give at this time, will definately settle the matter and the Indians abide by the same. I have the honor to remain,

very respectfully,
Joseph T. Carter
U.S. Indian Agent.

* * * * * * * *

[First enclosed petition:]

St Ignatius Jany 31st 1894

To the Hon. Commr of Indian Affairs
Washington D.C.
Through Maj. J. T. Carter
U.S. Indian Agent
Flathead Agency

For Cause we the undersigned in council has this day ask you for the immediate removal of Mr Alex Dow as a licensed trader. We are well satisfied he has not been an honorable man in his business matters on this reserve. A licensed trader should be above suspicion and too agressive.

[This petition had five pages of 115 marks and signatures. These included the marks of Michelle, Head Chief of the upper Pend d'Oreilles; Charlos, Head Chief of the Flathead; Eneas, Head Chief of the Kootanais; and Louison, Sub Chief. Also included were the marks of four Judges: Pattee, Eneas, Joseph, and Cilo; and Pierre, the Captain of police. Eight marks were identified as being on a "Committee": Alex Poirrier, Michell Pablo, Joe Decharem, Francois Elim-i-ohom, Domnick, Isaac, Michell and Black Blanket. Charles Allard's signature was on the petition, but Duncan McDonald's signature did not appear.]

* * * * * * * *

[Second enclosed petition:]

St Ignatius February 1st 1894

To the Honorable Commissioner of Indian Affairs
Wash D.C.
Through Major J. T. Carter
United States Indian Agent
Flathead Agency
Hon Sir

We the undersigned Chiefs of the Flathead Pend OReille and Kootani tribe of Indians of the Flathead ~~nation~~ reservation assembled in council have reasons to State that the Western and Northern boundary lines of this reservation are not surveyed as specified in the treaty of 1855 made by the government of the U.S. and the Flathead nation. we therefore pray to the government to send other surveyors and survey the lines over again and according to the treaty specifications. As the former surveys has been done without our Knowledge.

[The petition had four pages of 93 marks and signatures. These included all the chiefs and judges who had put their marks on the January 31, 1894, petition. This petition had the signatures of Duncan McDonald and Chas Allard.]

Document 50

Tsil Peh Arrested for Horse Theft on the Reservation March 15, 1894

Source: "He Is a Very Bad One," *The Anaconda Standard*, March 15, 1894, page 6, col. 1-2.

Editors' note: This was a case of the tribal police arresting an accused horse thief and his trial in Missoula in 1894.

He Is a Very Bad One
Old-Man-Afraid-of-a-Clean-Shirt on Trial at Missoula.
Why He Stole the Horse
His Feet Were Not Made for Walking —
One of a Desperate Gang of Indians in the Tolls of the Law.

Missoula, March 14. — The Indian, Tsil Peh (pronounced sil pe), who was tried yesterday before Judge Logan as United States commissioner, is one of the "bad men" of the Flathead reservation and his trial for stealing William Cahill's cayuse means more than the direct nature of the case would indicate. If he is convicted it will serve to quiet the persistent violation of law by the organized band of which he is a member and will do much to preserve law and order on the reservation. Tsil Peh is one of the sympathizers of the Indians who were executed in this county for murder, and is supposed to have been associated with them in their lawlessness during the period preceding their arrest, when they persistenlty [sic] defied the authorities and committed many deeds of violence and outrage. Ever since the conviction of the murderers, their followers and sympathizers, of whom Tsil Peh seems to be one of the leading spirits, have been guilty of numerous petty offenses, although they have been more careful than before their leaders were hung.

The theft for which Tsil Peh is now on trial, was committed last July near Arlee. The horse had been left picketed on the range, and when the owner went to get it one morning he found nothing but the picket rope which some one had untied from the horse's neck. The loss of the animal was at once reported to the agent at Jocko and the Indian police were instructed to keep watch for the missing steed. On July 8 or 9, Sam Pierre, a half-breed, while riding near the south end of Flathead lake, saw the horse picketed near an

Indian encampment. He inquired of a s.... named Millie as to the ownership of the animal and she informed him that it belonged to Tsil Peh. This fact was reported to Agent [Joseph] Carter, who was at that time clerk at the agency, and the arrest of Tsil Peh was ordered. He was finally discovered at the railway station at Ravalli by Duncan McDonald, who called Oliver Gebeau, one of the Indian police, and the latter made the arrest. Tsil Peh asked why he was arrested and was told that he was suspected of stealing a horse. He replied defiantly "I did it. What can you do to me?"

Policeman Gebeau turned his prisoner over to another officer who was to take him to the agency. He was brought to Arlee on a freight train and the policeman started for the Jocko agency with his charge. Just at the entrance to the agency square Tsil Peh attacked his captor and made his escape. He was not found again until a little more than month ago, when word was brought to Agent Carter that the fellow was at the house of a friend near the mouth of Jocko creek. The chief of police, Oliver Gebeau, and two other policemen were at once dispatched to secure the man. They succeeded in preventing Tsil Peh's escape from the house, but the man made a desperate resistance, defending himself with a knife to such good effect that he seriously wounded two of the policemen.

He was finally overpowered and was taken to the agency where he was placed in confinement. Here he admitted his guilt and offered to give two horses for the one that he had taken. He made threats that he would never be taken to jail as his friends would release him. His brother went to Agent Carter and informed him that if he valued his personal safety he would better release Tsil Peh and not attempt to prosecute him. He stated that Tsil Peh's friends would not permit the officers to take him to the train and said that he, himself, would wreak vengeance upon the agent. he was promptly locked up and has since made no further threats. Tsil Peh was brought to the county jail here, where he has been in confinement ever since.

The trial yesterday was a most interesting scene. Tsil Peh was brought to the court room by Deputy Sheriff Wood. In appearance Tsil Peh was anything but prepossessing. He is below medium height and has his hair cut in a sort of mop that hung loosely about his ears. He has discarded Indian attire and appeared in the court room clad in a shabby pair of trousers, a shirt that was so dirty as to be almost offensive, a ragged cowboy hat and a pair of moccasins. He was somewhat excited, although he feigned to regard the proceedings with insignificance. He, however, trembled violently during the examination of the government witnesses and his eyes roved restlessly about when he was not occupied in picking at the holes in his hat. He was seated with his back toward the door and whenever there was the slightest movement behind him he would turn his head quickly, but whatever transpired in front of him excited no outward demonstration. In his left ear he wears a battered gold earring, and on the right side of his neck, directly under his ear, are two ugly scars that look as if they had been made with a knife. He looks every inch a bad Indian, and his appearance, it is said, is sustained by his general reputation.

He seemed to regard Governor Leslie, the prosecuting attorney, with mingled malevolence and curiosity, and although he claimed to be able to understand no English, he seemed to be able to follow the course of the trial. At the conclusion of the government's evidence, Judge Logan asked Tsil Peh if he wished to tell his side of the story. He affected not to understand, and the question was repeated to him by Sam Pierre in the gutteral Flathead tongue. He said that he wanted to make an explanation, and was told to hold up his right hand. He seemed to understand the nature of an oath, for he nodded assent after the interpreter had repeated the legal form. Resuming his seat he proceeded to give his version of the theft of Cahill's horse.

He spoke in his native tongue, and his story, as translated by Sam Pierre, was as follows: "When my people made their treaty with the white people it was promised that they could ride on the railroad whenever they wanted to without paying anything. On the day I took the horse, I got on a train to ride and they told me to get off. I said that I would not and I was not going far. Then they threw me off, and I fell and was hurt. I saw the horse and did not want to walk so far, so I took the horse and rode back to Arlee. There I turned the horse loose. Some time after that my wife asked me where the horse was and told me that they would arrest me if they did not find it. I looked for it five or six days, but could not find it."

When asked if he had the horse near the lake where Sam Pierre saw it, Tsil Peh said, "Yes. But looked for him five or six days."

Oliver Gebeau, who made the arrest, is a tall, handsome half breed, weighing more than 200 pounds. He is an intelligent fellow and wanted everybody to understand that Tsil Peh did not escape from him, but from another policeman. Sam Pierre is also a half breed, with more of the French about him than of Indian and he seemed to hold Tsil Peh in supreme contempt. These two, with William Cahill, Agent Joseph T. Carter and the s...., Millie, will be summoned as witnesses before the United States grand jury in Helena. Until that body meets, Tsil Peh will be confined in the county jail at this place and it is hoped, for the sake of the county's reputation, that before he is sent to Helena he will be given a new shirt or else be compelled to wash the one he wears at present.

Document 51

Indians Spend Bitterroot Land Money in Missoula April 1894

Source: "It Was a Red Picnic," *The Anaconda Standard*, April 7, 1894, page 6, col. 3; "Lessons for Some Whites," *The Anaconda Standard*, April 9, 1894, page 6, col. 2.

Editors' note: This is a description of Salish Indians in Missoula spending the proceeds from the sale of their Bitterroot Valley allotments.

It Was a Red Picnic
Yesterday Saw Strange Sights on Missoula's Streets.
Lo Had Cash and Spent It
Many Thousand Dollars of Colored Rags Bought by the Wards of Joe Carter.

Missoula, April 6. — The people of Missoula have had a feast of color since early morning, and the occasion of it all way the payment to the Bitter Root branch of the Flathead nation their allotment for lands ceeded several years ago to the government. These Indians have since relinquishing title to their lands in the Bitter Root valley removed to the Flathead agency. This morning's overland train brought to town all the Indians entitled to receive this money. They were accompanied by Agent Joseph T. Carter, by whom the payment was done.

This morning, when the First National bank opened Mr. Carter occupied Cashier Keith's office, and promptly upon the opening of the doors the Indians crowded in and the payments began. Each received a draft on the United States treasury, which was immediately converted into cash at the teller's window. "Lo" would leave the window and immediately hie himself to nearest mercantile establishment, accompanied by his entire family, and buy whatever his fancy called for.

The young bucks invested in $6 Stetson cowboy hats, gaudy and expensive blankets, fine saddles, red handkerchiefs, cigarettes, tobacco and chewing gum. The dudes added sleigh bells to this equipment that stretched from head to heels so as to catch the eye of the copper-colored Hiawathas. The mature and middle aged men bought plows, spring wagons, harrows and harness, supplemented with the inevitable parti-colored blankets. The s....s ran wild on gaily colored handkerchiefs, calicoos, ginghams and blankets. The payment aggregated $18,000, and the checks varied in amount from $3 to $2,200. The recipient of the largest check was an old, wrinkled s.... 90 years of age known as "Marie Plessan," and she ranks easily now as the richest lady in her own right belonging to the tribe. After all the purchases had been made, accompanied by Agent Carter, the entire band wended their way with all the portable packages to the depot, and the rest of their plunder will follow by freight.

Soon after reaching the train the Indian police, by direction of the agent, began to search the braves for contraband whiskey. Some submitted to the search; other lit out to cache the liquor and on being overhauled smashed the bottles on the railroad track rather than incur the displeasure of the agent. About 6 o'clock the train pulled out, and happier and more contented lot of Indians never boarded a passenger coach.

* * * * * * * *

Lessons for Some Whites.
An Indian Boy Pays the Debt of His Dead Father.

Missoula, April 8. — There was one incident connected with the recent visit of Indians to this city which was a genuine surprise to those who learned of it. Among the Indians who had money was a lad of about 16 years, a son of Big Sam, old Chief Arlee's brother. He went to the office of the Missoula Mercantile company and paid $20 which had been owed by his father for six or seven years and which had long since been absorbed by the profit and loss account. But the boy insisted that his father told him when he died that he owed the firm $20 and the cashier must accept it. When this was finally done the boy went away happy and spent money like a prince. There is a moral in this tale for white customers but it is too obvious to need to be written.

Document 52

Duncan McDonald Laments Changes in Indian Life September 2, 1894

Source: "Good Old Days," *Western Democrat* (weekly) (Missoula, Mont.), September 2, 1894, page 2, col. 4.

Editors' note: Duncan McDonald was often a spokesman for tribal views. Here he expressed his regret at the loss of traditional Indian life.

Good Old Days.
Duncan McDonald Tells How the Indians Enjoyed Life.

One of the best known men in northern Montana, Duncan McDonald of Ravalli, is in the city with his son whose eyes were in need of treatment says the Spokane Chronicle. Mr. McDonald who is proud of his having a large per cent of Indian blood in his veins, was born in Montana forty-five years ago when there were only a few Hudson Bay trappers in the northwest. Most of his youth was spent among the Indians, and although he is now a well-read, thoughtful American citizen he still looks back with regret to the days of the blanket and tepee.

Once he went on the warpath with a crowd of young bucks who were out for horses and glory. It was in the middle of a bitterly cold February and the young men started out with an equipment of just one blanket apiece. They were forbidden to light a fire and lived on the scanty frozen food they carried out of camp. The dangers of being shot were nothing as compared to the dangers of freezing to death — but they enjoyed it.

"Yes, we're civilized now," said Mr. McDonald to a Chronicle reporter. "But I wish you could take your civilization and give up [us] the old days back again. Life was worth living then, every minute in the day — something to give excitement and keep one's blood bounding from morning till night. Give us back our buffalo and bears and deers and herds of horses and take your brass bands and electric lights back across the Mississippi again and you'll get our thanks."

"Improving the Indian's morality? Our people were honest in those days. You wouldn't find a faithless wife among the Indians then. One could leave things lying anywhere in camp and never worry about them. If anything was found it was taken to the chief and he returned it to the owner. Quarrels in the tribe were almost unknown, and as for cheating a tribesman, that was an infamy. Why, even the wars between tribes didn't really amount to much. Lots of times they would run along for months without anybody being hurt in them.

"And what have the white men done for the Indian? Taught him all kinds of meanness, made him as selfish and greedy as they are themselves, shut him up on little reservations and killed off all the big game. Why, they won't let us develop the wealth of the land we still hold. We must not even open the mines or cut the timber from the reservation. And then they tell us the Indians are lazy! Its like putting brains into a man's head and telling him not to think.

"Yes, sir, take your modern life and give us the old times again. Why, you don't even enjoy your own civilization — you know you don't."

And Mr. McDonald quit the subject in disgust.

Chapter 4

Documents of
Salish, Pend d'Oreille, and Kootenai
History Between 1895 and 1899

Document 53

Indian Farm Labor

January 25, 1895

Source: Joseph T. Carter to Commissioner Indian Affairs, January 25, 1895, letter received 5,294/1895, RG 75, National Archives, Washington, D.C.

Editors' note: Agent Carter referred to the importance of employment as agricultural laborers for tribal members in 1895. Some worked seasonally for off reservation farmers and others for tribal member farmers.

United States Indian Service,
Flathead Agency,
Jocko, P.O. Montana
January 25th, 1895

Hon. Commissioner Indian Affairs
Washington, D.C.
Sir:

Your letter dated Dec. 21st 1894 calling attention to the benefits accruing to Indians of both sexes, by placing them at service in the families of farmers etc.; and asking that I communicate my views as to the feasibility of carrying out these suggestions among the Indians of this Agency and school and to state what steps I propose to take in furtherence of this plan, "E" received and contents noted.

In reply I have to state that the plan suggested is substantially in force and being pursued upon this reservation with the excepting difference that thus far only adults have been thus employed and none attend the public schools in Winter.

Each summer a number of adult Indians engage with the white farmers in the vicinity of the reserve doing general farm work. A Still greater number are employed by the well to do mixed bloods and some even by the full blooded Indians who have made considerable progress and are accumulating property; some assisting in general farm work, others in herding and range riding. I do not think it feasible, scarcely possible to place children to work for white farmers outside of the reservation limits for several reasons. First, by inquiring, I find the farmers who would employ them are very few, second, they would learn little that they do not already Know, and third because of the storm of opposition from the parents, who with some truth say, the same ends can and are being accomplished within the borders of the reserve. A large majority, nearly all of the Indians of this Agency live in houses upon definite fenced holdings. The issue of rations is small, with the exception of issues to bands recently removed, scarcely larger than sufficient to support the poor and infirm and aged in a white community of like size. In the matter of Indian girls and women, a large majority are good and competent housekeepers, some of their homes being models of neatness. Most of the girls and young women, besides having a Knowledge of housework can read write and talk English can sew neatly and are in fact much further advanced in civilization that [than] the boys and young men. Of course this cannot be said of the members of Charlos Band, the Kootenais and Kalispels recently moved to this reservation but even with them progress is being made. Unless otherwise instructed it is my intention to pursue the plan suggested, but within the borders of the reservation, to persevere in encouraging the Indians to take up farms, fence, plow and seed them, dig irrigation ditches and strive to promote, in every way possible their efforts toward self support and independence. These ends are gradually being accomplished with slow sure strides I think as rapid as consistent, considering Indian nature Indian proclivities toward hunting and roaming. The old chiefs must die, they will not change, the old generation must pass away before self support can be a fully accomplished fact. Respectfully submitting my views in accordance with your instructions, I have the honor to remain,

Very respectfully,
Joseph T. Carter
U.S. Indian Agent.

Document 54

W. H. Smead Campaigns for Flathead Reservation Allotment January 29, 1895

Source: "The Flathead Reservation," *Daily Missoulian*, January 29, 1895, page 2, col. 1; "The Flathead Reservation," *Daily Missoulian*, February 3, 1895, page 2, col. 1.

Editors' note: Three years before being appointed Flathead Indian Agent, Smead was campaigning to allot and open the Flathead Reservation. Presumably some tribal members knew of Smead's 1895 political activity, and this would have complicated his reception on the reservation as agent in 1898.

The Flathead Reservation.

Senator W. H. Smead is the author of senate joint memorial No. 2. This is a memorial addressed to congress by the present legislative assembly of Montana, asking that lands embraced within the bounds of the present Flathead reservation be allotted to the Indians now on that reservation, in severalty, and that the remainder be thrown open to settlers.

The Flathead reservation contains an area of 3,600 square miles or 2,304,000 acres. There are on the reservation 1,300 Indians, including bucks, s....s and all papooses. Give to each buck, each s.... and each papoose 160 acres and it will make a total of 188,000 acres, leaving a balance of 2,116,000 acres of public lands for settlers, or 13,225 homesteads. This reservation also contains some of the finest agricultural lands within the limits of the state. It is well watered. The climate can not be surpassed. The Flathead lake, which is within its bounds, is a body of pure, clear water about thirty-five miles in length and having a maximum width of about eighteen miles, one of the most beautiful bodies of water in the world. This great mountain valley is crossed by only one range of mountains — the Mission range. This range of mountains is known to contain valuable deposits of gold, silver and copper, now inaccessible to the prospector and capitalist.

Should congress open this reservation it could at once furnish homes for 10,000 people. At least two thriving towns would spring up, one a trading town, the other a mining center. Besides the opening of this reservation would add millions to the wealth of Missoula and Flathead counties. This country is tributary to the cities of Missoula and Kalispell. Its development means wonders for them.

In the present depressed condition of affairs throughout the country, with thousands of unemployed, yet willing workers, it does not seem right that this vast domain should be left as a roaming and hunting ground for a few hundred Indians, when they can be well provided for and still leave over 2,000,000 acres of the public domain for the citizens of this land. By all means let the subject be pressed before congress and the nation until this desirable end is accomplished. Senator Smead is to be congratulated upon taking the initial step in this matter; and Missoula county is to be congratulated upon having such a wide awake and excellent man in its senatorial chair.

* * * * * * * * *

The Flathead Reservation.

Senate joint memorial No. 2, has passed the senate and is now pending before the house. It will undoubtedly pass that body and go before the national legislature. The matter should not be permitted to drop there. Plans should be prepared to press the proposition before congress to a successful ending.

The *Missoulian* believes that if the people of this section of the state were fully aware of all that the opening of this great reservation meant to them they would be untiring in their efforts to secure it. In the first place it is but just and right that the Indians now on this reservation should be cared for. As suggested in a former article on this subject, lands could be allotted to the Indians in severalty. This government has been expending each year for a long term of years thousands of dollars upon the education and training of the Indians. To what extent this has been successful, we are not fully advised. Granting that it has been a success, these Indians have surely reached that stage where they can, to a great extent, be self supporting and take lands in severalty. If this plan of spending thousands of dollars annually upon their training has not been a success, surely it is time to try something else. It occurs to us that 160 acres for each individual Indian now on the reservation is land enough for them. The government for several years yet would have to care for them through an agent as now. But this, we believe, would eventually be the best thing for the Indian. The Indian disposed of according to some plan that is both humane and in accordance with justice and right, let us consider what is still left for the settler. If all the 1,800 Indians now on this reservation were distributed over it uniformly there would be just two Indians on each square mile of territory. A reservation of 200,000 acres should be ample for them. This would give each Indian 160 acres of land and still leave 12,000 acres undistributed. But it would leave over 2,000,000 acres of territory for the settler. The very best agricultural lands belonging to the public domain have been taken up. Choice lands are rare. Of this 2,000,000 acres of land, at least one half cannot be excelled in any country. It lies well, is very rich, and above all is well watered. How long would it be before every foot of this land would be occupied by the intelligent and thrifty farmer, the great producer of wealth in this great country? Judging by the rush made but recently to similar tracts of land thrown open for the first time to settlement, all this country would be filled in only a few weeks or months. Can anyone doubt the material and permanent benefit it would be to Missoula, to Missoula county and even to the entire state, to have added at once to its territory a valley equal in area, natural resources and population to any in the state?

But we have only so far spoken of the agricultural possibilities of this region. It has been known for a number of years that minerals are to be found in the Mission range of mountains both gold, silver and copper, and it is not a mere matter of speculation to dwell upon the mineral possibilities of this region. In a short time this range of mountains would swarm with the miner and prospector, and doubtless many valuable and paying mines would be opened up.

Let there be united action in this matter.

W. H. Smead, Flathead Indian Agent, 1898-1904
Photograph by W. H. Taylor Studio, Helena, Montana
Source: Montana Historical Society Photo Archives, Helena, Mont.,
photo PAc 99-36.37.

Document 55

Charles Allard Tells of His Life and Buffalo Herd

March 4, 1895

Source: "They Are a Noble Lot," *The Anaconda Standard*, March 4, 1895, page 3, col. 1-2.

Editors' note: In this interview, Allard spoke of his life and the story of his buffalo herd on the Flathead Reservation.

They Are a Noble Lot
Speaking of Charlie Allard's Herd of Buffaloes.
Monarchs of the Plains
Interesting Chat With the Man Who Has Made a Success of
a Remarkable Business Venture

A famous Montana character is Charlie Allard of Ravalli, who is a guest at the Montana. Mr. Allard is famous mainly, perhaps, because he is one of the owners of the largest herd of buffalo in existence and no man living has given to these now rare animals, more patient study and attention than he. Though there are many other things which would make him famous were he less modest in telling his adventures and history.

He is still a young man at the age of 41; he has lived through hardships and braved dangers that would turn many a man's hair gray, and break a constitution, but Mr. Allard's hair is as black as coal, his eye as keen as ever, and though out of practice now, he can swing a lasso from the back of any bucking broncho that runs his range with accuracy and skill. His splendid physique perhaps is due to his ancestry, for he does not hesitate to say that the blood of Indian forefathers courses in his veins. He wears a broad-brimmed white hat and a blue flannel shirt, two articles of dress which have become as much a part of his personality, from his long life on the plains and prairies as cowboy and express rider, that he never discards them for the stiffness of a derby and the boiled article of civilization and discomfort.

Like many others of the prominent citizens of this state, Mr. Allard walked into it, but that was in 1866, and now he could charter a train of sleepers with a porter for every car if he chose to travel, but he is not luxurious in his tastes and accommodates himself to circumstance. The most convenient mode of travel, a foot, on the hurricane deck of a cayuse or on a cushioned seat in a palace car. He is a genial good fellow with a funny story of nature or a reminiscence that will entertain any hearer.

It was thus a *Standard* reporter enjoyed an hour's chat with him yesterday at the Montana. During the course of the conversation Mr. Allard told of his buffaloes and their history.

"The very first buffalo I ever saw I captured with my lariat," said he, "on the prairies of Kansas. I was younger then than I am now and I know a whole lot more about buffaloes than I did then, but I learned a great deal in one short half hour. I was in charge of a bunch of cattle down in that country for Demars in 1870, and, though I had never seen a buffalo, I knew one when I saw a huge bull on a knoll about a mile from where the cattle were feeding. He was going along very quietly and paid no attention to me when I rode up towards him on horseback. The horse I rode was a pretty good animal and used to buffalo hunting and was obedient to every touch on his rein. I had no weapon except an old-fashioned muzzle-loading revolver, and when I started to see the buffalo I was drawn by curiosity, but as I rode closer, a wild desire to capture the bull drew upon me and I determined to capture him at all hazards.

"I was handy with the rope in those days and as reckless a youth as ever straddled a broncho. So, as I rode up, I fired my revolver at the bull and missed him. The shot frightened him, however, and he started to run. I put spurs to my horse and followed as fast as possible. Only a moment was required to loosen the rope that hung from the pommell of my saddle, and I soon overtook the buffalo which, luckily for me, was old and clumsy, and in mighty short time my lariat was fast over both horns of the bull. Then I realized that I had caught a tarter, for, as soon as he felt the restraint of the rope, the bull showed fight. The line tightened and he wheeled about and faced me, standing for a moment pawing the ground, raising the dust in a cloud. Then he charged. His horn grazed my horse's flank, though I spurred him and he was trained to the business of dodging steers. Again and again I tried to get that rope about his foot, but he moved about so restlessly and charged so frequently that I was almost ready to cut the lariat and leave my prize when help, in the person a of a big, fat cowboy, who proved to be a bigger fool than I was, came upon the scene.

"Then we divided his attention between us and I managed to get the looked-for hold and in a few minutes the buffalo lay prostrate in the toils of my lariat. He could only struggle vainly and was powerless to rise when my pony settled back and snubbed him up as we do in branding steers.

"Then the other fellow left his horse and cautiously approached our fallen victim with his knife in hand. The bull kicked wildly and frantically and I feared he would prove too strong for my rope. Two or three times my partner retreated in mad haste to his horse, thinking the buffalo would break away, and if he had there would have been sure death to a man on foot. But the beast could not get up, and in a few minutes my friend sawed in two the hamstrings of the buffalo and we killed him at our leisure."

"It was about that time I conceived the idea of keeping a herd of buffalo, for at the rate they were being killed then I knew that some day they would become scarce and valuable. I captured four or five calves and kept them with our herd, but during the hard winter hay became scarce and I was compelled to turn them loose. Then I was never able to start out for myself, because every time I wanted to quit the boss raised my salary and thus persuaded me to keep on cowpunching. When I finally gave it up he was paying me $200 a month. Then I came to the Flathead valley. I had been wintering there every year for several years, riding the express route from Horse Plains to Mission for Clark Bros. during the winter season. I bought from the Indians a few head of buffalo which they had there in semi-captivity on the reservation. I paid them from $200 to $300 apiece for the animals and then I started into the business of raising buffalo. The herd thrived in all seasons. They had a range of from 30 to 40 miles north and south and were shut in on both side by wooded hills which made as good a fence as a man could build, for buffalo do not venture among the trees.

"The coldest storms of winter do not trouble them, for their thick shaggy coast are wind proof. During the heavy snows and blizzards they climb the hills and turning their breasts to the wind defy the storm. They feed where the snow is thinnest. Cattle are driven before a storm and will often go with a wind 60 or 100 miles from the accustomed range, unless they reach a sheltered spot. Horses turn their backs to a storm, but the buffalo faces it every time. They seem to keep in about the same condition of flesh the year round, and are as good eating in the spring as they are in the fall, and a buffalo steak is as fine a morsel as ever a man made a meal. About two years ago I purchased the Jones herd of buffalo, which was at Omaha. There were 31 of them in the herd and we paid, for I have a partner now, $18,000 for the lot. Marchiel Pablo, a well known cattle man, has joined me in the business and for the past year has had [illegible] charge of them, so that I do not know just exactly how many we have, about 140 I should judge now, and by next fall there will be fully 200 of them.

We have experimented in crossing buffalo with all breeds of cattle and the results have been most satisfactory. The Polled Angus stock, when crossed with the buffalo produces a magnificent animal. The fur is finer and closer than that of the buffalo and the meat is sweet and wholesome. We are procuring as many of these animals as possible, but will not put any on the market for several years yet. We are not selling any buffalo, either, for the reason that we need them all at present. We received letters every day from museums, parks and shows, wanting them in all quantities and though we might dispose of one or two singly we have no pairs to sell.

A good buffalo hide is worth $100 now in the market and heads bring from $200 to $500 when mounted, and the value of these is steadily increasing, so that buffalo breeding is as good an investment as real estate. Our herd is the only one I know about of any size. There is a small one in the Texas Pan Handle and these, with the few that roam in the National park, are the sole remnants of the thousands which roamed the prairies but a few years ago."

Document 56

Indian Leaders Fight With Agent Carter

March 5, 1895

Source: "Went on the War Path," *The Anaconda Standard*, March 6, 1895, page 6, col. 3; excerpt from "Their Hearts Are Bad," *The Anaconda Standard*, March 8, 1895, page 6, col. 3; "All at Liberty Again," *The Anaconda Standard*, March 14, 1895, page 6, col. 3; "Those Three Bad Indians," *The Anaconda Standard*, March 23, 1895, page 6, col. 3-4; Joseph T. Carter to Commissioner of Indian Affairs, May 7, 1895, letter received 20,518/1895, RG 75, National Archives, Washington, D.C.; "Will Walk Back," *The Kalispell Graphic*, May 15, 1895, page 2, col. 3.

Editors' note: Agent Carter's standoff with Louison and Charlo in March 1895, led to a complicated legal controversy. Three Indians were arrested and jailed in Missoula for the disturbance. Duncan McDonald hired a lawyer and got the accused Indians released on a habeas corpus petition, but they were rearrested by the U.S. Marshall. They were finally released by the U.S. Court in Helena when the government could not find any laws they have violated. See also Duncan McDonald's February 12, 1896, letter to a Missoula law firm for more information about the legal conflict.

Went on the War Path
An Indian Outbreak on the Flathead Reservation.
It Didn't Last Very Long
For an Hour or So Matters Looked Very Serious for Agent Carter
and His Few Faithful Servants at Jocko.

Missoula, March 5. — There was a miniature war at the Flathead agency last night, and for a time matters looked serious for Agent [Joseph] Carter and the handful of employes and Indian police that faced a crowd of angry Indians in front of the agency jail. Revolvers and rifles cracked and bullets whistled for a time, but the discharge of arms was a bluff and the resolute firmness of the little force under the agent won. The malcontents finally dispersed and three of their leaders are now confined in the Missoula jail. The disturbance was effectually quelled and it is not believed that there will be any further outbreak.

The trouble began about a week ago, during Agent Carter's absence from the agency on business. At that time, the tribe known as the Bitter Root Flatheads, whose lands are nearest the agency at Jocko, indulged in a war dance. The beating of tom-toms and the yells of the dancers were the first intimation that the agency people had of the intention of the Indians to perform this forbidden dance. Chief Clerk [Vincent] Ronan at once dispatched an Indian policeman to the dancers with the command to stop the dance at once. The command was obeyed, but, after the policeman departed, the dance was resumed as vigorously as ever and continued in defiance of the order from the agency.

Investigation showed that, after the policeman had returned to the agency, Louison, a medicine man of the Bitter Root tribe, had told the Indians to go on with the dance and pay no attention to the orders of the white man. Some of the young bucks then proceeded with the frenzied dance and there was considerable ugliness manifested toward the agent and his employes.

When Mr. Carter returned to the agency he promptly ordered the arrest of Louison and the medicine man was locked in the agency jail. This angered the young bucks of the tribe and they came to the agency office with the demand that their medicine man be at once released. If he was not allowed to go by the agent, they said they would batter down the jail and let him go themselves.

Mr. Carter's reply to this was that unless they at once withdrew and made no further disturbance, they would be locked up themselves. They paid no attention to this injunction, however, and at once hurried to the jail, where they effected an entrance and were hammering away at the cell door behind which the medicine man was locked. The prisoner incited them to use more force and his words gave them superhuman strength. They fairly threw themselves at the strong inner door and it seemed as if their purpose would be accomplished in a few moments.

All this had taken but a brief time and Agent Carter had meanwhile collected whatever men were available, white employes of the agency and a few Indian police. Arming this little force, Mr. Carter led them on the run to the jail, where the angry Indians were trying to release their medicine man. All of these Indians were inside the jail and to shut the outer door and cover them with the rifles was the work of an instant. They were commanded to desist and to surrender. This they did reluctantly and three of them who had been leaders of the crowd, where made prisoners. These three were Swash, Nicolla and Louis Coull-Coullee. They were handcuffed and bound and their companions sent away.

Agent Carter decided that, for safe keeping, he would send these three bad ones to the Missoula jail, and preparations were at once made to get them to

Missoula quietly. They were placed in a wagon and the team left the agency without attracting attention.

The bucks of the Bitter Root tribe were on the alert, however, and before the outfit had driven two miles, it was surrounded by 30 armed and mounted Indians, who, at the point of the rifle, demanded the release of the prisoners. This was done and the belligerent Indians returned to the agency, flushed with victory and uglier than ever.

They became boisterous and the situation was so critical that Agent Carter wired to the commandant at Fort Missoula for troops. The reply was that none could be sent without order from the department headquarters and a request was made for further information as to the cause of the trouble and the means of defence at the command of the agent.

Before replying, Agent Carter decided to try the effect of a bluff on the Indians. With an interpreter, he talked to the malcontents and told them that that was their last opportunity to surrender their men without getting themselves into trouble. If they did not turn over these three men, they would all be arrested, as troops would be there in a short time, unless they submitted peaceably. They could have their choice — surrender the men without trouble or have them taken by force.

The Indians took counsel among themselves and the more conservative prevailed. They decided to turn over the prisoners to the agent. This they did, and Mr. Carter reached here this afternoon with the prisoners in charge. Swasah, Nicolla and Louis Coul-Coullee are now safe in Sheriff McLaughlin's stronghold, where they remain sullen and looking as mean as coyotes.

* * * * * * * *

Their Hearts Are Bad
Indians Who Have Been Causing Trouble.
Three Real Bad Redskins
Incidents Concerning the Recent Outbreak at the Jocko Agency.

Missoula, March 7. — The three insurgent Indians, Swasah, Nicolla and Louis Coull-Coullee, who are confined in the city jail as a result of the outbreak at the Jocko agency Monday night, are sullen and morose and will say nothing to anybody. They are stoical in their indifference to all that goes on around them and accept their meals with ugly actions. All day yesterday an old s.... persistently loitered around the jail, begging to be allowed to see the imprisoned Indians. She says that one of them is her "pappoose" and she wants to talk with him. She has importuned everybody from the sheriff to the janitor to grant her permission to get inside the jail, but she has been turned away by everybody. After each refusal she goes away weeping piteously, but returns again in a few minutes, her tears dried, and waits for some one else to appear of who she can ask the desired privilege of seeing her son, who, though a big, strong buck, is still a "pappoose" to her, his mother.

* * * * * * * *

All At Liberty Again
The Three Rebellious Indians Discharged From Jail,
They Were Well Pleased
Judge Woody Advised Them to Go and Sin No More,
and They Wandered Outside and Joined in a Great Pow-Wow.

Missoula, March 13. — At 3 o'clock this afternoon Sheriff McLaughlin led a little procession from the county jail to the district court room. Behind him stalked in haughty dignity the three Indians, Swasah, Nicolla and Louis Coul-Coullee, who have been confined in the jail since the outbreak at the Jocko agency last week. Under Sheriff Curran brought up the rear, bearing the writ of habeas corpus issued by Judge Woody yesterday commanding the sheriff to show why these Indians were deprived of their liberty. The Indians paid no attention to anything that was going on around them, but marched straight on, well muffled in their gaudy blankets, two of them smoking cigarettes. They looked as if they had fared well during their confinement and were all sleek and cleaner than most of the reservation Indians.

All had good blankets of the customary high colors. Two of them wore white slouch hats, while the third had no head covering except his heavy black hair. Swasah is a tall, powerful looking young fellow, who looked like a Fenimore Cooper Indian. He wore regulation buckskin moccasins and looked as fierce and contemptuous as the wild Indian of romance is supposed to look. His companions were not so attractive, as one of them wore a pair of old congress gaiters and the other clumped along in a pair of heavy gum boots. The latter, as he threw back his blanket, disclosed a pair of gay breeches that looked as if they might have come from Herr Bandmann's theatrical wardrobe.

Entering the court room the Indians took seats and waited for the legal proceedings to go on. They were represented by Joseph K. Wood, who stated that the Indians had been held in jail for more than a week and that no charge had been preferred against them. The sheriff's return of the writ showed that the three Indians had been brought to him by the agent of the reservation and that he had been requested to hold them until a complaint had been filed. He also stated that he had to-day received a telegram from United States

Marshall McDermott, saying that a marshal would be here to-morrow with the complaints.

Judge Woody heard the attorney for the Indians and then examined the return made by the sheriff. He then ordered the Indians to be released. He told the aborigines to return to the reservation and behave themselves and then they wouldn't get locked up again. As soon as they understood that they were free the red men gravely shook hands with the judge and left the room as calmly as if they had not been in danger of going to the penitentiary for a year.

A few minutes past 3 o'clock a crowd of Indians had begun to assemble about the court house and when the three ex-prisoners came out of the building un-attended by an officer there were fully 25 of their friends waiting to receive them. The delegation was headed by the Indian judge who appeared yesterday to ask for the writ and the old fellow's green feather fairly bristled with delight as he welcomed the young braves whose loyalty to their medicine man had got them into such grave trouble. The crowd held an animated pow-wow for a few minutes and then went away to celebrate the release of the heroes.

* * * * * * * *

Those Three Bad Indians.
They Are Once More in Missoula's Jail.

Missoula, March 22. — The three bad Indians, Louis Coull-Coullee, Swasah and Nicolla, who were released from jail last week upon habeas corpus proceedings are locked up again. They were arrested at Jocko agency last evening by Deputy Marshal Haley and Bailiff Micklejohn, upon writs issued by the United States court. They will be arraigned here before United States Commissioner Smith as soon as Governor Leslie arrives from Helena. This will probably be to-morrow afternoon. Another Indian, Pierre, was arrested with them.

Marshal Haley came down from the agency this morning and, in speaking of this matter to a *Standard* reporter, he said: "There is a disposition on the part of some people to make light of the disturbance caused by these Indians. I find that it is really a serious matter. The three who were arrested on the night of the revolt at the agency are, unquestionably, bad Indians and since their release from the Missoula jail they have been worse than ever. They seem to be fermenting trouble all the time at the agency and they ought to be locked up where they can't stir up their fellows. Agent Carter deals very leniently with his charges on the reservation, I find. When he makes a complaint, you may be sure that there is some cause for it. There are many instances where he would be justified in proceeding against some of these turbulent spirits, when he overlooks the offenses entirely.

The four Indians were brought before Commission Smith this evening and the complaints read to them. They entered pleas of not guilty and the cases were set for trial at 2 o'clock to-morrow afternoon.

* * * * * * * *

United States Indian Service,
Flathead Agency,
Jocko, P.O. Montana
May 7th, 1895.

Hon. Commissioner Indian Affairs,
Washington, D.C.
Sir:

Replying to your letter Land 10,563.1895 dated March 18th 1895 also to your telegram dated May 3d 1895, I desire to report the sequel to the arrest of Louison as reported in my letter of March 4th ult.

In the afternoon a party of Indian demanded his release and upon being refused attempted to force open the jail overpowering the jailor. The leaders were soon overpowered and handcuffed. Upon starting them to Missoula for safe Keeping, a mounted and armed rescuing party numbering about thirty, overtook the team and and [sic] released the prisoners. I then telegraphed for assistance to the commander of Fort Missoula and pending his reply, sent word to the Indians who were concerned in the rescue, that unless the prisoners were given up, I would have each and all of them arrested and punished.

They thereupon returned the prisoners after filing off the handcuffs and I so telegraphed Col. Burt at Fort Missoula stating no troops would be needed.

The following day I brought them to Missoula and placed them in the County Jail and personally communicated the facts to U.S. Dist. Attorney Leslie.

A stress of work and matters calling for his attention prevented his filing a complaint against the culprits that day and in some way none was filed for about ten days. Meantime, during my absence at the Sub-station a Nez Perces half breed, Duncan McDonald employed two attorneys and secured the release of the Indians upon a writ of habeas corpus.

Returning and hearing of this proceeding I immediately communicated with Attorney Leslie; proper complaints were drawn, warrants issued and the culprits rearrested by Deputy U.S. Marshals assisted by the Indian Police.

The leader of the mounted Indians who rescued the prisoners, and notorious renegade named Big Pierre, was also arrested. All were arraigned and bound over to appear before the U.S. Grand Jury and are now incarcerated in the Helena Jail. The strong measures necessary in repressing these leaders has had a good effect and, exceptional peace and quiet as well as industry is to be noted everywhere notwithstanding the efforts of some Nes Perces, among them Duncan McDonald, Louison and a few sympathisers to forment trouble and discord. In this connection I desire here to state that Louison is the Nez Perces Indian referred to in your letter dated March 9, 1895 "Land" who has been allotted land as "6. Kol-Kol-snee-nee, 50 years of age. Brother of Elk who resides on Nez Perce allotment not yet approved." I earnestly urge that his allotment be approved and he moved upon it.

McDonald has always been a disturber if not worse as far back as the Nez Perce war as the correspondence in this office appears to indicate and seemingly cunning enough to protect himself. I simply mention this that the Hon. Commissioner may be advised of this mans character. He too is entitled to an allotment upon the Nez Perce reserve, his mother and sister each receiving allotments there, but as he has considerable money invested in improvements here, he does not desire to move and, while sometimes annoying, his conduct can be controlled.

On April 29th I was summoned to appear before the Grand Jury to testify in these cases. The Jury found indictments against three Indians but the U.S. Attorney, Ex Gov. Leslie was in doubt as to what law or statute would cover the offences; in fact feared they could not be convicted and punished under any. Not forseeing this contingency and Knowing that the indictments had to be drawn at once if at all, I telegraphed for advice in the hope that possibly similar cases had been brought to the notice of the Indian Office that would guide in this. However the answer not giving all the information sought, indictments were drawn against each under the statutes and rules of the Secretary of the Interior, which in the judgment of the U.S. District Attorney had been violated, as a failure to indict at the present time, would permit of their release upon a writ of habeas corpus. Had I doubted for a moment that the offence committed was not punishable under the U.S. Statutes I should have submitted the case earlier to the Indian Office for advice, and many other important matters pressing prevented an earlier report. I desire to reiterate that while some strong measures were necessary, it has resulted in exceptional industry, peace and quiet. A larger acreage has been plowed and planted than ever before in the history of this reserve. The progressively disposed are prospering. I herewith enclose vouchers for traveling expenses of self and Indian Police in taking prisoners to Missoula Jail also copies of telegrams sent at that time and later and respectfully request that the expenditure be approved and allowed and authority granted to pay for same from funds on hand under Incedentals in Montana. I have the honor to remain,

> Very respectfully,
> Joseph T. Carter
> U.S. Indian Agent.

* * * * * * * *

Will Walk Back.

The laws of the United States sometimes work great hardship on the people, says the Helena Independent. It is so in the case of Swasah and Nickola, two Flathead Indians. They were arrested by order of Agent Carter on the charge of riotous and disorderly conduct, because they wished to engage in a sun dance or some other festivity. While on the way to Missoula jail they were rescued by a number of indians [sic] led by Big Pierre. They were rearrested and brought to Helena, where they have been in the county jail since April 1. The grand jury refused to find any indictment against them, and yesterday, at the request of District Attorney Leslie, all proceedings against them were dismissed. They were accordingly let loose without money to pay their railway fare back to the reservation, and with the only alternative, to walk.

Big Pierre was indicted by the grand jury for his part in the rescue. Owing to the limited time Judge Beatty has to remain here and the delay in getting the witnesses to Helena he will be unable to preside at the trial of the case. He also said it would a hardship to keep Big Pierre until his case could be tried, and suggested, in case the Indian did not secure bail, that he be taken back to the reservation and be kept in jail there.

Document 57

Agent Peter Ronan Advised Against
Land Negotiations
April 24, 1895

Source: "Some Inside Facts," *Daily Missoulian*, April 24, 1895, page 1, col. 2.

Editors' note: In 1892 Congress passed a law providing for negotiations with the Flathead Reservation Indians to reduce the size of the reservation. After Agent Peter Ronan advised against such negotiations in 1892, the Indian Office moved on to try to convince other tribes to sell parts of their reservations. The *Missoulian* reporter was offended that Indian opinions had been considered and negotiations for the reduction of the Flathead Reservation were dropped "simply because a few Indians had prejudices in the matter."

Some Inside Facts
Your Uncle Grover Negligent In the Flathead Matter.
Ignored the Act of Congress.
He Never Appointed Commissioners to Treat With the Flathead Indians.

Annexed is a copy of the letter received by Hon. T. H. Carter from Thomas P. Smith, acting commissioner. Brief mention was made of it in the report of the board of trade meeting in yesterday's *Missoulian*. The letter contains some interesting information not heretofore made public and shows some reasons why the government has been negligent in conforming to or executing the act which contemplated the allotment of land in severalty to the Indians and the opening of the remainder of the reservation to settlement. It appears by the letter that the late agent, Major [Peter] Ronan, had advised that it would be unwise to undertake to treat with the Indians.

It would seem strange that a law passed by congress directing certain things be done should become obsolete and non-effective simply because a few Indians had prejudices in the matter. The law passed for a specific purpose. It directed the president to appoint commissioners to treat with the Indians. It appropriated money to pay the expenses of that commission. The purpose of the law was plain and the intention of congress was not observed, but Grover came to the conclusion that his opinion on the subject was paramount to congress and he simply ignored it. Cleveland thought in this matter, as in several other, that he occupied the chair simply to enforce such laws as suited him. The letter is as follows:

Hon. Thomas H. Carter, Helena, Mont., Sir — I am in receipt of your letter dated March 19. 1895, stating that in the act providing for "general incidental expenses of the Indian service" approved July 13, you observe an item providing for negotiations with certain Indians in Wyoming, and also the Flathead Indians and confederated tribes in Montana for the surrender of certain lands, etc., and the appropriation of the sum of $5,000 for the expenses of the commissioners.

Your request to be advised whether the negotiations with the Flathead Indians of Montana were prosecuted, and if so, with what results and if not whether the appropriation is still available.

In reply I have to state that no commission has been appointed to negotiate with the Indians of the Flathead reservation, Montana, under the act making the appropriation to which you refer, approved July 13, 1892, (27 States. 138.)

The office never asked for the appropriation of funds to negotiate with the Flathead Indians, and it was not intended that any portion of the funds referred to should be used for that purpose; so at least it was understood by this office.

The commission was appointed to negotiate with the Indians of the Wind River, or Shoshone reservation, Wyoming, but they were unsuccessful in their efforts. There remains a balance of the said appropriation amounting to $3,074.55.

For your further information I have to state that Senators Sanders and Power were advised by separate letters dated December 7, 1892, that the late agent Ronan was instructed August 15, 1892, to report whether it would be wise to negotiate with the Flatheads Indians for the cession of any surplus lands before the allotments should be made, or whether it would be better to have the lands surveyed and allotted first.

On November 6, 1892, the said agent transmitted his report to this office stating that the chiefs of the Flathead Indians bitterly opposed the allotment of land in severalty, and were upheld in their prejudices by most of the full blood Indians on the reservation; that no allotments had then been made to any Indians within the boundaries of the same; that great prejudice prevailed against a survey of any kind; that some of the younger and more enlightened Indians desired allotments and titles to their lands, but that they were silent upon the question inasmuch as it was unpopular to discuss the same; that nearly every head of a family on that reservation occupied definite, separate, though unallotted tracts; that their fences or boundary marks were generally respected, and that they lived in houses, the majority of their homes presenting a thrifty, farm like appearance.

For these reasons the agent did not believe it would be wise to propose negotiations with them for the cession of any surplus lands or attempt at that time to have the lands surveyed and allotted; that according to the views then held, the Indians would not listen to any negotiations looking whether to allotments in severalty or to cession of the surplus lands within the boundary of their reservation.

Very Respectfully,
[Sig.] Thos. P. Smith,
Acting Commissioner.

Document 58

White Traveler Through the
Flathead Reservation in 1895
June 4, 1895

Source: H. M. Kingsbury, "From Thompson to Kalispel," *Weekly Montanian* (Thompson Falls, Mont.) June 8, 1895, page 2, col. 1-2.

Editors' note: Kingsbury's travelogue in 1895 told of visiting with Duncan McDonald at Ravalli, the ferry at the Foot of Flathead Lake, and the buffalo (or buffalo/cattle hybrids) Charles Allard had grazing on Wild Horse Island in Flathead Lake.

From Thompson to Kalispel.
[by H. M. Kingsbury.]
Leona, Idaho, June 4th, 1895.

Editor Hendricks,

Dear Friend.

Thinking a few items picked up since I left Thompson might be of interest to your readers of the *Montanian*, here they are:

Leaving the N. P. Ry. at Ravalli, Mont., my route lay to the north. I stopped at Ravalli one day and two nights, the guest of Duncan McDonald who is the son of an old time Hudson Bay Co's. agent. Mr. McDonald has a fine place including a flourishing and extensive orchard which promises to yield upwards of 1,000 boxes of fruit this year. He entertained his guests with many interesting anecdotes and gave us an exhibition with his bow and arrows which he keeps hanging in his office. The bow is a remarkable piece of workmanship, being made of rams horn, it is perfect in shape and covered on the back with rattle snake skin. This bow, 40 inches in length, would drive the shaft 200 yards with ease. Mr. McDonald offered to bet five dollars that he could drive the arrow further into wood than a bullet from a six shooter could go, but no one took him up.

Well we are on the stage drawn by four horses and a few miles drive over a smooth road winding through rolling grassy hills, brings us to the Mission Valley, so named because here is located the famous Jesuit Mission of St. Ignatius. Here we see an exquisitely beautiful valley watered by Mission river and its tributaries, flanked on the east and north by the lofty Mission range

of mountains. Numerous farmes [sic] are noticed through the valley while the
prairies are stocked with countless cattle. The road is smooth and keeps an
almost air line direction north to Flathead lake which we reach about noon.
Here we find a few s.... men and numerous tepes of the red men. For crossing
the lake here the Indians have flat boats 30 by 40 feet long which they propell
by two immense oars a man to each oar. They sit in the bow of the boat and a
third man stands at the stern with a long oar in a socket, to stear [sic] the boat.
They can cross pretty easy if the wind does not blow. I saw a boat out in a squall
and it was swinging a good deal out of her course. Our stage ride is at an end
after a 32 miles ride. We must now take the steamer for our destination, but
no steamer is in sight and the telephone nor the telegraph are not on hand to
tell us how late she is. Soon, however, some one shouts "there she is." We look
and see a tiny speck at the horrizon [sic] in the north and are informed by a
resident that it is the steamer more than 10 miles away and that she will land
in about an hour. "Better late than never" and we are contented and spent the
time watching two young ladies catching fish. They have come in from the
country with their father and mother. They are good looking and their father
is a good looking polite man but their mother appears to be a halfbreed. They
proved their ability to fish by landing a large salmon trout. Gradually the little
speck has grown bigger and the steamer "Kalispel" is landing. The gang plank is
run ashore and an old crippled Dutchman wants to come ashore, we give him
a helping hand. Then three ladies appear and a baby, we carry the baby while
the cook helps the ladies to walk the plank. Then a lady with two pretty babies
is taken aboard and we quickly depart for Kalispel 65 miles to the north. The
beauty of the Flathead Lake can scarcely be described. Its peer can not be found.
Its rivals are few, nowhere in the heart of civilization, the world over, can there
be found a lake so large, so grand an altitude so great (2,500 feet) a climate so
superb. Its waters swarm with the finest fish in the world. Char, salmon trout,
rainbow trout, pike and white fish, and perhaps others unknown. Numerous
large rivers and brooks flow into the lake and all are swarming with the finny
tribes. The shores of the lake are lined with red men, fishing rod in hand, lazily
passing the hours away. In our voyage we touch at Wildhorse Island, (6 miles
long, and 3 miles wide) to leave some provisions for Moses, not the hebrew
of ancient fame, but a good looking full blooded Indian who speaks better
United States than a Londoner. Chas. Allard has placed his buffalo herd of 60
head on this Island and Mosses [sic] is their keeper. Separated from the main
land by a vast expanse of water, this is the one ideal spot on earth to keep a
herd of bison. The entire Island is covered with luxuriant and nutritious grass.
The bison were kind enough to be at the water's edge so we could have a close
view. This is the largest known herd of bison in the world and are valued at

1,000 dollars per head. I was told they are being successfully crossed with the Polled Angus cattle. Circling Wildhorse Island and touching at Dayton creek, takes us near 30 miles out of our course and we do not reach Demersville (the head of navigation) until 10 p.m. The Flathead river is a majestic stream and at Demersville 28 miles from its mouth the water is said to be 75 feet deep. The lake proper is 38 miles long and 15 to 23 miles wide and unknown in depth. Lofty mountaing [sic] lay to the east, high hills on the west, to the north and south the great Flathead valley, which like the lake is of marvelous beauty and unexcelled fertility. I saw corn raised at Kalispel, which is 17 feet tall, oats over 6 feet tall. Capt. Symons, government engineer, was in Kalispel when I was there, he has been examining the lake and rivers in order to estimate the cost of opening the river for navigation from the foot of the lake to Jocko. When this is done it will enable boats to sail from Kalispel and discharge their cargoes at the N. P. Ry. at Jocko. Capt. Symons says it is only a question of money as the plan is feasible and meritorious. The people at the head of the lake want a canal at the foot of the lake large enough to draw off the surplus water in flood time so as to avoid the widespread flooding of hundreds of square miles of valuable lands at the head of the lake, such as occured in the high water of last year. Capt. Symons remarked that "the government would not do that but would only work for the purposes of navigation." This is a country worth a long journey to see. The seeker after health, the sportsman and the lover of the beautiful and the rare in nature can all find their senses pleased and gratified. The round trip over stage and steamer is 13 dollars, and the distance traveled is 194 miles and in that trip we can see vast prairies, lofty mountains covered with snow, an immense lake, untutored savages in breech clouts, herds of bison, boundless forests, and majestic rivers, all in one day.

Document 59

Charlie Kicking Horse Attacked in Missoula Jail

July 7, 1895

Source: "He Was Kangarooed," *The Anaconda Standard*, July 7, 1895, page 6, col. 3.

Editors' note: The incident described in this article was outrageous. Charlie Kicking Horse was put in jail because he was needed as a witness in a court case, not because he was charged with a crime. In jail, he was attacked by the other inmates because he refused to turn over his money to them. According to the article, the jailers did not interfere with or try to stop the attack.

He Was Kangarooed
This Indian Was a First-Class Subject for the Kangarooer.
Would Not Pay the Fine
So "Shorty," the Judge, and the Swede Sheriff Put "It on" to Him Pretty Thick — Fun for the Spectators.

Missoula, July 6. — The whitewashed walls of the county jail have witnessed many an interesting sight and if they could speak could tell tales of thrilling interest — tales of tragic import, as well as of keen comedy.

There have been jollifications there and there have been scenes of mourning. Within the space enclosed by these walls has been played over and over again the whole scale of the gamut of human emotions. Wailing has been succeeded by laughter and happiness has followed misery. Chinamen, Indians, Ethiopians and Caucasions have all shared in the varied experiences that have transpired in Missoula's county jail and the incidents of their confinement have been as varied as the traits of the prisoners.

In all the history of the jail, however, it is doubtful if there ever occurred a more ludicrous incident than one which was witnessed last night be a few fortunate ones who happened to be in the sheriff's office after Sheriff Keim had arrested the men Houston and Holland, who are charged with cheating Indians. The policeman had had a stiff chase after the men and quite a crowd had been attracted to the scene. The two Indians, whose $3.50 Houston is alleged to have embezzled, were also locked up as witnesses and it was when the kangaroo court got hold of Charlie Kicking Horse that the fun began. The court made short work of Houston and Holland. They had no money and all that could be done with them was to put them over the barrel and attack them from the rear with a broom. This was soon accomplished and the court was ready for the consideration of the cases of the aborigines.

When Charlie Kickinghorse was searched the jailer found a whole bunch of firecrackers, six single firecrackers and $2.50 in silver. The possession of this money was the basis of the action brought against the Indian by the kangaroo court and the charge as formulated by the prosecution was the carrying of concealed money. A fellow who is serving a 60-day sentence was elected judge. His name is "Shorty," and he was as dignified as if he were presiding in Chief Justice Fuller's stead. A big Swede was made sheriff and the court was ready for business.

Some time was lost in finding an interpreter, as Charlie Kickinghorse could not speak English — or, at any rate, would not. At length a man was found who could converse with the red man and the trial began. There was no doubt that the Indian had been guilty of carrying $2.50 concealed upon his person, but he was given an opportunity to show to the court some good and sufficient reason why he should not be summarily punished for the dire offense. This he could not do. His explanation of how he came by the money counted for naught. He may have come by it honestly — if he did, so much the worse. No true jailbird would do anything like that. But there was, the court held, no valid reason why an Indian should be found guilty on the day after the Fourth, sober and with money in his pocket. Such conduct was radically wrong and merited the severest punishment.

The court, however, was disposed to be lenient, especially as the prisoner appeared to be somewhat ignorant of what was required of a man whose residence is the county jail. Accordingly, after due deliberation, Charlies Kickinghorse was sentenced to pay a fine of $2, although the court felt that he might err in not taking the odd 50 cents. He would for the sake of the family of the accused, run the risk of being considered too merciful and would make the fine only $2. The sheriff was instructed to collect the fine at once.

Charlie Kickinghorse had, by this time, become sullen and surly. He realized that it was useless to put himself in contempt of court and he said not a word. But he refused to pay the fine. In vain the sheriff coaxed him and the judge threatened. The horrors of the kangaroo punishment, as depicted by the interpreter, had no effect upon him. He would not give up the $2. Finding that all argument was vain, the court instructed the sheriff to prepare to inflict upon the prisoner the alternative punishment and the big Swede prepared.

The nature of this punishment is familiar to those who know anything about kangaroo courts. The condemned man is bent into such a position as will bring into prominence that portion of his anatomy which nature evidently intended to be spanked when it is not sat upon. Then a vigorous castination is administered, its extent depending upon the severity of the court. Now, as is well known, the Indian never covers that particular part of his frame with clothing. If he receives a pair of civilized trousers, he at once cuts out the seat and then drapes his blanket so as to conceal the defect.

In this respect, Charlie Kickinghorse is a true Indian. There was no protecting raiment to shield him from the blows of the sheriff's broom, when his blanket was removed and he was properly bent over. the bailiffs who held the prisoner hung on to him like grim death and the big Swede sheriff smiled audibly as he sized the splendid physique that was presented as a mark for the blows to be administered.

"All ready?"

"Yes. Let her go.

Whack!

"Ugh. Ugh."

Whack!!

"Ugh. Ugh. Ugh."

Another whack and the corridors of the jail echoed to the wail of the death chant of the Selish. Poor Charlie Kickinghborse thought that his time had come. Now subdued and now swelling forth like the wail of a lost soul, the cadence of the death song rose and fell. The kangarooed brave bade good bye to home and friends, to the scenes of his triumphs in the hunt and chase and was about to commend himself to the Great Spirit, when the big Swede let up. The dying brave arose and wrapped his blanket about his stalwart frame. But he didn't sit down — not much. He simply leaned the bruised portion of his anatomy against the cool brick wall and said it felt heap good.

Document 60

Duncan McDonald Possible U.S. Commissioner

August 4, 1895

Source: Joseph T. Carter, to Commissioner of Indian Affairs, August 4, 1895, letter received 33,331/1895, RG 75, National Archives, Washington, D.C.

Editors' note: Agent Joseph Carter was apoplectic over the possible appointment of Duncan McDonald as U.S. Commissioner to screen potential cases for the U.S. Court in Helena. McDonald had been a longtime opponent of Carter and was imbued "with Indian prejudices." Carter might be consoled if the appointment made McDonald a U.S. citizen which would allow Carter to force him off the reservation. On August 14, 1895, the Commissioner of Indian Affairs informed Carter that McDonald's appointment as U.S. Commissioner would not make him a citizen, but Carter could complain about the appointment to the U.S. Court in Helena. As far as can be determined, McDonald never finally served as U.S. Commissioner.

United States Indian Service,
Flathead Agency,
Jocko, P.O. Mont.
Aug 4, 1895

Hon. Commissioner Indian Affairs,
Washington, D.C.
Sir:

A few days ago I was notified by the U.S. District Attorney Preston H. Leslie that the U.S. District Judge for Montana, Hiram Knowles had appointed an Indian named Duncan McDonald, of this reservation a Commissioner for the U.S. Court. Mr. Leslie wrote further that he desired to see me about the matter.

It is the opinion of the U.S. Attorney that in the event of McDonald accepting and qualifying he becomes a citizen of the United States: can vote hold real property etc and by the same act severs his tribal relations with the Indians upon this reserve. This being the case I presume it my duty to remove him from it. If the Indian Office does not so hold I respectfully ask that the Hon. Commissioner authorize me so to do, as his presence here in the capacity of a U.S. Court Commissioner is a menace to good order, the progress and civilization of the Indians settled here.

In the event that this latter course is not thought necessary or best I earnestly urge that the matter be brought to the attention of the Department of Justice and the necessary steps be taken to have this appointment revoked.

It seems to me irregular wrong and to violate the rules and perogatives of the Indian Office and Department of the Interior, which prescribes how Indians may be appointed Officers in the service of the United States. I certainly have no objections to the Hon. Judge appointing any white man whom he may see fit to the position of U.S. Court Commissioner who may reside upon the reservation, in fact I think it would be wise to have one here; but to appoint an Indian who from some motive does his utmost to annoy and interfere with the government of this reserve seems at least unwise. The probable results can easily be forseen should this Indian be recognized as a Court Commissioner.

All cases of felonies perpetrated upon this reserve, larseny [sic], rape, arson and murder would have to be brought before him for hearing and it would be in his power to dismiss or bind over to the Federal Grand Jury, as he saw fit. Imbued as he is with Indian prejudices, justice could not be expected of him.

Surely this perogative is a grave and important function and should only be bestowed upon a capable and just man.

The Indian Police are now in pursuit of an Indian who last week murdered another Indian of this reserve.

Shall I have this murderer brought before this Indian for examination with the probability or even possibility of being dismissed and turned loose without being brought to trial.

Awaiting your advice and instructions I have the honor to remain,

Very respectfully,
Joseph T. Carter
U.S. Indian Agent.

Document 61

Montana Court Seizes Indian Cattle

October 17, 1895

Source: Joseph T. Carter to Commissioner of Indian Affairs, October 17, 1895, letter received 45,176/1895, RG 75, National Archives, Washington, D.C.

Editors' note: This case is an example of a tribal member being treated unfairly by a Montana state court. On November 8, 1895, the Commissioner of Indian Affairs advised Carter to have the Indian swear out a complaint in federal court against the constable for recovery of the ten horses taken. No record has been found of how the matter was finally settled.

Flathead Agency, Montana,
October 17, 1895.

Hon. Commissioner of Indian Affairs,
Sir:

A few weeks ago one of the Indians on this Reservation who is a farmer and well disposed, had a sick child and sent for a physician who resided outside the reservation. The physician came part of the way, heard that the child was dead, and turned about and went home. Afterwards he demanded of the Indian seventy-five dollars for his travel, which the Indian refused to pay; but proposed to pay a reasonable sum. The physician refused to take it, and sued the Indian before a Justice of the Peace outside the reservation, sent a constable into the reservation and served warrant and made return and got judgment, the Indian paying no attention to the Justice's court 60 miles away. Afterwards the Constable, at the bidding of the doctor came into the reservation levied upon ten head of the Indian's horses (worth $400.) and carried them off and disposed of them. Neither the constable nor the doctor ever applied or made known in any way to me the existence of such claim, nor did the Indian until after the horses were carried off.

The Indian in my judgment has been treated shamefully bad and should have redress. Can he bring suit for the trespass upon, and carrying off his property in his own name? or can he sue in the name of the United States for his use and benefit? Can he sue in the United States Court? or is he compelled to sue in the State Court? Please advise me fully as to his rights, and what I shall do in the premises. If suit can be brought, the United States Attorney will willingly attend to it.

Respectfully,
Joseph T. Carter
Agent FlatHead Indians.

Document 62

A Day at the Jocko Agency in 1895

November 1, 1895

Source: "On the Reservation," *The Anaconda Standard*, November 1, 1895, page 10, col. 3-4; "Indians and Horses," *The Anaconda Standard*, November 2, 1895, page 10, col. 3-4.

Editors' note: The *Anaconda Standard* reporter visited the Jocko Agency and reported on activities at the agency on a normal day. He also witnessed a roundup of horses on the reservation open range.

On the Reservation
A Day Spent at the Jocko Agency by a Reporter.
An Indian Agent's Trials
If You Think His Is a Sinecure, Try It Once — Petty Grievances of the Wards — Major Carter in Charge.

Jocko Agency, Oct. 31. — If anybody imagines for a moment that an Indian agent has a sinecure and that it is one long, continual picnic to be autocrat of a reservation, that man should spend a day as did a Standard reporter in the office of Major [Joseph] Carter at this place. He should observe carefully the incidents that transpire in that office from morning till night and note the variety of questions that are submitted to the agent. He should note the thousand vexations that arise; the silly disputes to be settled; the persistent efforts of the reds to get something for nothing; the little jealousies that have to be adjusted; the unreasonable demands that must be refused and yet refused in such a manner as to leave no rankling; that adjustment of disputes over land and fences and water and wagons and stock: the management of farms and mill and stock — he should note all these, and these are but a part of the whole, and he will wonder, as did the Standard man, how Major Carter can smile when the day is over. He will also probably be thankful to the fates that he has not been called upon the direct the affairs of an Indian reservation.

* * * * * * * *

Major Carter's office is a snug, handsome room and he states with pardonable pride that it was made by reservation labor. The lumber was sawed at the agency mill and was seasoned and dressed there as well. It is piece of work that would attract attention anywhere. The lumber is pine and tamarack and the two woods have been alternated with excellent effect in walls and ceiling, while the highly polished floor is arranged in a handsome inlaid design in which the two colors have been used artistically. The building cost the government practically nothing and is a remarkable exception to the majority of Uncle Sam's building ventures.

* * * * * * * * *

If, however, the visitor is inclined to envy Major Carter his comfortable quarters when he first sees them, all shade of that envy is banished and forever dispelled before he has remained an hour in the office. The Indian has troubles galore. He doesn't care to keep them to himself and he is not even satisfied to confide them to one of the efficient Indian policemen. He insists upon relating them to the agent and the variety and number of griefs that are unfolded in the agent's office during the day are bewildering indeed to a tenderfoot. But Major Carter and his clerk, Vincent Ronan, listen to these tales of woe with a nonchalance that is born of long experience.

* * * * * * * * *

"Wednesdays and Saturdays will be issue day at this agency after March 1, 1895," is the test of a notice posted in the outer room of the agency office and if the visitor chances to come to the reservation on one of these days, he will find his visit of especial interest. Not that the issue at present is very extensive — the "subsistence issue" for the past year was only $1.50 per capita for the reservation Indians — but there are always some of the agent's charges who are on hand to get what they can.

* * * * * * * * *

When the office is opened Saturday morning, Major Carter prepares with fortitude for the day's task. At his desk he attends to the routine work which must be done and at another desk Clerk Ronan is busy with his reports and the interminable red tape statements required by the department at Washington. But Major Carter is not left long alone. There is trouble at the sawmill and he goes across the agency square to straighten out the muddle of machinery. This done, somebody wants advice as to some horses. Instructions are given for this case and then the agent returns to his office. More troubles await him there. He finds a report that some of the Indians have refused to perform their share of the road work that is now being done on the reservation. This is settled quickly. A message is dispatched to the malcontents; "Tell them that until this work is done we will saw no logs and grind no wheat for them and if they will not do it, we will put them to work with a ball and chain on their ankles." The messenger departs and the major says, "We'll hear no more from them."

* * * * * * * * *

Now come Sophie Elizabeth, a clean, fine looking s...., with her baby in her arms. She is a graduate of the mission schools and is well dressed in civilized garb. She wants nothing for herself, but comes as interpreter for two Nez Perce women, who want some quilts.

"Their names?"

"They are two Marys. One is a widow and the other has no husband. They want some quilts."

A message is sent to the clerk in the storeroom to supply them and the two Marys, who are gorgeous in bright blankets and silk kerchiefs, trot out for their quilts. But they are very shrewd, and when the agent goes to the store room a few minutes later, he finds that they are receiving sugar and tea, beside the quilts. They know they are wrong, but they brave it out and not until they are told to skip, do they give up.

* * * * * * * *

They have evidently not expected to get any groceries for they have brought no sacks. But they are equal to the emergency and find a way to carry their supplies. One crooks her elbow under her blanket and, into the hollow framed in the blanket, the sugar is poured. It is secured by a string and into the crook of the other elbow goes the tea. The older s... is not so adept. She removes the kerchief that forms her headgear and bears away her provender in that. All secured, they move away, giggling and chuckling as the agent speeds their departure. They know that they really have no rights on the reservation, but they are bold in their demands. They are Nez Perces, and their reservation is elsewhere.

* * * * * * * *

As they move away, the agent sees old Antoine, a venerable brave, who is stone blind, squatted on the platform near the store door. He speaks pleasantly to the old fellow, who answers as cordially as an Indian can. Antoine wants a quilt and gets one. It is pale blue with the most gorgeous array of flowers sprinkled over it, but it is warm and Antoine cannot see the colors, so he will doubtless sleep warm under it. He doesn't hasten away. He simply gathers the quilt close to himself and waits to be led away. He doesn't say "thank you," but he looks pleased.

* * * * * * * *

How are you, Mrs. Marrigeau?" is the agent's greeting to an aged half-breed woman, who leads her little granddaughter by the hand. The child shows no trace of Indian blood. She is white of skin and speaks pure English. Her dress is that of any 5-year-old girl on the city streets. Her father owns a good ranch and has a big bunch of stock, but she wants some shoes and stockings, just the same. The wish is made known and the agent gives the order. The grandmother wants "a piece of glass to make a window." She knows nothing of inches but tells the clerk that there are "six; so," pointing to panes in a half sash, and she gets her glass.

* * * * * * * * *

Between times, Major Carter is busy with plans for the improvement of the roads on the reservation, and for the completion of the new roller flour mill, which will handle the grain of the Indian ranches. The old mill at the agency is also being rebuilt and about 30 new bridges are being put in. For all this work there is no appropriation, except for the new mill, and the work must be done by the reservation employes and the Indians. It requires unlimited tact and patience and is a discouraging task. "Here is an area as great as that of the state of Connecticut," says Major Carter, "and one man with no money must keep roads in order, build bridges and control 2,000 Indians." That sums up the whole situation. And still there are some men who think that the Indian agent has snap.

* * * * * * * * *

Indians and Horses
Over the Boundless Plain They Yell, Whoop and Run.
It's a Beautiful Sight
The Herds Are Separated and Those Animals Belonging
to Other Tribes Are Driven Off.

Jocko Indian Agency, Nov. 1. — Five thousand horses in a single bunch, rearing, running, snorting and shying, urged on by two score picturesque Indian and half-breed riders, sending into the air a cloud of dust that envelops and partially conceals the vast band of cayuses as the riders with swish of ropes, with shouts and yells, urge on the surging band of half-wild creatures before them. It is a picture seldom seen now and only possible in the unrestricted range of the reservation, a picture, if seen, never to be forgotten. The scene has an incomparable setting. In the background rise the rugged, majestic peaks of the Mission range; from their base stretches forward a dense, black area of timber and, in the foreground, the rolling prairie of the valley of the Pend d'Oreille river. Overhead the sky is clear, but above the mountains snow clouds hover and the rocky peaks are already silvered with the first white covering of the year.

But there is too much stir and activity in the group which forms the central portion of the picture, to permit of any lengthy consideration of the wonderful beauty of the scenery. The whole thing is so unusually picturesque and so attractive that it seems as if it must have been arranged as a show and the observer forgets the discomforts of the long, dusty ride across the reservation; forgets that his throat is lined with dust; forgets that the color of his clothes is concealed by the sifting of fine soil that has settled upon him in the ride from the agency; forgets that an hour ago he was lame and wary; forgets all but the interesting scene before him.

Picturesque and attractive as it is, the affair has not been arranged for effect. The reservation riders, with their red shirts and gay blankets, have not come out for their own amusement or for our entertainment. They find no particular pleasure in the dusty days and chilly nights, aside from the excitement which attends such a ride as they are engaged in. They are out upon serious business and we are fortunate that we have come upon them at this point. For five days these bronze riders have scoured the northern range of the reservation, driving before them every horse that was found in this long stretch of country. They have ridden across the rolling ground of the lower valley; they have searched the canyons; they have penetrated the dense timber of the foothills; they have climbed to the open parks on the mountain sides. From valley and canyon and hillside they have driven the half-wild horses and have gathered them on the banks of the Pend d'Oreille river for the cutting out.

Five thousand tossing heads, 10,000 vicious eyes, 20,000 tramping hoofs! Almost as far as the eye can reach are horses, horses, horses. There are steeds of every color and of every size. Nearly all of them are the mean, treacherous Indian ponies, some of them shapely and handsome it is true, but in every eye is a flash of wildness that betokens ill for the man who attempts to tame the owner. Here and there in the mass of horses that is being urged onward at a trot is a big, fine looking animal that evidences good breeding. But there are not many of these. They are nearly all cayuses of the cayusest order.

At one of the ranches on the banks of the river, there are three big, well fenced pastures and here the cutting out will be done. On the reservation there are now about 15,000 horses and of these it is estimated that fully 2,000 have no right to the Indian range. Most of these aliens belong to the Nez Perce Indians of the Umatilla reservation in Washington and, as they are cut out, they will be driven westward off the Flathead reserve. All other strays will be advertised and sold. This will do much to improve the condition of the range and it is for this purpose that this big roundup has been undertaken.

The band of horses now being driven toward the extemporized corrals has been gathered in the region north of the Pend d'Oreille river. As soon as the cutting out has been accomplished, the riders will cross the river and will round up the stock between that stream and Crow creek and there will be another separation at the Allard ranch on Mud creek. In addition to the removal of all alien horses, Agent Carter has ordered that all cayuse stallions may be disposed of, in order that there may be some improvement in the grade of horses raised on the reserve. Thus the roundup will accomplish a double purpose.

As we watch, the band of nervous, frightened animals is driven nearer and nearer to the fences which are to enclose them. The horses, many of them, have never been driven this way before. Some of them had never seen a man at close range until the riders routed them from their mountain pastures and hurried them into the valley. They are as wild as deer.

Now and then a startled creature breaks from the band and fairly flies out across the plains toward his home in the hills. But, swift as he is, the agile riders are too quick for him. Three of them have crossed his path and have intercepted his flight almost before we have realized what has been his purpose. Sullenly he is driven back to the herd. Again and again this performance is repeated. But the drive is inexorable and the band is driven steadily forward.

The riders are the most interesting feature of the scene. Quick, keen and daring in their work, they are here, there and everywhere at once. They are a motley lot. Every owner of horses on the range is represented. Indians, half-breeds and "s.... men" are all here, each in earnest in the work, for this is the one useful occupation which the inhabitant of the reservation really enjoys. Special Agent [F. M.] Corey of the interior department is at the head of the roundup, and stands in the novel position of an easterner, acting as foreman of an old-time western roundup. But he is possessed of indomitable energy and he is doing the work well.

With yells and shouted commands in French and English and Kalispell, the riders have bunched the herd for the night. The last stray colt has been driven in to hunt for its mother; the last rebellious cayuse has been forced back to the herd; the stragglers have been run in. The big band is ready for the hard work of to-morrow. The herders are posted and the night watch has begun. Tired and dusty and hungry, the riders hastily unsaddle their panting animals and hurry to the cook's wagon. There is plenty of food, coarse and of no great variety, but roundup appetites are not fastidious and the hungry fellows pitch in with vigor.

The show is over. The sun has sunk behind the hills and the cold breeze from the Mission mountains carries a chill with it. The lapse of excitement brings a return of the consciousness of bones aching from the long day's ride and certain suggestive sensations recall the existence of stomachs. Our horses' heads are turned toward the house where we will spend the night. We pause as we reach the height of a swell in the plain and look backward at the lights of the riders' camp. All is quiet now, except for the sounds of the restless herd and the voices of the night herders. Then we drop down into the lower valley and our horses are hurried homeward.

Document 63

Bitterroot Valley Medicine Tree

December 1, 1895

Source: "Old Medicine Tree," *The Anaconda Standard*, December 1, 1895, page 10, col. 1-2.

Editors' note: This was one of the early accounts of the medicine tree in the Bitterroot Valley and traditions surrounding it.

Old Medicine Tree
Under Its Branches Two Braves Meet in Mortal Combat.
It Is a Legendary Spot
Deeply Imbedded in its Trunk Is a Horn of Some Mammoth
Prehistoric Animal — A Receptacle for Offerings.

Missoula, Nov. 29. — Whoever has traveled over the old trail that leads through the upper Bitter Root valley to Ross' Hole has heard of the "Old Medicine Tree." Nearly everybody who has made the interesting journey to the head of this most beautiful valley in Montana has seen the tree and, if the traveler had any sentiment in his makeup, he has deposited his offering in the big horn that is imbedded in the tree, as was the custom of the Indians in olden days, when the red-man's gods were found in trees and rocks and rivers and when his deities had their abode, like those of the Greek and Roman, in somber canyon or rugged peak or shady grove.

There was never an Indian, were he Nez Perce, Blackfoot or Selish who passed this tree without making some offering to the Great Spirit, depositing his propitiatory sacrifice in the horn whose opening extended from the tree like that of a cornucopia. This horn was an antler of a monster mountain sheep or big horn, and, when white men first discovered the tree, had been there so long that it was firmly imbedded in the living wood, which had grown around it and made it almost a part of the tree itself. Now the growth of the tree has nearly covered the horn and but little of it is visible.

With this horn of plenty have been deposited articles of great value as well as trinkets, dear only to the dusky maiden or brave who, anxious to appease the Great Spirit, left as an offering that which was to her or him a great sacrifice. Beneath this tree gaily painted braves have assembled on the eve of a battle and have sought the assistance of their god in the contest of the morrow. Here have gathered hunting parties to pay homage to their deity that buffalo and deer and elk might fall before their flint-tipped arrows. Here the young novitiate in war has come alone to pray for strength and skill that the ordeal which was to establish his standing in his tribe. Here, too, has come the lover with his petition for success in his amorous suit. Here have anxious wives, mothers and sweethearts united in an entreaty for the successful return of absent soldier husbands, son and lovers. Here has been poured out the tearful invocation of the wronged maiden, whose anguish-wrung heart found comfort in communion with the god of her people. Here has been offered the supplications of the red men for generations and each petitioner has left within the horn some offering as evidence of the sincerity of his prayer.

An air of romance hangs about the place. It is a hallowed spot, even as the pagan temples of Greece and Rome are objects of veneration. If the god to whom these rude prayers were offered was not the true one, the petitions were sincere and, in these days before the advent of the Black Robes with their message of peace and good will, the Indians worshipped, as they thought, in the true religion. But there is not so very much romance in the composition of a cowboy and the early riders after stock in the Bitter Root rather discouraged the use of the medicine tree by the votaries who had been accustomed to leave their offerings at this rustic altar. Old timers in the valley say that when the tree was still in use by the red men, the cowboys whenever they were in the vicinity of the place would always "race for the old tree." The first one there was always sure to find something to reward him for his effort — beaded buckskin, carved clay or some other quaint Indian offering. The Indians were reluctant to abandon their ancient custom, but the cowboys were too much for them. No Indian wanted to play the votary to a cowpuncher, so the Old Medicine Tree was eventually abandoned and not stands alongside the trail to Ross' Hole, a monument to the devotion of the aborigines.

There is an interesting story connected with the tree and the manner in which it was set apart as a thing sacred. It was told in early days by the Indians and was recently repeated by an old timer to a Standard man. Many years ago, a party of Nez Perce braves was journeying down the Bitter Root valley on the trail to the buffalo hunting grounds. They had crossed the divide and were making good progress down the valley. As was their custom they had their women with them to skin the game and cure the meat. Among these women was a maiden whose beauty was so great that it had made her famous throughout the Northwest and her suitors came from many tribes.

There were but two of all her lovers who found favor. One of these was a handsome brave of her own tribe and the other was a valiant warrior of the

Blackfeet. She loved her tribesman, but her father, a chief, favored the Blackfoot brave and the question of her marriage seemed fair never to be settled. But the old chief finally said that the two rivals should meet in personal combat at the first opportunity and that the victor should receive the hand of the peerless beauty.

As the hunting party neared the spot where stands the Old Medicine Tree, a solitary Indian was seen approaching from the opposite direction. It was the Blackfoot lover, who was riding ahead of a hunting party of his own tribe, bound for the deer haunted mountains of the Bitter Root range. He knew of the edict of the old Nez Perce and but little time was lost in the preparations for the duel, which all knew would be a fight to the death. The weapons were to be tomahawks and the combatants were soon ready. It was a moment of awful suspense. Each of the braves was the recognized champion of his tribe and the duel was certain to be a splendid exhibition of skill.

For more than two hours, says the narrator, these two braves fought beneath the tree. Their movements were as quick and graceful as those of a cat and their weapons met and parted in many a stroke and guard. The contest was a terrible one. Both were badly wounded and from many a gash the blood dripped to the ground. But fortune favored the stronger lover, and a swift stroke of the Blackfoot hatchet stretched the Nez Perce upon the ground. The favorite lover was killed but the chief-father was pleased with the result and foresaw as a result of the contest, a powerful alliance between his tribe and the Blackfeet. The girl went, a weeping bride, to live among strangers. Beneath the tree, where he had fought so valiantly, the Nez Perce was buried and soon after, the big horn placed in a cleft and the "Old Medicine Tree" became a shrine.

This is the story as it was told to the Standard man. What became of the unhappy bride is not stated. But the tree is there and the big horn, now imbedded in the wood, gives substance to what may or may not be a myth.

Document 64

Growing to Be a Salish Woman

1895 plus

Source: Adolf and Beverly Hungry Wolf, *Children of the Sun: Stories By and About Indian Kids* (New York: William Morrow and Company, Inc., 1987), pages 30-32; Bob Olson, "Mrs. Combs Visits Home," *The Missoulian*, July 14, 1967, page 10, col. 4-8.

Editors' note: These two interviews with Mary Ann Combs (or Coombs) give some bits of her life story as a Salish Indian woman. See also the 1975 interview with Coombs about Chief Charlo in Robert Bigart and Joseph McDonald, eds., *"You Seem to Like Your Money, and We Like Our Land: A Documentary History of the Salish, Pend d'Oreille, and Kootenai Indians, 1875-1889* (Pablo, Mont.: Salish Kootenai College Press, 2020), pages 396-400.

Training of a Flathead Girl
[by Adolf and Beverly Hungry Wolf]

Our family used to have an adopted grandmother among the people of the Flathead tribe, who live south of us, in Montana. Mary Ann Combs was born in a tipi along Montana's Bitterroot River, in 1881. For the first ten years of her life she was among those few Flatheads, with her parents and other relatives, who shunned reservation life in favor of their ancestral wilderness homeland. In her old age, eighty or ninety years later, she was the last one of her tribe who had received the traditional training that brought her from childhood to becoming a woman.

Mary Ann grew up in the lodge of her grandparents, who wanted to make sure she would learn to be a woman in the true, proven, old Flathead way. Thus, when she reached puberty, they asked a highly respected old woman to be her guide. This woman, Mrs. Ninepipe, was noted for being a hard worker and a good wife and mother, as well as being kind and helpful to others in the tribe.

Mrs. Ninepipe went to visit Mary Ann early on the first morning of her instructions. She began with a lengthy prayer, asking that the girl have a long life as a good woman. Everyone who knew Mary Ann felt that this prayer came true. The woman gave Mary Ann additional blessings by painting her face with a red-colored earth that her people considered sacred.

Then she said, "You have to watch me and see how I life. I don't flirt or run around with men. I work hard to gather roots and berries, and to prepare all the meat that my husband brings home. I save everything I can and don't waste things. I know that my husband provides the family with food and protects us, so I follow his orders like a dog does its master, and I do what he wants me to do."

For the next four days Mary Ann stayed with Mrs. Ninepipe and did exactly as she was told to do. She was required to work hard during that time and she was not allowed to rest. Her father and mother warned that she should obey everything the old woman told her if she wanted to have the old woman's virtues in later life.

The people near her were part of a hunting camp of four lodges. She was required to bring a load of firewood to each of the lodges every day. She carried these loads on her back, in the old way. She was also told to bring the water supply for each lodge. In addition, she was required to do all the cooking in the lodge of her parents, without help from anyone else.

She said, "That old woman told me the reason she wants me to keep busy and working is so that I don't start out being a lazy woman, else I would have scabs all over my body — even on my face — and I would become lousy and filthy and would always want to lie around. I was pretty scared about being this way, so I kept busy all the time I was with that woman.

"She taught me to prepare bitterroots the right way, and she told me never to be careless about it. She said to watch so that I don't waste food, or let it get overcooked. She showed me how to make our traditional blood soup without breaking up the blood too much. She said that if I was careless making this nutritious soup, the blood would turn into water.

She told me not to warm my feet by the fire, else they would grow large as I got older. She said to warm a rock and hold it to my feet instead. You can see that I have small feet. She also told me that if I had any lice, I should take one and stick a pine needle through it and then stick the pine needle into the ground by the fire to roast the louse. She said that way I would never be bothered by lice, and she was right.

"Every morning I was told to get up very early and wash myself in the creek and put lots of water on my hair so that it would grow long and heavy [Mary Ann's thick, white braids still hung below her waist when she was in her eighties]. I was told not to wash with warm water or in a basin. That is why I still go down to the little creek behind my house every morning to wash."

Mary Ann was also given instructions for having children. She should never eat the flesh of the black bear of her breasts would go dry. Also she was not to pick berries from bushes in which grizzly bears have fed, else the child she was carrying would always have saliva running from its mouth, like a bear.

She was told different ways of giving newborn babies certain characteristics, according to Flathead belief. To make a baby grow up quiet and gentle, she was to take the heart of a partridge, mix it with a certain white clay, and frequently rub the mixture on the child's chest. To make the child active, industrious, and grow up to be a good food hunter, she was told to crush a bunch of ants and mix them with white clay, to be rubbed on the child's chest. To make children brave, they should be rubbed with mixtures containing the hearts of hawks or eagles. To make them strong, the mixture should include part of a bear's heart. To make them good hikers and climbers, she should use the heart of an elk. Her husband, Louie Combs, had been rubbed with a mixture that included a chipmunk's heart, which made him always slim and frisky.

Mary Ann said she continued helping old Mrs. Ninepipe for the rest of her life, in thanks for the guidance given her while she was young, In her old age she believed that if the young people of today were still given such strict and direct training at the hands of the elderly wise persons, they would grow up to have more respect for life and better behavior.

* * * * * * * * *

Mrs. Combs Visits Home
by Bob Olson
Missoulian Correspondent

Stevensville — "When I am sad, I can't stand it. I come here to pray and to think of the old days and of my folks. I don't know if I feel better or worse."

These are the words of Maryann Topsseh Combs, [in1967] an 87-year-old Salish Indian Woman who makes a yearly pilgrimage to St. Mary's Mission in Stevensville.

As a child Mrs. Combs lived in the Bitter Root Valley where she and her people gathered the native bitter root flower for food. Her people lived in the Kootenae Creek country near Stevensville, and her tribe generally hunted farther south near Darby, since the meat was better there. From their home on Kootenae Creek, they often attended Feast Days at the old St. Mary's Mission.

Although her eyesight is failing, she continues to make moccasins, winning a blue ribbon for her work at the 1966 Ravalli County fair. Shew also makes her own clothing, including those she is wearing in the photographs.

History Teacher

Living in Arlee now, she is a teacher and interpreter for college people who come to the area to study Indian history.

Mary Ann Combs
Source: Toole Archives, Mansfield Library, University of Montana, Missoula,
photo 85-0214.

"We are losing our language, our customs, our people are nearly all gone, and our own children no longer speak our tongue," she said. In an effort to save the vanishing Salish culture and history, she readily talks with anyone interested in the Indian people, and is a willing a cooperative subject for the photographer.

A highlight of her 1967 pilgrimage was gathering the roots of the bitter root flower west of Victor, Montana. The Indian people used the roots of Montana's state flower for food and occasionally for medicinal herbs.

The trip to St. Mary's Mission today is vastly different from her trips as a child. In those days she and her family would travel by foot or horseback, camping as necessary along the way. Today, she boards a bus at Arlee and is in Stevensville in a few hours.

Welfare Not Wanted

When informed that she was entitled to welfare aid, she said, "I don't want welfare; I just want what's coming to me from the Bitter Root," referring to the land which was taken from the Indians but was never paid for. However, Mrs. Combs will receive a payment for her peoples' land in the Bitter Root Valley due to recent legislation which made possible a cash payment in addition to the land given the Indians years ago in exchange for the Bitter Root.

She still has her original parcel of land in the Jocko Valley near Arlee. She continues to live on her husband's government allotment in her small cabin, which she keeps in immaculate condition.

During her recent visit to the Mission, she passed an apple tree which had been planted by Father [Anthony] Ravalli when he was at the Mission many years ago. "My mother's apple tree," she said and tenderly fingered the small green apples which were growing on it. She said that her mother had picked apples from it when they lived in the Stevensville area.

Document 65

Examples of Indian Honesty

January 15, 1896

Source: "One Honest Indian," *The Anaconda Standard*, January 15, 1896, page 10, col. 1; "Old Mrs. Ninepipes," *The Anaconda Standard*, January 17, 1896, page 10, col. 3.

Editors' note: In January 1896 the Flathead Agency made payments from the sale of Bitterroot Valley allotments. The newspaper carried these articles as examples of the honesty of the Salish Indians.

One Honest Indian
He Is Anxious to Liquidate a Debt He Contracted 20 Years Ago.
A Pay Day at the Agency
Disbursement of Another Installment of Proceeds of the Sale of Lands
on the Old Bitter Root Reservation — Incidents.

Missoula, Jan. 14. — There was an interesting scene enacted at the Jocko agency on the Flathead reservation that was witnessed by a large number of interested spectators, including many from this city. The occasion was the disbursement among the members of Chief Charlott's band of another installment of the proceeds of the sale of lands on the old Bitter Root reservation, formerly occupied by Charlott and his tribe. The amount paid out to-day was $8,800, which makes the total sum received by the Indians $27,000. The total appraisement of the land on the old reservation is $97,000, as made by General [Henry] Carrington, so that the Indians still have a large sum coming to them. The amounts received by the Indians to-day varied from $7 to $1,100.

One of the men who received the money was the Indian, Thomas Cosaha, whose portion was $415.44. He deposited $400 with Major [Joseph] Carter, the Indian agent, and used the balance for household supplies. He received his money last night and this morning he came back to settle some old debts that he had contracted in the Bitter Root country. He said that 20 years ago he owed a man in the valley about Corvallis $20. He did not know the man's name, but he says he had a store there. He wanted the agent to find him and pay him the $20. From Cosaha's description of the man it is supposed that he is Jerry Fay, who did business at Grantsdale and who is now in Gibbonsville. Cosaha stated further that he had for 13 years owned [sic] James Cowen of Corvallis $6 and this sum he sent to Missoula by one of the visitors at the agency. This was done this evening and Cosaha will probably sleep easier to-night.

Another amusing incident of the disbursement was one in which Johnnie Lumphrey was actor. He stood by as an Indian woman received $1,100 and his copper skin turned brassy as he saw the money counted. Said he: "That is more money than I ever saw before. If I had that in a poker game I would raise them $50 better." The Indians naturally had a little celebration, but it was a quiet one. Most of the money has been spent by them for improvements on their ranches and in paying old debts.

* * * * * * * *

Old Mrs. Ninepipes
She Vainly Sought to Defraud One of Her Creditors.
But She Finally Yielded
Chief Charlot Prevailed Upon Her and After a Consultation the Money was Reluctantly Turned Over.

Missoula, Jan. 16. — Yesterday's Standard gave some of the incidents of the payment of the Bitter Root Flatheads of the proceeds of the sale of their old reservation, that went to show that the Indian is honest in his business transactions, despite his reputation to the contrary. As a matter of fact there was but one instance in which an Indian sought to defraud his creditors. In all other cases, the red men seemed anxious to find the men whom they owed and to square their debts as soon as possible. The single Indian who sought to evade the payment of a just debt was a woman, the Widow Ninepipes. She was among those who received large sums and she wanted to hold on to all she got. She did not deny her debt, but she stated emphatically that she would not pay it and gave only a woman's reason for her refusal.

It appears that several years ago a half-breed, Baptiste Matt, sold a ranch to a son of Widow Ninepipes, for which the widow agreed to pay $500 when she received the payment for her Bitter Root land. Matt turned the account over the Alex Dow, who conducts the store at Arlee, and Widow Ninpipes agreed to make the payment to him. But when she received her money on Monday evening she wanted to keep it all. Mr. Dow was in a quandry. His money was in sight, but he couldn't touch it and he very much needed the $500.

Persuasion and threats and arguments counted for nought. The widow made her statement and would say no more. Her ultimatum had gone forth and she proposed to abide by it. She sat glum and sullen and held on to her money.

At last, as a final resort, Mr. Dow sent for Charlot, the venerable Bitter Root chief, and asked him to use his influence with the woman, who is of his tribe. Under ordinary circumstances Charlot is the last man in the world to look to for aid. He is grouty, ugly and suspicious usually but he had just received his portion of the cash and was in good humor. He consented as readily as was consistent with his dignity as chief and was conducted to where Widow Ninepipes remained obdurate and sullen. The nature of his errand was soon made known and the widow weakened a little for the first time. She said she would pay $200, but no more. This was not what was wanted and the old chief knew it, so he asked that Mr. Dow's agent, Widow Ninepipes, an interpreter and himself be taken to a private room where they could be quiet and alone.

This request was granted and the queer company passed into an inner room, where the Indians seated themselves on the floor and talked "heap medicine." After they had discussed the situation fully, Charlot assumed a dignified pose and spoke, in part, as follows:

"Woman, I am chief of your tribe. The honor of the tribe rests with me. I am held for your honesty and I am blamed if you do not pay your debts. You owe this money. You must pay it. I am an old man. Soon I must die. I cannot die with the burden of your debt upon me. I am your chief and I say you must pay the money."

This produced the desired effect. The widow yielded and produced her money. Then followed an interesting scene. The woman's money, $1,500 in all, was poured out upon the floor, all in gold and silver. Over it bent the old woman, 80 years of age, her wrinkled face twitching with anxiety lest she lose some of her hoard and her hands stretched forward as if to save the treasure. Near her were the others watching the count, which progressed slowly. It was like wringing blood from the crone, but she paid. Old Charlot affected indifference but his satisfaction was ill concealed.

Document 66

Charlo Questions Accuracy
of Land Sale Payments
January 25, 1896

Source: "Charlot's Grievance," *The Anaconda Standard*, January 25, 1896, page 10, col. 1-2.

Editors' note: Charlo's questions about proceeds from the sale of part of his ranch in the Bitterroot Valley presumably were answered by the Missoula Land Office.

Charlot's Grievance.
He Nourishes the Belief That He's Getting to Worst of a Deal.

Missoula, Jan. 24. — Chief Charlot and some of his head men of the Bitter Root tribe of Flatheads are in town today with a burden of trouble. The old chief will probably never recover from the treatment which he received 10 and 15 years ago from the treaty commissioner, who accomplished the transfer of his people from their Bitter Root reserve to the Jocko agency. Charlot feels that he and his people were deeply injured by these officials and has never forgiven the white race for this injury. It is doubtless true that some of the promises made by General [Henry] Carrington at the time the transfer was made have never been fulfilled, and the grouty old chief has some reason for his hostility.

However this may be, the old man blames everybody who is white for the sins of General Carrington, and is a hard man to get along with. To-day he and his followers went out to Fort Missoula and held a consultation with Colonel Burt, whose aid they sought in righting their wrongs. The exact nature of their complain[t] is not made public. Colonel Burt said to a Standard reporter this afternoon that he did not think it was wise nor honorable to publish the matter. All that could be said was that Charlot and his men had presented their grievances to Colonel Burt and had asked for advice.

Later in the day Charlot called at the land office and had a long interview with Register Evans. From what he said there, through his interpreter, it appears that he thinks that he has been getting the worse of it in the distribution of the money received by the government from the sale of the land in the old Bitter Root reservation. Judge Evans was able to satisfy him in a measure by showing him that only half of his ranch had been sold, and that he still had money coming for the remaining 80 acres. The old man believed, he said, that his whole ranch had been sold and somebody had held out half the money.

In appearance, the old chief has changed but little during the past three years, since a Standard reporter interviewed him at his home near Jocko. He looks a little older and his eyesight is failing him. But there is still the same sturdy figure and the same stern, determined face. He has discarded the silk hat that he has worn to Missoula of late years, and to-day wore a broad-brimmed light felt hat. He always attracts attention, wherever he goes. His face indicates superiority over the average Indian, and he is, all in all, a queer mixture of intelligence and stubbornness.

Document 67

Imposter Government Agent Arrested
on Flathead Reservation
January 29, 1896

Source: "Corey a Queer Duck," *The Anaconda Standard*, January 30, 1896, page 10, col. 1; "Cory Convicted," *Evening Republican* (Missoula, Mont.), June 12, 1896, page 4, col. 2.

Editors' note: F. M. Corey arrived at the Flathead Agency in 1896 with papers and a claim to be a special agent of the Interior Department. While there, Corey rounded up trespassing horses from the reservation range and helped enforce Indian Department rules. According to Carter, Corey gave all the fine money he collected to Carter to be deposited in the U.S. Treasury. It turned out that Corey was an imposter, but no motive for the deception was ever given.

Corey a Queer Duck
His Recent Business on the Reservation Is Much of a Mystery.
He Is Mum as an Oyster
United States Commissioner Smith Places Him Under Bonds to Await
Examination Next Tuesday — He is Quite Ill.

Missoula, Jan. 29. — F. M. Corey, the man who is believed to be a bogus government agent, was arraigned this morning before United States Commissioner Smith and was placed under bonds to await examination next Tuesday, when United States Attorney Leslie will be here to conduct the examination. Corey is quite ill and he was not taken from the county jail on this account, Commissioner Smith going to the sheriff's office for the arraignment. Corey seems to be suffering from a light attack of pleurisy. He still maintains his stoical silence, and will vouchsafe no information regarding the motive for his peculiar conduct and is indifferent to his present predicament, apparently, although he admits that he is in a tough place.

There is some difference of opinion as to Corey's true character. Some are inclined to believe him a fanatical fellow, who desired to be of some assistance to the Indians of the reserve, and took this means of doing it. The stronger, opinion, however, seems to be that he is a thoroughbred crook and that he has made a considerable sum of money while posing as a special agent of Hoke

Smith. He has turned over to Major [Joseph] Carter, as stated in the Standard today, about $800, but it is estimated that he has collected in the neighborhood of three or four times that amount. This would have made his sojourn at the Flathead reservation a most profitable one, had he not lingered too long. It is this fact that makes it seem that he may not be such a rascal after all. He must have known that the fact that he was an imposter would be discovered as soon as Major Carter communicated with his department chiefs.

Corey is a peculiar man. He impressed all who had business with him in his assumed capacity of special agent, as being a man who was honest to a fanatical degree. He always insisted upon absolute correctness in the minutest details of his business, and he was as exact himself, to all appearances, as he required others to be. In his work he was active, energetic and tireless, and it seemed at times as if he were made of iron, so great was his endurance. On the big horse round-up, which he organized and conducted, and which resulted in ridding the reservation of about 2,000 horses that had no right there, he was in the saddle longer than the experienced riders who were with him, and he rode back and forth, here and there, all day, with a feverish nervousness that kept everybody jumping all the time. His executive ability was remarkable, and his familiarity with the methods and regulations of the Indian department, made it comparatively easy for him to successfully practice his deception.

While he was at work on the ranges, he succeeded in collecting from some of the oldest and boldest trespassers who have allowed their stock to graze on the Indians' land. From one of these men, one who had always defied the authorities, and who had never paid fine or range fee, he collected nearly $200. This is but a single instance of his success in protecting the Flathead tribes from the encroachment of whites and other Indians. As the Standard stated to-day, the Flathead reservation is without doubt greatly benefited by the operations of Corey, even though he be a fake.

His presentation of a letter of introduction from Major Lane of the Washington reservation and his familiarity with the rules of the department and the conditions prevailing at the Flathead reservation made his story so plausible that it is not surprising that he deceived Major Carter and the reservation employes. His information regarding the reservation was so complete that it seemed impossible that he could have obtained it from other than official sources. He knew what the department had said regarding the infringement of the rights of the Indians by outside stockmen, and he knew just how to go to work to prevent any continuance of it. He not only knew, but he did it. He acted promptly and effectively and, whatever portion of the fines and fees that he collected stuck to his fingers in passing through his hands, he earned all that he made in this way. His experience is one of the strangest stories ever told of reservation life, and there is much curiosity as to what he will say when he is examined. Commissioner Smith fixed his bonds at $1,500.

Corey has retained Hal S. Corbett as his attorney. He sent this evening for Charles Allard, at whose ranch he made his headquarters during the round-up. It is not known what he wants of Allard, but it is supposed that he has some papers and documents there. Marshal Davidson returned to Helena this evening. To-day he had all the sheriff's office looking for the man who stole his overcoat. The garment was found this afternoon at the Florence hotel, and he went home contented.

* * * * * * * *

Cory Convicted.

F. M. Cory will be remembered as the queer individual who completely deceived Major Carter of the Flathead reservation by representing himself to be a special agent of the department of the interior. He was tried yesterday in the federal court at Helena and was found guilty of impersonating a federal officer and collecting money on the reservation. He will serve six months in jail for these offenses and there is another count yet to be tried.

Cory was confined in the Missoula jail during the winter, where he won the confidence of the officials by his quiet behavior. His case is peculiar and opinions differ as to whether or not he filled his pockets with funds enough while on the reservation to repay him for undergoing punishment. Certain it is that he collected and paid to Major Carter more money than it has cost the government to prosecute his case. It was the major's report of these collections which led to the unmasking of Cory. It is thought by many that the man has a rapidly running lot of wheels in his cranium.

Document 68

Duncan McDonald Complains about
Flathead Agency Affairs
February 12, 1896

Source: Duncan McDonald to Messrs. Bickford & Stiff & Hershey, February 12, 1896, enclosure in letter received 9,381/1896, RG 75, National Archives, Washington, D.C.

Editor's note: Duncan McDonald laid out tribal complaints about Joseph Carter's administration of Flathead Agency affairs. He also gave the Indian side of the conflict between Carter and Louison and Charlo in March 1895. The letter was very hard to read but has been reproduced here as accurately as possible. Some periods have been added to the text.

Ravalli, Mont., Febry 12th, 1896

Messrs. Bickford & Stiff & Hershey
Dear Sirs

It is with sorry that I enter this complaint against our Indian Agent Mr. Joe Carter of the Flathead reservation. We have tried every way shape & form to reach our grievances to the Indian Office. as all transactions have to go through the hands of Indian Agent & our prayers for his removal has never reached the Indian Department. First we complained to the Military officers three times but we have been directed back to the Indian Agent to make proper complaints. Which is the very man we want removed also his gang of employees. Second we tried to reach the U.S. Grand Jury in Helena & we were arrested for trying to reach the said Jury. We have written to Washington through our Agent which is also a failure. Now how in the name of God could we do to join hands with the whites harmonously. he the agent has been using his authority too excess or exceeding his authority to be abusive.

First st trouble he pulled down the fence of an Indian by the name of Paul Andre twice & threatened which said Indian threatened back with a rifle if Mr. Carter pulls down his fence again & same Indian notified the chiefs that he would Kill the agent.

2d The writers fence also was pulled down by the same Agent to make a public high way when the old road was always open & better road & because a bridge was washed away during high water and it was my work that we have a bridge by my house and at the same time my field has been fenced for six years. he reaches his hands & pulls my fence down which I protested & he treatened to put me in jail. said enclosure cost me 500.00. And if I dont get redress for this I will enter a suit against the government. I was one of the men caused to be arrested by him because I wanted to go before the United States grand Jury.

3d He put an Indian Sub Chief by the name of Louison who was once a Judge of the Courts of Indian offences because he the Agent sent some Indian police to Stop an Indian dance which we call it a sham dance. After the said Indian police left the dance the said Louison made a speech & told the dancers now boys. Those police have come to you for nothing *because* you will not respect the agents authority nor our chiefs. And *while* you are dancing and when you are through quit for good, tomorrow is the beginning of Lent. I dont want you to dance any more. Agent Carter puts this man in prison influenced by his ignorant interpreter not explaining the meaning *because* Although the Agent was told by half bloods that Louison did not say that his authority was worthless this affair came near causing an outbreak. Because one Indian by the name of Su-ah-sah told the Agent to release this sub Chief as he did not mean any harm. Su-ah-sah said you remember two or three weeks ago I made a wooden sleigh & I came to you to get an order to have my slegh ironed because I insisted you called me to get out you dirty Indian son-of-b. and I did not feel hard of you. On this conversation he threatened & ordered Su-ah-sah to get out of the office or he would be imprisoned. Said Su-ah-sah went to the Jail and this charge he was imprisoned & two other Indians because they were spectators in the scuffle when Su-ah-sah was arrested. The Agent puts three Indian prisoners in a buggy & started for Missoula City. Charlos the head Chief of the Flatheads ordered some of his Indians to stop the Agent from taking the prisoners off the Indian reserve. As there is two Jails on the reservation. Also Judges of Indians offences he cannot see why he the Agent wants to take the Indians off as there was a place on this reserve to try prisoners and if found guilty they could be imprisoned. Sure enough by the command of the Chief some Indians ran after the Agent & brought back the prisoners to the chief, in this case. The Agent threatened to get the troops and have them all rrested if Charlos insisted for the troops to come as he would call on a hearing before the commanding officer but the prisoners would rather go to the County jail than to have this harmless Chief get into trouble. The said prisoners were locked up for nine days in Missoula without a hearing. I employed a lawyer to have them released which he did under the Habeas Corpus proceeding. This enraged the Agent & threatened he would put me off the reserve. I cannot see why as long as I am doing this through the proper channels of the law I should be removed as one of the prisoners was a relative of mine & me Knowing he the Agent started all these troubles. I was sure they were badly treated & unessary. He the Agent meaness & bull headedness he had them re-arrested and taken to Helena, and put the government to a lot of unessary expenses. They were all discharged without a trial. In this trouble the Agent Knocked one Indian down with his rifle & called him names.

4th I was present at a council at the office when the Chief and Judges demanded the discharge of Vince Ronan a brother-in-law of said Agent because he tried to have an intercourse with said Head Chiefs Charlos daughter-in-law. Said Agent Carter never in the least paid any attention. his answers were most impertenent on several occassions. this clerk attempted & also tried to down the wife of Joe Barnaby in a room to have inter-course before she could get the goods she earned by labor. This is common occurences with the clerk. As the Judges & Chiefs have been told by the Agent that he was the big boss no matter how many Chiefs & Judges on the reservation this makes us tremble with anger.

5th Pierre Pims who is captain of the police gave whiskey to Catherine wife Mechelle Finley and Mary Theresa wife of Pascall got them paralzed drunk and boasted that he did not intend to give them whiskey for nothing. connections he wanted from them and made an attempt but failed. they the women complained to the Chiefs & Judges & Carter refused to listen. & numerous of occurrences which makes the tribe grieved & ugly. What I have said can be proven & sworn too. Another time the said Indian Agent Kept a man by the name of Mr. Corey as special Agent. the said Corey was furnished U.S. Indian police by Mr. Carter since Augt/95 until Feby. 96 he turned up to be impersonating U.S. officer. he was arrested by Carter. This is no excuse as the gentleman ran with Carter six months before he was arrested. he cannot make any excuse. Indians Chiefs & Judges demanded credentials from Mr. Corey. he refused to furnish in presence of Mr. Carter. This operation of Mr. Corey & backed by Carter with his U.S. Indian police caused a great loss of horses among Indians. as I Know lots of old people are unable to have their horses branded. All the unbranded animals are put in field & are dying off fast. one family have lost about 100 head by the work of Mr. Corey. And J. Carter. And as his actions have been proven very bad suspicious we demand his discharge & Vince Ronan Pierre Pims Capt of the police & Bonome Gebeau (Henry Matt for bringing whiskey every chance they get). I am urgently requested by the head men for this good feeling of the government to have this man removed forthwith.

I remain
Yours truly
Duncan McDonald

P. S. The Indian Judges of Indian offences it seems their credentials is Kept away from the same Indian Agent. If the Indian office at Washingto make Indian Agents call elections once a year say July 1st it will eventually that educated Indians will get to the front. then the Government will unquestionably get along smooth. It is the duty of this gentleman to have ignorant class as he can cheat them better as his character is well Known in Western Missoula Co. what Kind of a gentleman he is.

Document 69

Whites Attack and Murder Indians in Kalispell

February 14, 1896

Source: *The Inter Lake* (Kalispell, Mont.), February 14, 1896, page 8, col. 3; "An Indian Woman Shot," *The Inter Lake* (Kalispell, Mont.), February 28, 1896, page 4, col. 2; "A S.... Shot," *The Anaconda Standard*, March 2, 1896, page 10, col. 3; "Wicked Joshing," *The Anaconda Standard*, March 4, 1896, page 10, col. 3; *Flathead Herald-Journal* (Kalispell, Mont.), March 5, 1896, page 8, col. 2; Joseph T. Carter to Commissioner of Indian Affairs, April 10, 1896, letter received 14,317/1896, RG 75, National Archives, Washington, D.C.

Editors' note: In 1896 a number of violent attacks by white people on Kootenai Indians in Kalispell were reported. Susan Kiona (or Melisse), an aged Indian woman, was murdered in an alley in the city. No record was found of any white people being punished for the crimes.

A number of boys, most of them large enough and old enough to be considered young men, were annoying parties of Indians last Friday evening, hooting at and snowballing them. The Indians were simply going quietly from town to their tepees in groups of four or five. The young scamps attacked all indiscriminately and were not particular whether the snow balls struck men or women. There is no great love for an Indian loose in this country, but a summary stop should be put to such proceedings. The boys are old enough to know better, and to be punished if the thing is continued. Some of these days they will attack the wrong Indians and two or three of them will get beaten to within an inch of their lives, if nothing worse happens. Then we will all get righteously indignant, or we will be expected to get into that condition, and demand the severe punishment of the Indians. A good rawhide, vigorously applied, would have been a proper and good thing for those boys last Friday. It is unfortunate that it is so, but there are a half dozen boys in Kalispell, boys nearly young men, who are a pretty tough lot, and who will surely get themselves into trouble sooner or later if some severe measures are not adopted with them.

* * * * * * * *

An Indian Woman Shot.

An old Indian woman was shot in town Tuesday afternoon, and is lying in a precarious condition at the camp in the woods below town. There is considerable uncertainty as to how the shooting occurred. The s.... was first discovered lying on the street in a helpless condition. She soon recovered enough to start toward the camp and went several blocks, and then fell on her face, unable to move. A number of Indians were gathered around her and through one who talked English it was learned that the s.... said she had been to the kitchen at Landis' restaurant where the cook had given her something to eat. As she went away from the building some one had struck her, she supposed with a club, knocking her down and cutting her back. She had bled profusely and the blood had run down all over her clothes. A number of ladies who discovered her condition got her wrapped in a blanket and the Indians carried her to the camp. Later it was found that instead of being struck with a club she had been shot, apparently with a 22 bullet, and presumeably [sic] one of the small cartridges used for target practice.

Two young men were placed under arrest Wednesday charged with having done the shooting. Their names are withheld by request until after the preliminary examination now in progress, is concluded. No one believes that there was any intentional shooting, or that if the persons under arrest were concerned in it at all that it was anything but an accident caused by the glancing of a bullet when they were firing at a target.

It is an unfortunate affair all around and if there is not there should be an ordinance forbidding any shooting within the city.

* * * * * * * *

A S.... Shot.

Missoula, March 1. — On Tuesday evening, Feb. 25, an aged Kootenai Indian woman was shot in Kalispell. She was in the rear of a Main street tailor shop about 5 o'clock in the afternoon when she received a bullet in her back. She stumbled and dragged herself to Main street and was there met by the city marshal, who first thought she was intoxicated, but seeing the blood upon her hands and dripping from her clothes, inquired what was the matter, and she replied she thought some one had struck her with a club, but could not tell who, saying she saw no one. Some Indians assisted and carried her to their camp, where it was found she had received a shot from a small caliber pistol or rifle. The next morning the county physician visited her and it was reported she will probably die, the bullet cutting the intestines.

From the circumstances told by an intelligent Indian named Riley, it would seem that this is not the first time that Indians have been shot at in that vicinity. The facts were brought to the notice of County Attorney Logan by Indian Agent [Joseph] Carter, who was in the city, and warrants were issued for the arrest of the suspected parties.

* * * * * * * *

Wicked Joshing.

Missoula, March 3. — Major Carter spent yesterday in the city on business. In speaking of the shooting of the old Indian woman at Kalispell a week ago, Major Carter said that, as far as can be learned, a number of men have been in the habit of shooting at Indians from behind a door in which there was a loophole. The bullets fired were of 22 caliber, but still not pleasant to receive. The old woman who was shot was an inoffensive creature, and when she was wounded she was attending to her own business. Missoula is bad enough, but even here practical joking never reached the stage where it is considered funny to shoot men and women, even if they are Indians.

* * * * * * * *

Susan Kiona, the aged s...., mentioned by us last week as having been accidentally shot on one of the alleys of the city, died from the effect of her injuries at the Indian camp east of town last Saturday night. Her companions of the camp during Sunday sewed the body up in a gunny sacking and buried it in a shallow grave near by. After doing this they reported the fact of her death to the authorities. Early on Monday morning Constable Klinginsmith dug up the body and brought it to McMahon's undertaking rooms in this city where Dr. Macdonald held a post-mortem examination. At the same time Judge Nash, acting as coroner, impanneled a jury and proceeded to hold an inquest. The inquest occupied all day Tuesday, a large number of witnesses being examined. The young men who were last week hastily arrested for the shooting caused the attendance of witnesses whose testimony cleared them from the charge. The jury found the deceased came to her death from the effects of a gun-shot wound inflicted by some unknown person, and they exhonerated the parties under arrest from all blame in the matter.

* * * * * * * *

United States Indian Service,
Flathead Agency,
Jocko, P.O. Mont.
April 10, 1896

Hon. Commissioner Indian Affairs
Washington, D.C.
Sir:

Last week the City Marshal of Kalispel, Montana complained to me that a number of Kootenai Indians were camped about the city, that they were drinking and were frequently intoxicated, that he was reliably informed that the whiskey was furnished them by a certain city saloon Keeper, that he was almost certain of obtaining sufficient evidence to secure a conviction and asked my cooperation. He said he was unable to compel the Indians to leave the vicinity and appealed to me to get them to return to the reservation, that he apprehended serious trouble. Two saloon men of that place are now under bonds to appear before the U.S. Grant Jury at Helena for selling liquor to these Indians. Upon inquiry I learned that there are a number of Kootenai Indians camped there eking out an existence by fishing, sawing wood and doing odd jobs about the town. One of them came to me and related to me the following account of the Killing of an old Indian woman, by one of the citizens of that town.

On February 25th last, an old woman named Melisse was passing in the rear of a tailor shop, which fronts on the main street; while walking through a wood yard, in the rear of this shop, she received a rifle bullet in the back. She stumbled and crawled to the main street there an officer thinking her intoxicated stepped up to arrest her, but seeing her bleeding, asked her what was the trouble; she replied she thought some one had struck her on the back with a club, but that she saw no one. Two Indians assisted and carried her to the Indian camp where it was discovered that she had been shot. Two days afterwards she died. An Indian named Riley informed the City Marshal that he had been shot at from the same place, that the parties in the tailor shop had a hole in their back door about four inches in diameter through which port hole they frequently fired upon Indians. The City Marshal investigated, found the hole in the door as described by the Indian and arrested one of the proprietors of the place.

The Marshal has since informed me of subsequent proceedings in this case, that although he was satisfied the shooting was willful and malicious, no evidence to that effect could be obtained. An inquest was held upon the body of the woman the exact wording of which he did not remember but that it was to the effect that her death was caused by an accidental gunshot wound.

Although the facts here related were brought by me, to the notice of the County Attorney, Sydney Logan, I am informed that the man arrested was allowed to plead Guilty to the charge of "Shooting within the city limits" fined $25.xx and turned loose.

It is not perhaps pertinent to this case to go over the long list of wrongs and murders related to me by this Indian, as perpetrated by white men of that locality upon Indians, where in every case the guilty parties have gone unpunished, while swift sure punishment, sometimes lynch law, is meted out to the Indian, but I think it would be wise at this time to compel the Indians to return to the reservation and thereby avoid any possible trouble. I therefore respectfully request that authority be granted me to proceed to Kalispel for the purpose of inducing these Indians to return to the reservation.

As a further reason, I feel that this is important as Spring is at hand and it is most desirable that these Indians be encouraged to put in a crop, stay at home and take care of it after planting.

I Know that many of them are destitute and in want and all live a long distance from the Agency.

Our seed wheat and supplies are exhausted, therefore, I have enclosed an estimate for an open market purchase of wheat (seed), and supplies sufficient to Keep these people from starving until their crops are harvested. Unless some provision is made for their subsistence I am satisfied it will be impossible to Keep them upon the reservation.

I therefore respectfully urge that the necessary authority be granted.

I have the honor to remain,

Very respectfully,
Joseph T. Carter
U.S. Indian agent

Document 70

Baseball Popular on the Reservation in 1896

May – July 1896

Source: "Flathead Agency," *Daily Missoulian*, May 29, 1896, page 3, col. 1; "Jocko Base Ball," *Daily Missoulian*, June 27, 1896, page 3, col. 1; "Indians Play Ball, *The Anaconda Standard*, July 27, 1896, page 10, col. 3.

Editors' note: Baseball became a popular sport on the reservation in the late 1890s. Teams were organized at St. Ignatius and the Jocko Agency.

Flathead Agency.
Spring Has Awakened Every Thing Into Life on the Reservation.
What Is Going On at the Mission — Game of Base Ball
Between Pupils and Agency Boys.

Agency, May 28. — (Special to the Missoulian) The Flathead reservation looks its best at this time of the year. The many rains have brought out the grass and wild flowers and the beautiful valleys and dells are in their Sunday garb. The many cattle and horses that roam the hill sides are fat and sleek. The Mission range is yet densely covered with snow. Settlers who have resided at the Mission for 16 years have never seen the snow as low on the foot hills at this time of the year.

Indians have begun rounding up their horses, which is wild sport for the red man. Orchards at Ravalli and Mission are in bloom and a good crop is looked for. Garden truck is looking well. The many late rains have given grain a good start and everything looks encouraging.

Superior Father [George] de la Motte, has in practical operation the new acetylene gas for stereopticon light. He claims it is the first in the west. He has made it a thorough study and says it is not at all dangerous but a much better light than electric.

The Mission has about 400 Indian children who are learning different trades and receive a common schooling under the able care of the father. A visit to the Mission is at all times interesting. Mayor Alex Demers, who owns the Mission store postoffice and the city government in general, with his estimable wife, is always ready to welcome his many friends and make their visit pleasant.

Last Sunday was a red letter day for the pupils of the Mission. On that day took place the long expected base ball match between the school boys and their old friends from the Agency, commonly called the Jocko boys. It has been the talk of weeks and had more interest for them than their books, or arithmetical problems.

Notwithstanding the threatening rain all marched enthusiastically to the base ball ground, which is the pride of the Reservation. For upwards of three hours did the battle last, the respective opponents being cheered on by their supporters, with such exulting shoutings, only as Indian pupils can give.

It was clear from the beginning that the Jocko boys could not hold their ground against the sturdy Mission boys so careless was their play. What a triumph for the Mission boys to knock four pitchers out of the box and more so when at the end they scored 48 to 1.

The well earned victory was more important to them than the issue of the forthcoming presidential campaign and so enthusiastic are they over it, that to add fresh laurels, they are prepared to meet them again on June 7, when it is expected that again will the home team uphold its reputation as the best in the Flathead Reservation.

Great praise is due to Captain Langevin for the excellent training he gave his officers. On the other hand, it is a source of pleasure to state that Captain Matt's team took their defeat in a gentlemanly spirit, no harsh feelings being aroused, and by their good conduct on the field they merited the approbation of the many spectators.

The Mission boys are now ready to meet all future comers and to try their dexterity. Address all communications to St. Ignatius Industrial School Base Ball team.

* * * * * * * *

Jocko Base Ball.
The Mission Team Again Defeats the Boys from Jocko.
Great Game — Lasts Four Hours and Only Ended Then By an
Approaching Storm.

Early in June the St. Ignatius Mission boys opened the base ball season by transmitting a friendly challenge to the Jocko boys. The latter in due time accepted, only to meet defeat. The full account of the match appeared in the Missoulian at that time. A return game was arranged and in due time the Jocko boys again crossed their bats with the St. Ignatius team. This game, like the first, ended in triumph for the home team, the score being: St. Ignatius, 29; Jocko, 9.

The Jocko boys, undismayed, determined once more to try conclusions with the Mission team and another game was arranged to take place Sunday, June 21. The morning of the eventful day finally arrived, but not so the anxiously looked for ball team. However, about noon, when their coming was almost despaired of, the Jocko boys arrived, ready for the fray. They meant business and came prepared to "play ball." Excitement ran high. The home team hurriedly donned their uniforms and badges and took their places in the arena.

The game was one of the most exciting ever witnessed here and not for a second did the rival teams cease their vigilance. However the first crucial hour soon passed, leaving the St. Ignatians in the lead. Thereupon the Jockos lost heart, believing that fickle fortune had deserted them indeed. The pitchers for the home team, L. Paul and Marcine, did good work as usual. The local cranks have dubbed them the "cyclone pitchers," a title which they have fully merited by their spirited work.

For four hours the game continued until finally the threatening storm brought the battle to a close with the Mission team again victorious. And now the home team, elated with this success, is prepared to meet any and all comers. They anxiously look for a challenge from the Missoula nine. They can promise any visiting team a hearty welcome and as fine a ball field as may be found in all Montana.

Below we append the score by innings and the names of the home team with their respective positions:

Agency.......0 3 3 6 4 1 1 — 18
Ignatius.....5 1 1 15 5 5 0 x — 31

A. Delaware, center field; John Salais, short stop; James Savage, second base; M. Langevin, catcher; W., McLachlan, right field; O. Morrigean, first base; W. Asselyn, third base; George Uno, left field; Louis Paul, pitcher.

* * * * * * * *

Indians Play Ball
But They Put Up As Poor a Game As Any Team on Earth.
They're All Full Bloods.
Half-Breeds Can't Go In Their Class — The Spectators Enjoyed It, and the Missoula's Helped Them to Make 11 Runs.

Missoula, July 26. — [T]he biggest crowd of the season turned out this afternoon to see the baseball game between the Missoula team and the nine from the reservation. The audience in the grand stand was immensely amused for three or four innings, but the game became very monotonous after that.

The aboriginees cannot play ball a little bit. They have a good idea of the theory of the game, but they are sadly deficient in practice. They wait for a high fly to drop before they go after it an are too lazy to put any ginger into the game at all. When a swift ball is thrown, they are at a loss to know what to do with it. Campbell pitched for the Missoulas and Pequinney was behind the bat. There was not much chance for field work, but Babbitt won the honors of the game by making a phenomenal catch of a pop-up fly back of second base. In the sixth inning, Hammond and Harpster went in as a battery for the Indians and for two innings there was a little interest in the game. Only seven innings were played. It was a novel game, anyway, and the crowd had more fun than it would have at a circus.

The Indians rode down from the reservation last night and this afternoon when every one in the grand stand had given up seeing them and the management was about to call no game the players appeared on horseback galloping across the prairie towards the ball grounds. They came with blankets and broad hats, but threw off the former when they went into the field. Two of them had red caps that they thought more of than they did of the game and would stoop to pick them up whenever they came off, as they did invariably when their wearers tried to run. One buck had a pair of baseball pants that he had picked up somewhere, and he was the star of the aggregation. All of the players were full bloods and they would not let any half breed players have anything to do with the game. It is said that there are some fair players among the half breeds, but the captain wouldn't have any of them in the team. If Campbell had not tossed the ball to their batters they would not have made a run. As it was, they managed to get in 11, by the help of the infield of the Missoula, who let them run around while they held the ball. The score was:

Missoula.........3 2 4 1 0 3 2 — 15
Flatheads.........1 6 1 2 0 1 0 — 11

Missoula is a little late, but just to show that she is all right, she will hold a ratification meeting Friday evening at the court house yard. It is to be a non-partisan affair, and it is thought that there will be a big turnout. There has been much discussion of the condition of affairs to-day and there is no little dissatisfaction expressed over the action of the populists. Judge Reeves is scored by all for his statements at St. Louis and populists are the most bitter in their criticism of him.

Document 71

Bishop Brondell Greeted in Style

August 12, 1896

Source: J. F. Nugent, "Nugent in Montana," *The Daily Iowa Capital* (Des Moines, Ia.) August 18, 1896, page 4, col. 6.

Editors' note: Baptist Kakashee and a large delegation of mounted Indians greeted Bishop John Brondell on his arrival at Ravalli and drive to St. Ignatius for the St. Ignatius Day celebration in 1896. The escort ceremony, firing of guns, and St. Ignatius Day celebration were major events in the church calendar in 1890s St. Ignatius.

Nugent in Montana.

St. Ignacius Mission, Montana, Aug. 12. — Editor Capital: I wanted while in this country to see something of the Indian and learn something of the vexed Indian problem. Seven or eight hours' ride through the most enchanting scenery brought us to the Bitter Root valley. By the way this is called Bitter Root because the bitter root grows here in abundance. I tried to get some of the roots, but all I could get was a description. Before the advent of the white man to this country, the bitter root was the Indian's bread stuff. It is a small root like a carrot, and is ready for use in June. It has no leaves to amount to anything but throws up a tiny stem topped with a beautiful pink flower. It would seem as if the power who made the buffalo grass for the buffalos made the little flower merely to flag the place where the children of the forest should dig for their bread. After another hour's ride we reached Revalley where we took carriages for the mission. The mission is five miles from the station. It was the 31st of July. The 31st of July is St. Ignacius' day and Ignacius day is the Patrick day of the Indians on this reservation. Bishop Brondell of Helena had invited us to wait for this occasion and to accompany him on his confirmation tour to the mission. As soon as we arrived at the station our carriages were in waiting and in a few minutes we were on our way for "Ignace." Revally has a population of five, four besides the station agent. Here Clark's Fork rolls rapidly through its stony and winding channel. The great shady mountains tower majestically over the river. Between the winding river and the foot of the mountains flow the coaches of the Northern Pacific. Thirteen coaches thoroughly equipped for comfort and filled with tourists sweep through here every day. It is a current of human life, a stream of tourists. After we started in the carriage I noticed Indians mounted on their ponies in the nooks and corners around the station and the willows on the river bank. In an instant they all fell into line, or rather into a squad behind and on either side of the carriage. The day was warm and the road dusty. Our road for the most part lay through canon, gorge and valley. It has been the custom for the Indians on occasions of this kind to meet the bishop or the "big black gown" at the station and escort him to the mission. As we drove on, Indians coming to meet us turned and swelled the rank. When we were about half way we saw the top of a hill on our road covered with Indians. They were drawn up in line on either side of the way and holding their horses by the bridles. As the carriage came up they took off their hats and knelt for the benediction. The carriage drove slowly and the bishop imparted his benediction to both sides, alternate as he passed along. In a twinkling the whole crowd was mounted. I noticed that neither children or women needed any assistance to get into the saddle from the level ground. They all hooked their toes into the stirrups and pulled themselves up with a jerk and were mounted. With our kind of boots and shoes this could not be done. We had now about three miles to go. The procession was made up. It was too dusty for the Indians to ride before our carriage, and they were too anxious to ride behind. So the escort took the form of wings and flapped on either side. On we went the carriage in the road and the Indians on either side, sometimes up above on the mountain side, and some times down below us in the canon. To someone in a balloon 5,000 feet above us it must have looked like some fabled bird with a black body and wide butterfly wings skimming slowly near the earth. Never did a butterfly have half the colors that were displayed on the wings of our escort. Every color and form of head gear, blankets spotted and barred, striped and plain, hair with ribbons and bands, moccasins with beads, necklaces and ear rings, all were there in grotesque and lavish profusion. Even here and there might be seen the Easter bonnet. Of course it was not easy to tell which way the bonnet was going, whether it was passing from a lower stage of formation to a higher perfection through evolution, or whether it had reached perfection several Easters ago, and was now degenerating and apparently was well along on the home stretch. Still to an experienced eye the rudiments of the Easter bonnet was there. Not a word was spoken. Not a sound but the clatter of the horses' feet on the ground and the click and clink of their shoes on the rocks. The younger Indians would come closer to the carriage and watch us with vague expressions, but apparent delight. The young people were all bare head and all chewing gum. It was very amusing to see the children crowding close to the carriage much as the boys in the parade crowd around the clown's cart. The chief "John Baptist" rode near the carriage. He and the bishop were the only two big men in the procession. The one represented a people and a power that began, we knew not where, but which is destined to pass with the present generation. The other represented a power which has endured 2,000 years nearly and must undoubtedly extend to the end of time. Side by side, silent and dusty the two chiefs rode. One clad in the purple the other in the cast away garments of civilized life. Several of the Indians had fire arms, and fired salutes as they rode on. After we arrived at the mission the bishop held a reception in the church. This reception consisted in a few prayers, singing a few psalms and the kissing the Episcopal ring. At the close of this the bishop made a short address to the Indians. He spoke in English. Falth [sic] [Jerome] d'Aste, an old missionary, stood beside him and turned it into "flathead" as the bishop delivered it. Flathead or calispee is the language of the reservation. There are so many interesting things here and so many things about the Indians and the management of the Indian, that I think I'll write another letter on points of general interest concerning the civilization of the Indian.

J. F. Nugent.

Document 72

Montana Tries to Enforce State Game Laws on Indian Hunters August 16, 1896

Source: "To Call a Council," *The Anaconda Standard*, August 16, 1896, page 10, col. 1.

Editors' note: Montana refused to recognize tribal hunting rights in the 1890s and tried to force Indian hunters to follow state game laws when off the reservation.

The Call a Council
Major Carter Will Instruct His Wards in the Game Law.
Hunting Off the Reserve
The Matter Is in the Hands of the Department at Washington and a Settlement Is Looked for Before Long.

Missoula, Aug. 15. — Last spring Game Warden Booth, it will be remembered, placed some Indians under arrest for hunting out of season. It will also be remembered that the Indians did not stay arrested, but went back to the reservation as if the hand of the law had not been placed upon them. A formal demand was made upon Major [Joseph] Carter for the delivery of the Indians, and he decided to refer the matter to the department headquarters. Here the subject has rested ever since early spring and there has been considerable discussion as to whether or not the Indians had a right to hunt outside their reservation in conflict with the state game law.

Mr. Booth is in receipt of a letter from Major Carter in which the latter quotes the following from the instructions of the department: "You should further assure the officers that it is the earnest desire of this office to prevent the Indians from giving annoyance to the settlers adjoining their reservation, and also from leaving the same for the purpose of hunting in violation of the game laws of Montana. Further, you should say to them that you will call your Indians in council and again carefully instruct them in regard to the provisions of the game laws, and that they will certainly lay themselves liable to the consequences of the prosecution by state officers if they violate such laws; that you will use your best endeavors to prevent them from repeating the offense and that this office hopes that you will be able to adjust this matter amicably and without prosecution in the premises. It is thought that when the officers fully understand the intention and wish of this office to protect them as far as possible from the annoyance of the Indians and to have the Indians respect the game laws of their states, they will not insist upon prosecuting the Indians that have offended, inasmuch as it seems they did so under a misunderstanding owing to the intermeddling of Mr. —— in giving them a letter relative to hunting which they understood to be a permission to hunt as much as they pleased. In the present case I think it would be well for you to officially inform Mr. —— that he is not again to give any Indian or Indians such permission, as in doing so he will likely render himself liable to prosecution."

Major Carter adds that he intends to call a council as desired by the department. The gentleman mentioned in the letter as having issued what the Indians thought was a permit a is [sic] well know business man of the county.

Document 73

Salish and Crees Fight Over Gambling Losses

December 2, 1896

Source: "Red Men at Outs," *The Anaconda Standard*, December 2, 1896, page 8, col. 1.

Editors' note: Friction over gambling arose between Salish and Crees camped near Butte in 1896. No further information was found about how the tension was resolved.

Red Men at Outs
Flatheads and Crees Quarreling Over a Band of Horses.
There May Be an Outbreak
The Flatheads Lose Their Horses and Game by Gambling
and Are Now Trying to Recover Them.

Trouble is reported among the Indians who are camped about four miles south of Silver Bow. The trouble is trifling as yet, but the Indians are beginning to make heap talk and it is possible that they may get to shooting each other, as all are armed to some extent. The trouble is between a camp of Flatheads and a camp of Crees and Chippewas. The Flatheads left the reservation at the time of the Wild West show in Butte. Most of these Flatheads have found their way back to the reservation, but one lodge has been hunting and wandering about ever since, and when the snow started in, they selected a spot near Silver Bow and concluded to spend the winter. They had collected quite a little game, and with 35 head of horses which they possessed, they hoped to get through the winter in comfortable shape. Lately, however, a band of Crees and Chippewas arrived, part of the same band that has camped at Silver Bow every winter for several years. These Indians were transported across the border into Canada, but as soon as they got over there they started back and are with us one again.

The Flatheads and the Crees got along well together for a time, but they got to gambling and the Crees, it seems, won the 35 head of horses from the Flatheads and also some of the game they had taken for the winter. This has left the Flatheads destitute. Worse than that, the Flatheads now claim that, although the Crees won the horses, they have since won them back in a square game, but they refused to give back the horses. The Flatheads are not strong enough to attack the Crees openly, numbering only five braves and four s....s while the Crees have 22 braves. The Flatheads have tried several times to steal back their horses, but the Crees keep close watch and the Flatheads have been unable to accomplish anything.

In one of the raids of the Flatheads to recover their horses, night before last, two or three shots were exchanged and, although no one was hit, the exchange has served to heighten the feeling on both sides. The Flatheads are desperate and, although woefully inferior in point of numbers, are goaded on by hunger and by the belief that an injustice has been done to them, and apparently they have nearly reached a point where they are willing to take any chances in order to revenge themselves on the Crees. The Crees keep a steady watch and do not hesitate to shoot at anyone who comes too close to the band of horses, which they hold and which they claim they won fairly.

The Flatheads yesterday laid their case before Major Tom Burke, general Indian agent for Rocker and part of Burlington, who had something to do with getting them off the reservation to participate in the Wild West show, and Major Burke was unable to do anything himself, but wrote a letter to Major [Joseph] Carter of the Jocko reservation advising him to remove the Flatheads back to the reservation before they get into serious trouble.

Document 74

Commission Tries to Buy Part of Flathead Reservation March 25, 1897

Source: "Council Is Ended," *Daily Missoulian*, March 25, 1897, page 4, col. 2.

Editors' note: The negotiations on Flathead in March 1897 were the opening salvo for the Crow, Flathead, Etc., Commission which was trying to convince the Flathead Reservation tribes to sell part of the reservation. Charlo and the other tribal leaders refused to sell any land. See also article from September 27, 1898.

Council Is Ended
Commissioners Have Two Big Talks with Reservation Indians.
Chief Charlos Opposed to Relinquishing Any Lands
— Another Pow-Wow Next Summer.

United States Commissioners Col. J. B. Goodwin and Benjamin F. Barge, in company with Indian Agent Major Jos. T. Carter, came to Missoula last night from St. Ignatius Mission, where they held their second preliminary council with the Flathead Indians relative to securing some of their lands. Chief Charlos was at both councils and the propositions laid before the Indians were submitted through an interpreter, although a great many of the Indians understand the English language. The councils held at both Arlee and St. Ignatius Mission were for the purpose of the commissioners laying before the Indians what the government wanted and would do in case they will relinquish part of their domain, and now that the commissioners are away the Indians can discuss the matter among themselves and when the next council is held the latter part of spring or early in the summer they will be in a position to decide intelligently.

Both commissioners are favorably impressed with Chief Charlos and while he is not in favor of relinquishing any of the lands of the Flathead reservation they think before the next council is held the chief will have changed his mind and look upon the proposed purchase as one looking to the betterment of the Flatheads. The majority of the Indians on the reservation are Pend d'Oreilles, next in number the Flatheads, and the others Kalispels, Spokanes and Kootenais.

The Indians, the commissioners say, are in good condition and without doubt the most intelligent they have yet visited.

Col. Goodwin, wife and two sons leave today for Fort Hall, where they will join Commissioner Chas. G. Hoyt, who is now negotiating with the Bannack and other tribes. Commissioner Barge will return to the Flathead agency with Indian Agent Carter and visit certain portions of the reservation where there are large numbers of the Indians, enquiring into their condition and gleaning a description of the valleys, etc.

Document 75

Flathead Reservation Indians Perform in Rodeo at Anaconda June 20, 1897

Source: "The Great Indian Carnival," *The Anaconda Standard*, June 20, 1897, page 4, col. 5-7; "Heap Big Indian Carnival," *The Anaconda Standard*, June 25, 1897, page 3, col. 2-3; "Indians As They Live," *The Anaconda Standard*, June 29, 1897, page 3, col. 1; "Could Not Unseat Him," *The Anaconda Standard*, June 30, 1897, page 3, col. 1.

Editors' note: These articles and advertisement publicized an Indian rodeo and performance presented by Flathead Reservation Indians in Anaconda in June 1897.

Heap Big Indian Carnival.
The Flatheads Will Show Anaconda Some High Jinks.

But a few years have passed since the red men held possession of the mountains and valleys of Montana in quietude, undisturbed by the advance of the white man and the progress of civilization. Many there be who are yet residents of this vale of tears who remember well the time when the Indians were their nearest neighbors. Yet so rapid has been the increase of population that in a quarter of a century the Indian has been herded to the reservation, and the pale face knows him no more except as a wanderer, a gypsy-like stroller along the highways. The rising generation views him with contempt and sees naught in the blanketed buck and lean cayuse to approach the heroic brave and the fleet steed he rode in the tales of adventure the old-timer tells or history narrates. But the stories are true: it is only the change in times that has worked the metamorphosis in the Indian. He is still a picturesque character, untutored and wild, a child of nature and clinging to his old customs with a tenacity that is not equaled.

The camp of the Flathead band that is west of the city, on the hillside overlooking the race track, is a scene that brings to the mind of the old-timer days of long ago, and the village has been visited by many curious and interested spectators. But the Indians do not give visitors a hearty welcome. Their dogs bark at the heels of a white intruder as savagely as the town dogs bark at the

THE GREAT INDIAN CARNIVAL

At Anaconda, Mont., June 27, 1897,

UNDER THE AUSPICES OF JUANITA COUNCIL.

Two Performances, Afternoon and Evening, at 2:30 and 8:00 p.-m.

500 INDIANS

Under the Direction of CHIEF ISAAC of the Flathead Nation, in Original Indian Life, Consisting of and Showing

Genuine Indian Marriage
Genuine Indian Gambling
Riding Bucking Horses
Foot Racing
Fancy Arrow Shooting
Indian Cattle Killing
Peace Dance

Stealing and Recapturing Horses
War Dance
Sham Battle
Locating, Breaking Up and Relocating Camp by Squaws
Squaw Racing
Athletic Sports of All Kinds

A Novel Feature, an Indian Quadrille and Dance. Realistic, Spectacular and True to Nature

A GRAND STREET PARADE AT 12:30

With 500 Indians in War Paint and Dress Will Parade the Principal Streets of the City

The Evening Performance Will Conclude With a Grand Sham Battle

Between Opposing Tribes. Participated in by all the Indians. Such a Display Never Before Witnessed in the Great Northwest.

Admission to the Grounds, Adults 50c, Children 25c.

Excursion train leaves Butte on B. A. & P. at 10 a. m., 1:15 p. m. and 5 p. m., returning at 3 p. m., 8:30 and 11:30. Fare for round trip, $1.00.

"The Great Indian Carnival"
Source: *The Anaconda Standard*, June 20, 1897, page 4, col. 5-7.

dusky visitor in the alleys of the city. The white man in an Indian camp gets little satisfaction and sees few sights of Indian life as it really is.

On next Sunday, however, the Flathead band, under the leadership of Chief Isaac, will give one of the rarest entertainments that has ever been seen in Montana, a realistic reproduction of the life of other years, the wild, weird ways which they love in spite of irresistible power that binds them to quieter lives and a dependent existence upon the bounty of the government.

They will show how they captured the mustangs on the plains, how they stole ponies and how they fought their battles. The camp will be moved from one site to another, the s....s doing the work.

The young Indians will ride, as no white man ever does, the wild cayuse without saddle, brid[l]e or girth, picking up articles from the ground while at full gallop, shooting firearms under the horse while they ride head down on the side of the animal. It is reckless, dangerous, but the young braves love the sport. Last Sunday one of them while practicing had his leg broken by the horse falling upon him. Dr St. Jean set the leg and the rider is now confined to his tepee with the limb.

Another interesting feature is to be the Indian marriage, stealing the bride and ending with the peaceful settlement by the exchange of ponies. Indian gambling, so ably described on the Missoula page of the Standard last Monday morning, will be illustrated by the tribe, with whom it is still the most popular method of gambling.

A central figure in the group is an aged Indian and his s...., both of whom are more than 100 years old. He is the medicine man of the band and will "make medicine" for the performance on Sunday, invoking the Great Spirit and driving all "evil ones" out of the camp.

The war dance and peace dance will be given by the entire tribe, a company of several hundred redskins, and these alone are sights which no one should miss seeing, as it is the chance of a lifetime.

All railroads are giving excursion rates, one far[e] for the round trip, and special trains will be run via the B., A. & P. to accommodate the Butte visitors. The Indian peace carnival, given by the Indians themselves, is an enterprise that has never been undertaken before in Montana, and its success is assured.

* * * * * * * *

Indians As They Live
A Brilliant Opening for the Carnival Last Night.
The Great Spirit Invoked
War Dances and a Sham Battle — Fancy Trick Riding
and Broncho Busting
— The Flatheads and the Carroll Club Will Play Ball To-Day.

It was a hot show. The Indian carnival put up sport enough last night to satisfy everyone in spite of a few unfavorable conditions, which necessitated a partial change of programme. The parade in the evening before the exercises began attracted a large crowd and was most favorably commented on.

The crowd at the grounds just about filled the big grand stand without crowding and was enthusiastic and sympathetic from start to finish. Electric lights illuminated the enclosure and made it almost as bright as day and revealed a weird and novel scene. At right angles to the grand stand, in two parallel lines, were the smoke-stained tepees of the Flatheads. Outside of the tepees played the hopeful offspring of the noble red man, while innumerable dogs of all kinds and conditions joined in the sport. Through the open flap of the tepees could be seen the s....s bending over the fires and busied with the numerous duties which fall on the shoulders of the unfortunate female Indian. The bronchos were either scattered over the ground feeding or were tethered near the tepees. The bucks, gaudily arrayed in brilliant and striking colors, walked slowly around, wrapped in their blankets and traditional dignity. It was a striking scene, a bit of native savagery in the heart of civilization.

The visitors to the carnival were permitted to wander about the Indian village, thoroughly satisfying their curiosity, which was not resented by the Indians.

At 3:30 the carnival opened. The old medicine man, who is said to be fabulously old, so old in fact that the memory of man cannot recall his birth, then slowly walked to the center of the space between the two rows of tepees and, waving a mystic wand, began a weird incantation to the Great Spirit, responses to which were uttered in the shrill voices of the s....s. This over the bucks, headed by Chief Isaac, all on prancing, bucking bronchoes, began a march around the encampment. All were magnificently dressed, according to the Indian standard of taste and affluence, and their faces were daubed and fantastically worked in various colored paints, which, in the glow of the electric light, made a striking appearance.

An exhibition was then given of Indian trick and fancy riding and a number of difficult feats, such as picking up a handkerchief while riding at full gallop, caught the crowd and brought out the applause. Twin did some good work, but was not at his best. There were plenty of bucking bronchos and the crowd went wild over both the intentional and involuntary exhibitions of the Indian pony's ability to cork-screw himself into every conceivable position.

After this feature of the programme, a big fire was built in front of the grand stand and bucks stripped off their superfluous clothing to get down to the hot work of the carnival, a genuine Indian war dance. The s....squatted around one side of the fire with blankets pulled up over their heads and ranged themselves on the other side awaiting the signal. The old medicine man stepped to the front and waved his feathered wand and began a weird monotonous chant accompanied by a peculiar drum beat that resembled Chinese music, while the s....s took up a mournful minor as a refrain. Headed by the chief the Indians began their strange dance which many a time in the past has been the prelude to bloody war. Slowly at first, keeping perfect time to the fantastic chant of the medicine man and the s....s, the dance began. Then the pace quickened, the music became faster and louder and the dancers bending and twisting their bodies in rhythm to the music, uttered sharp, fierce cries. Faster and faster came the music until the dancers dispersed in an apparent frenzy of a mad desire for blood and war.

The sham battle was a hot affray while it lasted and was particularly vivid and realistic. The exhibition of Indian wrestling was a big feature of the evening and captured lots of applause. The closing event was the famous American quadrille introducing steps that would make Lole Fuller's tights turn green with envy.

To-day there will be another grand parade at 11 a.m. The carnival will open at the grounds at 2:30 p.m. with a ball game between the Carroll club and a nine of Indians and will be followed by an entire change of programme, introducing features such as horse stealing, breaking camp by the s....s, a peace dance, fancy arrow shooting and the principal features given last night. In the evening another programme will be presented.

* * * * * * *

Could Not Unseat Him
Twin, the Flathead Rider, Does Some Fancy Riding.
They Had a Sham Battle
Indians Give an Exhibition of Horse Stealing and the Way an Attack Is Repulsed — Ball Game Between the Indians and Carroll Club.

The opening feature of the Indian carnival yesterday was an exhibition game of baseball between the Indians and the Carroll club. The few innings played were closely watched by the spectators and good plays were heartily applauded. While the Flatheads did not play an errorless game they showed themselves to be hard hitters and good sprinters. When the exhibition closed it looked as if they would have had the best of it in a nine-inning game.

Following the ball game the usual carnival opening was made. After the opening parade Twin and others gave a clever exhibition of trick riding, daring feats catching the applause of the crowd. Handkerchiefs and gloves were picked from the ground with the horses at a dead gallop and there was some fancy bareback riding done that would put circus men to blush.

A man who owned two fine looking black horses led them into the enclosure and put up a good bet that no Indian could ride either of them. This was just the kind of a snap that Twin was looking for and the challenge was immediately accepted. One of the black horses was led forward and after some difficulty was saddled and bridled. This accomplished Twin vaulted into the saddle. The horse gave a snort and then scattered the crowd in its mad rush for anywhere. Finding that it could not be relieved of its burden by simple speed it started bucking and for 15 minutes did its best to throw Twin, who kept his seat through all the cork-screw movements of the beast, and finally made the horse understand that it had met its master.

The man who made the challenge was not satisfied and Twin accommodated him by riding the other horse without bucking strap or bridle. It was no use. Buck as the horse would, and some very artistic bucking was done, Twin could not be unseated, and won the deserved applause of the crowd.

An exciting exhibition of horse stealing and a sham bat[t]le was then given and the programme for the afternoon finished.

In the evening a fine programme was rendered to a large crowd and the carnival brought to a close.

Document 76

Indian Domestic Conflicts Spill Over Into Butte

July 17, 1897

Source: Joseph T. Carter to Commissioner of Indian Affairs, July 17, 1897, letter received 29,725/1897, RG 75, National Archives, Washington, D.C.; "A Gay Indian," *The Anaconda Standard*, September 7, 1897, page 10, col. 1.

Editors' note: This case was an example of law and order problems on the reservation in 1897. On September 2, 1897, the Commissioner of Indian Affairs declined to authorize the payment of Little Michel's medical bills and on December 18, 1897, he also refused payment for La La's bills.

Department of the Interior,
U.S. Indian Service,
Flathead Agency, Montana,
July 17th, 1897.

Honorable Commissioner of Indian Affairs,
Washington, D.C.
Sir:

I have this day received a communication from the Sheriff of Silver Bow County informing me that a Flathead Indian named Law-law had been seriously wounded by another Indian, that the shooting had been done near Butte City and that Law-law had been taken to the County Hospital for treatment and that the County Commissioners wished me notified and informed that the government would be held for caring for Law-law.

To this letter I replied that I would promptly report the matter to the Department and would be guided by the advice and instructions of the Honorable Commissioner.

It has also come to my knowledge that the same Indian who shot Law-law, also shot and seriously wounded another Indian named Little Michel at or near the town of Phillipsburg, Montana.

The Indian who did the shooting is named Pierre Joseph and was on the police force at this Agency. Upon receiving the first news of the trouble the Indian Police were started in pursuit of Pierre Joseph. He was promptly arrested and brought to the Agency where he now is in custody awaiting the action of the authorities of the places where the trouble took place; my understanding of the law to be that Indians while off their reservations are amenable to the state laws and to be tried in the state courts.

As yet I have but Pierre Joseph's account of the affray which I have every reason to believe to be true.

Law-law and Little Michel ran away with the wife of Pierre Joseph. They were overtaken at Anaconda, Montana by pierre [sic] Joseph who demanded the return of his wife, but was driven off, Little Michel attacking him with a heavy weapon. The next day Law-law and the wife of Pierre fled to Butte but were overtaken and when Pierre Joseph came up to Law-law the shooting commenced. Law-law fell shot through both legs. Pierre Joseph then took his child and rode to Phillipsburg 50 miles distant and upon coming to an Indian camp was accosted by Little Michel who had ridden over from Anaconda.

Little Michel asked Pierre Joseph what he had done to Law-law, Pierre Joseph replied that he was probably sick. Comprehending that some injury had been done his partner, Little Michel attacked Pierre Joseph with an iron flute made from a gun barrel, striking him with the weapon. Pierre Joseph pulled his pistol and shot Michel in the leg. Little Michel is a renegade Indian and has served a term in the state penetentiary [sic] at Deer Lodge. Law-law who has a wife upon this reservation has been a well behaved Indian, and well to do.

As we have no hospital upon the reservation and the wounded men can scarcely be moved without endangering their lives, I trust that instructions may be sent to allow the County authorities to take care of these Indians until they can be safely brought to their homes. If so instructed vouchers will be taken for their care and keeping and submitted for approval. I have the honor to remain,

Very respectfully,
Joseph T. Carter
U.S. Indian Agent.

* * * * * * * *

A Gay Indian.
La La Who Was Shot in Butte Is a Red Skin Lothario.

Missoula, Sept. 6. — The gay young Indian who created so much trouble on the reservation by his familiarity with the wife of another Indian, and who subsequently eloped with her, leaving his own wife, only to be shot at Butte, while the Indian police were after him, has recovered from the effects of his wounds and is once more sporting around at the agency. He regards himself as a hero, rather than in his true light of a thorough rascal. He wears all of the finery that he can load himself with and poses in such striking attitudes that he makes a decided impression upon visitors and upon the susceptible maidens of his tribe. The older Indians regard him with contempt, according to the statement made the other day to a Standarde [sic] reporter by Michel, the old interpreter, whose sightless eyes almost flashed as he heaped abuse upon the head of the gay Lothario.

According to Michel, La La's wife is a good woman and deserves much better treatment than she receives from her spouse. La La, however, holds his wife in much higher esteem since his recent difficulties and conducts himself more carefully than he did in former days.

"When La La was shot," said the blind interpreter, "he sent word to his wife that he wanted to come home and asked her to send him some horses, so he could get back. His wife would not do it. If he wants to come he can come home the same way he went. That woman took him. She can bring him back. Then, bye and bye, La La came here and then he sent word to his wife that he wanted to come to their place. He was sick from the shots. She said that he could come home when he was the same way that he left. He could wait till he was well and then if he wants to come home he can do so."

So La La had to remain at the agency till his wounds were healed and then he went home to his wife, humbly and to all appearances, penitently. But his subsequent actions do not convey the impression that his repentance was sincere. He has, anyway, a light hold on the affections of his wife.

There have been several elopements and similar escapades on the reservation within the past year and Michel, in speaking of them, said: "All the trouble has come in the last 15 years. Before that we never had anything like this. I think that all the trouble comes from one woman. She keeps talking to the other women all the time and she makes all this trouble. It is too bad. She is a bad woman."

In connection with the La La affair it is told, and there is a photograph to prove it, that a well-known young lady from Missoula's society circles, while visiting at the reservation some months before the elopement took place, mounted a pony behind the gay La La and had her picture taken in that position. It is not necessary to state that copies of this picture are not freely circulated.

Document 77

Clairmont Boys Meet the Indian Court

September 14, 1897

Source: "Queer Indian Justice," *The Anaconda Standard*, September 14, 1897, page 10, col. 1.

Editors' note: The case of the Clairmont boys was an interesting commentary on the operation of the Flathead Reservation Indian Court. The judges struggled without DNA evidence, but were unwilling to allow lawyers and white justice procedures to complicate their work.

Queer Indian Justice
The Court Sentences Three Boys for the Same Crime.
Have No Use for Lawyers
Attorney Dixon Appears for the Young Men
— They Ordered Him to Go Away
— Will Appeal to the U.S. Court.

Missoula, Sept. 13. — J. M. Dixon went to Butte this evening to appear before the federal court in behalf of some Indian clients of his who are now in confinement. The case is an interesting one in many respects, as it shows how the Indian courts operate. Some time ago Louis Clairmont came down from the reservation to enlist Mr. Dixon's services in behalf of his three sons, who had been sentenced by the Indian court.

It appears that the three boys had been unduly familiar with the daughter of "French Ed," a well-known s....man of the reservation and the girl found herself in a condition that was unfortunate for a young woman with no husband. The court of the Indians was convened to consider the case, with old Antoine, the chief justice, presiding. The court deliberated at length, but was unable to fix the responsibility for the condition of the girl, further than the author of her shame was probably one of the Clairmont boys. Which one it was not possible to determine. The court, however, was determined to punish some one for the crime and, in order to be sure and get the right one, all three of the boys were sentenced. The oldest was givens three months' imprisonment and $300 fine; the second two months and $200; the third 30 days and $30. Here the matter rested till Clairmont here called upon Mr. Dixon. The attorney said that he could not do anything with an Indian court, but the father was so insistent that he finally consented to go up to the reservation and see what could be done.

He accordingly appeared before the court and, through an interpreter, informed the judges that he had come simply to talk the matter over. He wanted the judges to consider what they had done and release the boys. The judges mumbled together and finally Michel, the blind interpreter, delivered their decision to Mr. Dixon.

They said that the lawyer must go away. Lawyers were bad people and always making trouble. In passing the sentence that they had, they had simply been carrying out the instructions of their great father in Washington, who was the lawyer's great father, too, and they could not do anything else. A lawyer is like and race horse and an Indian like a cayuse and the Indian cannot enter with the lawyer. He is not in the same class. Further than this, they would say nothing and Mr. Dixon now seeks the aid of the federal court in freeing his clients from their peculiar position.

Document 78

Missoula County Attempts
to Tax Mixed Blood Indians
October 31, 1897

Source: Joseph T. Carter to Commissioner of Indian Affairs, October 31, 1897, letter received 46,325/1897, RG 75, National Archives, Washington, D.C.

Editors' note: This an early example of the many cases of Missoula County efforts to tax mixed blood residents of the Flathead Indian Reservation. On November 10, 1897, the Commissioner of Indian Affairs wrote Agent Carter that for mixed bloods living on the reservation, "none of their property real or personal and no matter how acquired is now subject to taxation." Despite this decision, the conflict with Missoula County over taxes was to drag on for many years into the twentieth century.

United States Indian Service,
Flathead Agency,
Jocko, P.O. Mont.
Oct. 31st, 1897

Hon. Commissioner Indian Affairs,
Washington, D.C.
Sir:

An effort is being made by the County Assessor of Missoula County to levy taxes upon the personal property of a number of mixed blood Indians living upon and belonging to this reserve. Also upon the personal property belonging to the Industrial school at St. Ignatius.

Notices have been sent to about 40 or 50 families and the tax aggregates several thousand dollars. I enclose a sample one sent to Oliver Gebeau, who is my present chief of police and who was born upon this reservation.

The assessment of these people was done surreptitiously, the assessor going to a certain traders store and getting from him the information upon which this levy was made.

The people who have received notices have applied to me for advice and protection and as the notice threatens to confiscate their property they are much exercised over it.

I spoke to the U.S. District Judge about the matter and he expressed the opinion that if these mixed bloods sustained tribal relations here they were not taxable.

The trouble is they are taxed and I am satisfied from the character, manner, disposition and expressed sentiments of the County Assessor that an attempt will be made to collect the tax whether lawful or not. Some of the people will probably be worried, harassed, and bullied into paying this, (in my opinion) unlawful tax; others will be put to the expense of defending costly lawsuits, unless some steps be taken by the Department to protect them. I therefore most earnestly urge that I be advised at as early a date as possible, whether or not these people are to be considered and recognized as Indians, and if not are they taxable citizens, and such other advice and instructions as the Hon. Commissioner may deem proper.

In reference to the St. Ignatius Mission School; the personal property taxed is the cattle, milk cows and horses necessary to feed the children there taught and to run the industrial farm of that institution of learning. I have the honor to remain,

Very respectfully,
Joseph T. Carter
U.S. Indian Agent.

* * * * * * * *

Treasurer's Office
Missoula County.

Page 70
Line 3

Missoula, Mont., October 1, 1897.

Oliver Gibeau

Your taxes for the year 1897 amounting to $6.64, are now due and payable at this office. If not paid on or before the first Monday in December 1897 at 6 o'clock p.m., the law makes and addition of 10 per cent, to the amount of said taxes, and requires that property upon which taxes are delinquent, shall be immediately advertised for sale, or seized and sold for the payment of said taxes and costs.

Respectfully,
Alfred Cave, Treasurer.

Please bring this notice with you, as it saves time in finding your name on the Tax Book, in giving the page and line. Remit in Cash, Bank-Draft, Express or Money Order.

Document 79

Gambling Violence Put an Indian in Missoula Jail
November 7, 1897

Source: "Lost Another Friend," *The Anaconda Standard*, November 7, 1897, page 10, col. 1.

Editors' note: No information was found to explain the first part of this article, but the fight between Joe Lumphrey and Poker Jim, Isaac, and Joseph over a gambling game was an example of violence in the Indian community.

Lost Another Friend.
"Poker Jim" Is in Jail and Will Stay for Some Time.

Missoula, Nov. 6. — Deputy Sheriff McCormick has lost a friend. He lost his room mate last month, but discovered that his chum was married and that was all right. But the friend that he has lost this time will not continue to stand as well as did the other. Dougal is willing, but the friend is not. "Poker Jim" is the Indian who the other day wanted to present Dougal with a s...., but the offer does not stand good any more. Poker Jim is in jail, and his erstwhile friend is the man who placed him there. Worse than that, he is liable to stay there for a long time. It was about 2 o'clock this morning when Joe Lumphrey, a well-known half-breed, presented himself at the county jail and asked for assistance and protection. He walked with extreme difficulty and his left ear looked as if it had been run through a sausage machine. He was bloody from head to foot, and his appearance would convey the impression that a new Indian war had broken out. Joe told his story as follows:

He had been playing cards with Poker Jim and two other Indians named Joseph and Isaac and fortune had smiled on his hands. He had won so many pots that he excited the ire and suspicion of his companions. One of them left the tepee and returned in a minute with a club, which he proceeded to use with telling effect upon the person of Lumphrey. The other two reds joined in the affray, and when they got through with poor Joe he didn't know whether there had been another earthquake or whether a cyclone had struck him. As soon as he collected his wits and took an inventory of his members, he proceeded to hobble down the Rattlesnake and up to the county jail, where he enlisted the services of the doughty Dougal.

The two returned to the tepee, where the card game had been played, and the officer without ceremony pulled Poker Jim and his companions out of bed and took them to warmer quarters at the county jail. They protested and Jim told Dougal that it was all a mistake. He insisted that he was a good Indian and that Joe Lumphrey was a liar. It required all of the Selish that deputy could command to convince the three that they must go, but he finally accomplished his purpose and lodged them in the steel cage.

This forenoon the whole crowd was taken up to Judge Myers' room, where Joe Lumphrey grunted and groaned and rubbed his sore spots, while the others laughed at him. No interpreter could be found and the case was continued till the afternoon. Then the justice of the peace heard the tale of the game and its sequel and took the matter under advisement till Monday, when he will sentence the others.

Document 80

White Woman and Tribal Member
Fight Over Belongings
December 10, 1897

Source: Joseph T. Carter to Commissioner of Indian Affairs, December 10, 1897, letter received 53,471/1897, RG 75, National Archives, Washington, D.C.

Editor's note: On November 18, 1897, Mrs. M. D. Gregg, a white woman, complained that Mr. Morrigeau had kept some of her belongings which had been washed out of her wagon while crossing a river on the reservation. The affair was complicated, but indicates the type of friction that occasionally arose between the races in the 1890s.

Department of the Interior,
U.S. Indian Service,
Jocko, Flathead Agency, Montana,
December 10, 1897.

Honorable Commissioner of Indian Affairs,
Washington, D.C.
Sir:

I am in receipt of "A" 49456, '97," in which you say, — "I herewith enclose a communication from Mrs. M. D. Gregg, under date of 18th instant, relative to the loss by her of certain cattle, clothing, etc.," — "I will thank you to investigate the matter and return inclosure with report and recommendations in the case."

Replying, I desire to say that, I received a communication from Mrs. Mitchell, alias Mrs. Gregg, complaining of the loss of her clothing, but the inclosure forwarded by you contains the first complaint or mention of the loss of her cattle.

Immediately upon the receipt of her letter, I investigated the matter and found that Mr. Morrijeau, who is the same party she refers to as "Mosier," found one of the sacks she lost, containing a jacket only, and he informed me that he had loaned Mrs. gregg [sic], alias Mrs. Mitchell, through sympathy, a blanket, a mackintosh, and an oil-skin covering or robe; that she promised to return them upon her return, but, though she drove through when returning, she made a detour to avoid passing their door, as they supposed to avoid returning the borrowed articles; that he concluded this woman (a stranger to him) intended to steal and keep the articles that he had loaned her. I advised him to write to her again, and tell her to send the articles she borrowed to Mr. Sloan, a relative of Morrijeau's, which she agreed to do in her letter to me, and I advised Morrijeau to send the sack he found to Sloan. I am now advised by Mrs. Morrijeau that she did again write to this woman and can hear nothing from her; that she failed to return the borrowed articles. She (Mrs. Morrijeau) or her children, are not wearing any of this woman's clothing, and are ready and willing to return to her what they found, but would like to get back the articles this woman borrowed of them.

Morrijeaus are half-breeds, good, kind, honest, well to do people, of exceptionally good character, and it does look as though Mrs. Gregg, alias Mrs. Mitchell, is the delinquent, and should consult some attorneys to defend, rather than prosecute. There is no doubt but that she borrowed the articles mentioned and has not returned them, for she so admits in her letter to me, although she makes some lame excuse for not so doing, saying she was mis-directed, which I doubt, as she had before traveled the road, and there is no other road through the reservation which does not pass by Morrijeau's farm, though by going over a mountain or crossing the river above, one can avoid passing their door, but must pass by their place, and in sight of their house.

The cape or jacket found is not of sufficient value to pay the postage of the letters written about it, while the goods she borrowed and holds, of Mr. Morrijeau's, are of some value. I was sorely tempted to forward the cape found to the Indian Office, to show how exaggerated and unreliable are these complaints and alleged grievances from whites on the border of the reserve.

Of even day with this letter, I have written Mrs. Gregg, alias Mrs. Mitchell, and enclose you a copy of the letter, which will settle the matter, I think.

Although three years have elapsed since the alleged loss of her cattle, I will promptly, upon receipt of further information, investigate and report further in the matter.

Very respectfully,
Joseph T. Carter
U.S. Indian Agent.

Document 81

Christmas at St. Ignatius, 1897

December 24, 1897

Source: L. Kenny, "The Indians at St. Ignatius Mission, Montana: Extracts from a Letter of Mr. Kenny," *Woodstock Letters*, vol. 27, no. 1 (1898), pages 82-84.

Editors' note: Kenny visited St. Ignatius Mission for Christmas in 1897 and described what he saw. Note the role of Baptiste Kakashe, the church chief and chief of police at St. Ignatius.

The Indians at St. Ignatius Mission, Montana.
Extracts from a Letter of Mr. Kenny.

What shall I say about the Mission, First get a *constructio loci*. A long valley, about ten miles in width, and fully fifty in length; enormous and very steep mountains form its eastern wall. First ranges, comparatively mere hills, with real mountains behind them run less regularly along the west. To the north, the plain in some places continues even as far as the eye sees. The southern edge is an uneven spur joining east and west.

Near the southwest corner of this valley, you see the Mission, — one large frame house, and the immense brick church very like the Church of the Sacred Heart at Chicago. All the rest are frame buildings. There is the boys' school taught by scholastics; the Providence Sisters' school for large girls, and the Ursulines' kindergarten for girls and boys. Around these are a multitude of out-buildings, the largest of which is our mill. Around these again lie in promiscous disorder some fifty or more ramshackle huts and shanties in every stage of ruin. This is the town of St. Ignatius. The huts belong to the Indians and are inhabited about once a week. But I didn't mention the emporium of our city: De Mers' hotel, store, post office, butcher-shop, and a little of everything else. Near De Mers' are four neat frame houses.

Our school has about seventy boys, the best natured boys I ever saw. They range in years from twelve to eighteen; in class from 5th reader — two are in the 5th — down. They are called Indians, but they might as justly be called French Canadians; all races are well represented in this 'glomeration. Take five or six full bloods, and as many half breeds out, and the rest of the pupils look as much like any public school boys as do any other parochial scholars. There are unmistakably Hibernian faces, a couple of perfect little tow heads, the olive skin and boöps of Italian skies, a little Solomon Levi nose, and one representative of Africa's woolly-headed tribe; but Paris prevails.

My idea in regard to the Indians and Catholic Missions are in a perfect seething of instability. My first impression was cold disappointment. We have heard such persistently repeated praises of this mission, that probably our notions went of themselves beyond those of the writers or speakers. Certainly I was completely deceived either by myself or by others. I think it can be safely said that the Flatheads are as near to what is usually meant by civilization as they were sixty years ago, no more. But it is hard for us to get out of our Protestant way of looking at things. Civilization need not precede Christianity, as all history proves, and as I realized only at the Christmas midnight Mass.

From sixty miles or more through snow and rough weather whole families of these wild people came to assist at the Mass. Their dwellings on Christmas eve were such as surely made them realize the stable at Bethlehem. The whole nation, save Charlot's band, were here. Baptiste harangued his people at the entrance of the church just before midnight. At 12 they fired a volley and crowded into and really packed this huge church.

The singing and the solemn high ceremonies, the decorations and the crib were just as you see everywhere. Not until holy Communion time did I perceive the crowd. Then up the aisle came the procession, — the men on one side, brawny, eagle-eyed, wild fellows; the women on the other, little emaciated creatures. Baptiste, the chief, received first, then he stood at the sanctuary gate motionless as a statue, a symbol effecting order. I thought I had never seen a man look nobler in all my life. Such an eye, such an unconsciously grand face, such a pose, and, not least, that luxuriant grey hair standing up from the forehead and thence falling in venerable locks down on his shoulders. Meanwhile his people were approaching the railing, the men in blankets of every possible color and mixture of colors, the women with the little papooses tightly swathed in blankets to their backs. There the little copper face peeps out six inches above the mother's heads and coos at the priest when he distributes the heavenly manna. Three fathers were more than an hour in distributing holy Communion; and all this time I was lost in contemplation of Christ — the meek, the tender babe of Bethlehem — coming unto these wild untamable bosoms, and of these strange beings coming unto Him. "Thou hast hidden these things from the wise and prudent, but hast revealed them to the little ones. Yea, Father, for so it has been pleasing in thy sight," I thought. This is the sight, I believe, this is the fact, which takes the breath away from Catholic witnesses and drives them into rhapsodies about the Indian's virtues such as seem pure mendacity to dull onlookers.

Christmas afternoon I met Francis Saxa; this last name is a corruption of Xavier. Old Ignace who went to St. Louis so often to get priests to come among these people, and finally got Father [Pierre] De Smet to come, on his second trip took his two sons with him and had them baptized in our church there. Francis Saxa was one of those boys. He was then ten years old, and that was before 1840. As a child, how often I had heard of those brave Indians that came those thousands of miles for the black-gown! How little I then thought of ever seeing the face of one of them. As he stood before me, I felt a thrill of delight, such perhaps as was that of Napoleon's men when 4000 years were looking down upon them. I felt contemporaneous with Noah, — I was looking ancient history in the face.

Through Father Superior I gave him a print of the new St. Francis Xavier's Church in St. Louis. When Father [George] De la Motte gave him the picture and said in Kalispel: "This is the church in St. Louis which replaces the one in which you were baptized," the old man kissed the picture and burst into tears. We were pained, but relieved when he explained, "Father, I wept because that is where I first saw the fathers." How much Jesuit history weaves around this man! He is not a Flathead but an Iroquois. It was the faith implanted by Father Jogues and his companions that sent those delegations to St. Louis.

Pray for me,

L. Kenny, S.J.

Document 82

Hamlin Garland Described Life
on Flathead in 1897
1897

Source: Extract from Hamlin Garland, Notes on the Flathead Reservation [1897], Hamlin Garland Collection, Special Collections, University of Southern California Library, Los Angeles, item 49-2, pages 112-126.

Editors' note: The notes are impressions Garland recorded in his note book about his 1897 visit to St. Ignatius town and mission, and a mixed-blood fiddle dance. They provide a sketch of life at St. Ignatius in the late nineteenth century. The manuscript was hard to read but is reproduced here as accurately as possible.

The early descent wild. the wide beautiful valley of the Mission. the fine fences ditches splendid fields of grain. birds singing. a feeling as if late June.

The Mighty Mountain behind. Spotted with snow naked for two thousand feet of top. the topped covered by big clouds like sombreros. the hills smooth and grassy to the west and south. the splend peaks behind over which the sun streams.

We came soon to ranches fenced with rail fences and watered by the Mountain water. the crops were excellent. Roads much trod.

The Mission. Around the Mission are grouped a village of small huts and shanties. the Church looming over all like a Mexican village. the store of logs was filled with half-blood Indians in Cheap American clothes.

We ate at the little [illegible] in which was not a single white man but our selves. full-blood Indian women Some children quarter bloods. Out side I saw Indians. blanket draw s[illegible]tualy to their Chins Stalking solemnly about.

the whole place a jumble of half-bloods, quarters. Cootenai. Cour de lain. pend oreille and flat head people. the faces of a dozen tribes.

It is a half way station on the road to civilization. Here is every shading of advance. the Indian with blanket and feathers. the Indian in American dress with moccasins and uncut hair and the Indian shorn and wearing boots. Their trail along the grades.

The Mission is a village which began as a camp of teepees. passed into a permanent Camp and at last into a regular village of log huts. surrounding the

Church and boarding school. Which are enclosed in a big fence instead of the adobe walls of the south west.

A Pend Oreille splendid in gay Color. a green ribbon [illegible] about his head. rode about on a splendid horse looking for bright eyes.

Boys with shinny blue-black hair and black eyes strolled by in complete Indian dress together with boys in long trousers and black dress.

Gay young half blood girls of denim. Not many pretty or graceful. all awkward and self conscious.

Some old women seemed Scotch Irish in type tall and bony. two monstrously fat.

Groups of superb young riders danced and swooped about the streets most with wide white hats buried by ribbons of gay colors. Some with Vests Shirts and Trousers of American make but retaining the blanket. their hair in braids bound with ribbons or weasel skins. Splendid leggins mixed with Calico Shirts. bordering mugguns and diagonal trousers.

In this way they type forth the change which has come to them.

They are at the far end of their own spenldulous civilization and beginning on the crudest border End of the Whitemans dress and Manners. They are doubly cursed. they must give up a life based on nature and occupy one based Artificial distinctions and prejudices. Some of the men part their hair on one side and Carry it in a sweeping curve up over the head binding it with a ribbon. A fine fashion. One man mounted on a fine horse wore his hair thus and used a light green ribbon.

Others gayly painted with shell disks swaying on the ears.

Some touch of vivid Color appeared on all the dresses.

A party of Visiting Crees "Canada Indians" rode up one with a battered hat adorned with feathers.

Carlisle students halty and bright.

The half blood women all dressed like awkward country people. Sauntered around as aimlessly.

the sorry old nags or the trilling race. driven by frisky half-bloods. They could not possibly trot a mile in seven minutes. The French ability to come off a small affair with great show of enjoyment.

The greater number of the people are half-breeds of french parentage but there are a good many scotch mixtures and some few Irish.

The best farms are naturally run by the half-breeds or s.... men. One of the S.... men was in town with a load of berries.

the Language is a difficult arrangement of little lisping clucks and clicks and gutterals. the tl sounds are often heard as Tl-Cootena. Tlook. tlrsh. tleck.

It is not a question of ceasing to be an Indian and becoming a banker or political leader. a merchant. it is a question of ceasing to be a free man. equal in privelges in order to become poor cowboys, ranchers. eating at the third table of white men. hired men and renters.

So it is that many of them persist in being Indians in rags rather than cow-hands in denims.

At night the swift rush of Mission Creek sent us to sleep. the Crickets Chirped. the Cloudless sky was scentietant with slow [snow?] and the mighty peaks loomed on us portentious as storm clouds sharply cut as steel disks.

[Here is a crossed out section of two paragraphs that might be about a different subject.]

<u>the dance</u>

the dance took place in one part of a double shanty. Its one window was darkened and as we passed on through the slab door we came upon them dancing an old fashioned square dance. Candles were stuck high up on the log walls. the room was just large enough for one set and allowed for a row of seated on-lookers. It was roughly floored and had logs running across the ceiling.

At first glance all the people were dark. They were half-breeds all. most of them were dancing heavily and lumpishly. the girls were painfully awkward and dull. the men were decidedly better but they were likely uncouth country boys and struggled with the figures of the dances amid good natured laughter.

There was a powerful lack of women. There were two dances and the question was at which one will be the most women.

The men were handsomer than the women. There was only one fairly pleasing women.

At a glance it was like looking in on a dance in the middle seats on the early theaters. It was primitive and rude and good natured.

Some of the young fellows had enough puck to go through the figures with a certain deftness. the fiddler played the same old tunes of the people of the old time west.

Contrary to my expectations my presence did not disturb them they lumbered away quite as if no white people were looking on.

I could not help thinking of the deft bound of moccsined feet. the stream of feathers. the flury of foxes tails in the Indians native dance. They were so wild graceful suggestive and free and this was so awkward.

It has one compensation the women came into it and in many of the old dances the women had no part.

<u>Church Service</u>

people streamed in. people in blankets. people in Cheap Calicoes. Little girls in red or bron or green robes girdled by beaded belts. The men all on one side. the dipper of holy water. the blanketed figures Kneeling on the floor.

The soft voice of the intoning priest. the clear childish voices of the choir boys. The drama and movement of the service. the clanging staccato chant.

The dramatic orator in the Chinook tongue. a priest of great power and eloquence.

I wondered what these grown men thought of the music so different from their own.

Document 83

Jesuit Scholastic Described Life on Reservation

1897

Source: Thomas C. McKeogh, "The New Scholasticate Amid the Rockies," *Woodstock Letters*, vol. 26, no. 1 (1897), pages 71-80.

Editors' note: In 1897 a scholasticate or Jesuit training center was located at St. Ignatius Mission. McKeogh wrote about life and sites on the Flathead reservation and described many aspects of Indian life at the time. The letter also included an extended postscript about the burning of a school building at St. Ignatius by a twelve-year-old mixed blood named Ben Murray who had recently arrived at the school. The postscript has not been reproduced here.

The New Scholasticate Amid the Rockies.
A Letter from Mr. T. McKeogh to a Woodstock Theologian.

Dear Brother in Christ,

P. C.

We are tenting to-night on the old mission grounds snugly encamped amid the mountains. Spurs of the main range of the Rockies, cloud-capped and "white with the snows of endless centuries" wall us round in this smiling valley — the rendezvous of the tribes. The mountains look but a ten minutes' walk distant, yet one must go a long way, fully ten miles, to undeceive the judgment. Though nestling at the feet of these giant peaks, we are still "high up," probably not less than 3000 feet above the level of the sea. So you can see we move in high society out here, though our lot be cast among the Flatheads. The mountains tower a good 8000 feet above the plain. I will not wary you with an imperfect description of these sublimely imposing cliffs: they must be seen to be appreciated.

We pitched our tents, and our valises, about noon on Sept. 27. All the mission welcomed us in a style that badly hacked the old saw, "There is no place like home." And this brings me to speak of our new mountain home. New home it may be appropriately called. Seven new stately buildings — standing testimonials that our fathers have not been idle in these out of the way parts — replace the log cabins of half a century ago, and give the place the appearance of a thriving settlement. These buildings look strangely out of place with their surroundings — with the rude tépees and squatty Indian huts that dot the landscape to the right and left of them, with the wild mountain crags that hem in the horizon line around and about them, and with the fields of grain and stretches of open prairie extending fully thirty miles in front of them to Flathead lake. A stone's throw away stands the old log cabin that sheltered the pioneer fathers from withering chinooks and freezing blizzards — when not buried with their dusky wards in the fastness of the forest.

Three of the main buildings are the property of the Sisters of Providence, in charge of the Indian girls from the ages of nine to twenty-one. Many of the girls remain with sisters until they get married. In addition to an elementary education, they are taught music and drawing, beside receiving practical instructions in sewing, cooking, and the various other arts that go to make young ladies useful as well as ornamental in the kitchen.

The two buildings across the way are occupied by the nuns of the Ursuline Order, and the tots and totesses of the kindergarten. The scholastics are anxious to have us see an exhibition of the papooses. They tell us that the good sisters accomplish wonders with the little ones. The Ursulines do the washing for our community, as also the sewing and mending (except the shoes), and are wholly dependent on the fathers for their support and maintenance. Not so, the Sisters of Providence. They have an appropriation from the Government, and the produce and yearly profits of a large farm. These sisters never turn their back on the plow; they came out here to live and to stay.

The large boys' school, a roomy building, three stories high, is under the management of two scholastics. Mr. Darcy does all the teaching, and Mr. Piet all the perfecting, and strapping if need be. The boys are classed off in four divisions. Two divisions have school in the morning, and the other two in the afternoon. In order that idleness may not have place in our house, while one division are at their books, the others are at work at the various trades in the Industrial Shops building. Master mechanics, hired for the purpose, give them practical lessons in the different crafts and oversee their work. Specimens of the handiwork of some of the Indian boys would do credit to much paler complexions and older heads. About twenty-three boys have been here all summer — poor orphans who had no home to go to, whom the fathers, in their charity, kept with them and cared for. As they go to and fro in very orderly ranks, clothed in blue jean pants and waist, one cannot help comparing them to "the boys in blue." Next Monday, Sept. 21, is the opening day of the new school term, when all the others are expected to return. Last year they registered 90 boys and 300 scholars in all, counting in the boys and girls of the sisters' schools. The boys are mostly half-breeds, sons of a French Canadian father a s.... mother. The half-breeds seem to be much harder to get along with than the full-bloods — especially the older half-breeds. They have all the vices of both and the virtues of neither, and cause the fathers no end of annoyance by stirring up a spirit of discontent among the more simple and better meaning full-bloods. They take scandal a readily as they take an unbranded steer. It seems to be a toss up with them which they will take first. This spirit of wholly indifference of theirs obliges Brother Campopiano, at the cost of much labor, to brand his steers every twelvemonth. This propensity to take scandal is the reason too that nothing stronger than tea or coffee is drunk at table. I soothe the old brother by telling him that we will have lots of "cold snaps" in the winter time. This, too, most likely, is the reason for the long shed-like jail, just opposite my window, over among the Indian huts. John Baptiste, an old Indian, stalks about the premises under the twofold title of "Chief of the Flatheads," and "Chief of Police." He has eight policemen under him, to keep the peace of the village. The Government pays him $18 a month, and his subordinates ten dollars. When they catch a culprit, they put him behind the bars, and keep him on bread and water for six or seven days, should he refuse to work. The maximum punishment is ninety days in this shed. They have a court, all of whose decisions must be referred to the Agent for approval or disapproval. Cases of drink and disorderly conduct, gross violations of the rules of the Reservation, gambling, immorality, are tried in this court. Horse thieves, murderers, etc., are taken to a higher tribunal of Government appointment. At Christmas time, I understand, they have a "distribution of premiums," i.e., a public flogging, before the assembled tribes, of the desperately wayward ones.

Their mode of gambling is very primitive and Indian-like. It consists in passing a small stick from hand to hand as rapidly as possible, and guessing which hand it is in. They keep up a humdrum song during the whole game. The lucky guesser wins the stake — usually a horse or a blanket. If they should have money, they play for it.

But I have not yet finished the enumeration of the buildings. Besides those mentioned, there are many other detached structures strewn over the premises. Such are the blacksmith shop, tin shop, wagon shop, saw mill, grist mill, bakehouse, milkhouse, carriage house, stock barn, and long shed for agricultural implements. There is also a storeroom, stocked with groceries and merchandise, with which Brother Campopiano pays off the Indians and half-breeds, who work for him on the farm.

The principal building is the scholasticate. It has a frontage of 120 feet, and is nicely set off by a well-kept lawn, artistically laid out in winding gravel walks, and ingeniously wrought flower beds of various designs, fragrant with the aroma of sweet scented asters and pansies. The house is 90 feet deep, with two wings, each 90 by 30 feet; it is steam heated, supplied with bathrooms, and all the late improvements conducive to health. It has some thirty-two or -three rooms. Water is conveniently at hand in each corridor, being forced through the house by heavy pumping machinery in the tower building close by. The theologians occupy the third wing facing northwest, and the philosophers are domiciled in the southeast wing. The philosophers are doubled, trebled, and some five or six of them lead an ascetory life. Each theologian has a room to himself. The rooms are large, decently and comfortably furnished, but not very lightsome. There are fifteen philosophers and nine theologians, including the three Missourians. The philosophers are just beginning their second year, and will be taught again this term by Fr. Chianali. Mr. Cardon will teach the philosophers physics, chemistry and mechanics. Rev. Fr. Superior (Fr. De la Motte) will teach morning dogma at 9 A.M. on Mondays, Tuesdays, Wednesdays and Fridays, and will lecture on "De Deo uno et trino," "De Deo Creatore," and if time permit, will also see "De Verbo Incarnato." Fr. Brounts is to teach evening dogma at 5.20 P.M. on Tuesdays and Fridays; he explains "De Ecclesia" et "De Romano Pontifice." Fr. Brounts is also professor of moral. Class at 10.30 A.M. daily; repetition on Wednesday at 5.20 P.M. and "Casus Conscientiæ" on Saturday at 9 A.M. Elocution every Saturday at 5.20 P.M. for an hour. Fr. Superior delighted our hearts yesterday by announcing in his opening instruction that there will be no dictation. We will follow Hurter's Medulla closely. Some one jokingly remarked that instead of circles we will have "round ups" twice a year.

Just now we are enjoying short vacations, which mean an hour's walk in the morning from 9 to 10, and two hours' recreation in the afternoon from 3 to 5. The rest of the day is devoted to free study. The long vacation of the scholastics this year consisted of a ten days' outing under an open tent near Lake McDonald, ten miles distant. We all went on a picnic to this lake a couple of weeks ago. It is a fine sheet of water, a mile and a quarter long and about a quarter of a mile wide, literally walled in between two ranges of massive rocky cliffs, that rise perpendicularly from the water's edge to an enormous height. It is fed by the glacier and the melting snows buried in the bosom of the mountains. The glacier is immovable, and plainly visible from the lake — at least a mile and a half of it — though seen from the distance, it has the appearance of a snow-drift bank about 100 yards long. A few of us unmantled to take a plunge in the inviting crystal waters of the lake; it was like a plunge through a hole in the ice in the winter time. A "memorare" recited in the early morn against sudden and unprovided death must have saved us. However, we were much refreshed when we got out. But did we walk to the lake? Not all of us! Six of us almost flew there on Indian ponies that lope like the wind. Mine must have loped like the late St. Louis cyclone, leastways I was all twisted up in a knot when he had spent himself. The flying was all on the cayuse's part, on mine it was somewhat of the nature of the tumble of a jumping jack with a small boy at the string. I yelled "whoa," but I found to my woe that that in Indian meant "go," for he only ran the faster. Just as he would be on the point of slowing up, the other scholastics would come dashing behind him on their ponies, only to start him off again at a breakneck pace, or rather lope. After a while things got so exciting that I forgot my fears, and came in ahead, but it wasn't my fault! And the slowing up! Just when I looked forward to a little respite — that's the time the little fellow began to shake dice with the disjointed bones of my loosened anatomy. I thought he would never stop slowing up. It is needless to say I returned in the wagon! Still I had a nice time — so did the cayuse!

Last Friday they induced me to go on another expedition to the agency of Arlee, twenty miles away. I rode one of the wagon horses this time. There was little racing and flying as we followed the mountain trail, climbing, climbing, now to the right, now to the left, with the Rockies very little above us, until we were actually in the clouds. It was really a novel experience to be physically in the clouds. Our horses were panting and steaming, and their muscles fairly quivering from the exertion. We were cold with our sweaters and coats on, and had to dismount and dance a little warmth into our feet. And oh, the panorama that lay before us in the valley and cuddling mission below! It was a gorgeous sight! The scenery all along our route was most picturesque and romantic. Our way led through the Rattle Snake Cañon. We didn't get poisoned, but were very very badly rattled. We were right royally treated at the agency by Father Dethoor, with whom we took dinner. After dinner he took us over and introduced us to Chief Charlot, and had the old chief give us names. To one he gave the name "tuft-of-hair," another he christened "spectacles." When he came to the last one in the party, he looked him over for fully three minutes, the later posing the while a la mode Delsarte. Then he shaded his good eye, began to laugh heartily, and duffed him "Psaie," at which the old s.... burst out into a loud guffaw. We afterwards learned that it meant "crazy." You must know that the Indians have a strange way of designating or distinguishing people. They know no names except the baptismal names. They either call a person by his first name, or nickname him after some peculiarity that they notice about his person, for example, "father with the wart on his nose," or, "father of the swollen face." They call the scholastics "soon to be priests," and the sisters "the holy women." The scholastics are addressed as "fathers," by the boys, and make no objection whatever to it. The scholastics are not a class hard to please. They seem perfectly satisfied with everything and everybody; ever ready to go out of their way to do one another a good turn — hard workers apparently, with a kind word for their neighbor, and close observers of their rules. Charity is the ruling spirit of the whole house. It actually lives here. The piety and religious deportment of the scholastics are truly edifying. All wear beads and Roman collars. They hail from nearly every quarter of the globe; the majority of them are American born and from the East.

What have we out here in the wild West in the way of recreation? Many more sports than you have in the "effete" East. We have bathing and boating, horseback riding, base-ball, hand-ball, tennis, foot-ball, coasting and skating. There is a creek about five minutes walk from the house, fairly alive with speckled trout. This creek, a mountain stream, also runs the grist mill and saw mill, supplies the stock with water and irrigates the fields. The Indians and half-breeds do most of their fishing, if you may call it such, at night, by the bright light not of the moon but of a blazing chunk of pitch, cut from the green pine tree, and set burning at the prow of the boat. The fish, attracted by the brilliant glow over the face of the water, come up from the depths to take note of the light, and gather in schools about the boat, only to find themselves suddenly thrust through the throat, or the back, by a long spear, with a "big Injun" at the other end of it. The Indians have little trouble in landing their catches; the fish drop dead in the boat as soon as they recognize their captor. Just how skilful the Indians are with this instrument of slaughter, you may gather from the following notice that we saw tacked to a tree at St. Mary's lake, back of the mountains, in one of our Thursday outings there. It read something like this: —

<blockquote>
"Caut FisH
187 in Too days
Spekeld Trout and his Brudder."
</blockquote>

They showed us some of the big catch, beautiful mountain salmon, weighing on an average from six to eight pounds.

Oh, but we have a magnificent ball field! They have so much land here that they have to "sthack it up," as the Irishman wrote, when he first saw the hills of Montana. We also have a fine lawn tennis court, but the scholastics are strangers to the game as yet. Occasionally the scholastics go on long walks, or rather long climbs up to the mountain tops, where roam the mountain goat, deer and grizzly bear. Many of the Indians are away hunting them for winter provender.

As for variety of amusement I have loads of it every day. My window looks out on an Indian village that you pay ten cents to see at the zoo in Cincinnati. I can see a Buffalo Bill Wild West show free of charge whenever I please to turn my optics on it. Indian pony races, lassooing and riding wild bucking horses, and rounding up kicking steers are every day scenes. Such things are common. If any tourists come this way, I think I will rent out my window.

"How is the weather up here?" I hear you ask. Substantially and accidentally different from most of your eastern cities. The air is remarkably dry, fine, and invigorating. The damp days do not seem to affect one here as elsewhere. A peculiar phenomenon about the rain here is that it wraps the mountains in shrouds of snow — in striking contrast with its vivifying effect in the grass-robed valley below them. The weather here just now is about the same as at Beulah or Waupaca — cool in the mornings and evenings, and warm during the day. Last year, the scholastics say they played base-ball nearly up to Christmas time. I have also heard it said that the thermometer sometimes indicates 45 degrees below zero.

I have yet to say a word about the only brick building of the mission — the church. It is a neat Gothic structure, containing 1,000,000 brick made on the grounds, and put up at a cost of $45,000. It is reckoned the finest church of its kind from St. Paul to San Francisco. There are but few benches in the church, and most of them without backs — the Indians, true to their squatting propensities, preferring to kneel and sit on the floor. A sermon of ten minutes is preached in English at the high Mass on Sundays and holy-days and is followed by one of equal length in the language of the Kalispel. The scholastics are called upon on some few festive occasions to preach in the church. Fr. D'Aste, the "father of the golden hair," as the Indians poetically style him, besides being the spiritual father of the community is also "the Black-Robe chief of the Mission." "Much he teaches the people, and tells them of Mary and Jesus," assembling them every evening in the church to learn and recite their prayers in common, both in English and Indian. They also pray in concert before and after Mass. One prayer after another is recited without a halt in the voice or a change of key or pitch. The Indians here keep the first Friday very holily and solemnly. On this day quite a large number of them receive Holy Communion. It is a novel and picturesque sight on these mornings to see the altar railing lined with Indians, the men on one side, and the women on the other — all arrayed in showy and richly colored blankets. It was new to us to see a s.... receiving holy Communion with a papoose on her back. The old chief, John Baptiste, of whom I spoke before, is one of the first to receive. Immediately after, he takes a position, beads in hand, at the foot of the altar steps. Erect he stands, as straight as an arrow, his arms folded, his long iron-gray hair falling loosely over his shoulders, chief like, and marshals the braves to the right and to the left in case of confusion. But there is no confusion. It is really edifying, and a matter of agreeable surprise to see how orderly and modestly they go and return from the sacred banquet table. Nor can one help recalling with affection sympathy, admiration and love, the memory of those early fathers of the Society, whose untiring zeal and self-sacrificing charity, brought these children of the forest so near to their God. "Requiescant in pace!" rises the prayer, unbidden, to our lips. This duty of marshal was assigned to the old chief by the fathers to be exercised only on great feast days, such as Christmas and Good Friday, when the different tribes for miles around assemble at the mission for services, and there are as many as 600 or 700 holy Communions. But old John is proud of his office, and keeps it up at other times to. If an Indian should so far forget himself as to keep his blanket up over his head, the doughty chief ascends the altar steps and pulls it down. On the first Friday, the Indians, men and women, also sing some of their hymns, taught them by the fathers. The girls of the Sisters of Providence sing the high Mass on Sundays, and sing it well. It is astonishing how well they pronounce the Latin. They tell us that at De Smet the old men and women know the whole Mass by heart. On the feasts of the saints of the Society the scholastics do the chanting. By the way, the scholastics have a good choir and glee club, and are just starting an orchestra.

You should see our congregation at high Mass on Sundays. It is decidedly a mixed one. A glance from the gallery is rewarded with a truly unique and picturesque sight. Below you is the wailing papoose, strapped to its young Indian mother's back, and just opposite its half-breed papa. There are the uniformed wee tots of the kindergarten, and the boys and girls and old maids of every and any age. Unlettered s....s and scarred warriors are here, piously telling their beads. Mingled with the children are refined sisters, yes, and white-veiled novices — clothed in the sombre livery of their Master, and offering their young pure lives to do the Master's work in these isolated parts among the lowest of his creatures. Black-robed Jesuits, too, are there, the tender, youthful, aspiring philosophers, and wise looking, expectant theologians.

It would edify you to see the Indians visiting the graves of their dead after Mass, in the little graveyard, near the church. The Indians, it seems are dying off very fast. Father D'Aste buried fifty-two or -three since the 1st of January last. The mixture of savage and civilized life has a debilitating effect upon them. They eat all the sugar and sweets they can lay their hands on, and drink tea and coffee by the potful. Nor do they know how to eat; but bolt their food, and stuff themselves until they are literally too full for utterance. They always act in the living present, and let the morrow take care of itself. Bad food, uncleanly habits, want of proper ventilation in their log cabins, and in not a few cases, dissipation and immorality, are, doubtless, other causes of the yearly long death list. Another reason is their sweat baths, and sweat houses. These latter are what would be called by us "childrens' play houses." They are small round huts the shape of a hollow sphere cut in two, made of osiers or willow twigs stuck into the ground and bent over at the top until they meet. These are covered with leaves or blankets until they are airtight. In a hole in the centre they build a fire and put in it big boulders and heat them until they are quite hot. Then they close up the opening, throw water on the boulders, and lie around in the steam stark naked. They are soon dripping with perspiration, and then run out and plunge into the ice-cold waters of the creek or river as it may happen to be. Then they lie around on the bank without a stitch on for hours. It is suicidal, isn't it? Many of their deaths, the fathers say, are most edifying. They die in great sentiments of piety and religious fervor. So anxious are they to have the priest with them when sick, that they send thirty or forty miles for him if they have but a cramp in the stomach. Once they receive the last sacraments they no longer wish to live.

We had the pleasure of witnessing an Indian funeral the other day. The Indians walk in procession to the graveyard. A surpliced acolyte with a black wooden cross leads the way; then come the s....s two and two, followed by the men two and two. Next follow the officiating priest and two acolytes with censers. The litter carried by four men closes the mournful train. As they go, they sing a most weird funeral dirge, — an old war song to which the fathers have put pious words. After the interment of the body, the next in order is what you would call a pow-wow — the s....s sit around the grave, and wake the echoes with their groans and lamentations. This lasts some ten or fifteen minutes and is followed by prayer, and ends up in another long wail. The civilizing influence of religion has altogether done away with the barbarous custom, which they tell us, is still prevalent among the Crow Indians — namely, that of slashing their faces and arms with sharp knives, and cutting off the joints of their fingers by way of manifesting their sorrow and bereavement. The graveyard is not an unsuitable place to close the career of this long wail of mine — the graveyard, where all things of "earth earthly" come to an end.

Yours in Domino,
Thomas C. McKeogh, S.J.

Document 84

Questionable Death of Spokane Jim

February 9, 1898

Source: "It May Be Murder," *The Anaconda Standard*, February 9, 1898, page 10, col. 2.

Editor's note: Deaths and possible murders were a frequent part of newspaper coverage of reservation affairs in the 1890s. No further information was found of the outcome of this investigation.

It May Be Murder.
An Investigation Will Be Made Into the Death of "Spokane Jim."

Missoula, Feb. 8. —Two weeks ago there was a story in circulation here of the alleged suicide of "Spokane Jim," an Indian living on the reservation near St. Ignatius mission. The incident was of note as it is not often that an Indian takes his own life. Alex Demers come down from the mission Saturday and to a Standard reporter said that there are strong doubts as to the cause of Jim's death being the hanging that was supposed at first to have been done by himself. There are doubts so strong that it is likely that the remains will be exhumed and an investigation made. Mr. Demers gave the following story of the death of "Spokane Jim," as it is told at the mission:

"The fact of his death was first made known by his wife. She told the neighbors that she had found him dead, hanging from a rafter in their own house. She said that they had had a quarrel the night before and Jim had driven her out of doors. He locked the door behind her and she was forced to sleep in a shed back of the house. In the morning she determined to get into the house and went to the door and knocked. She received no answer and then kicked the door open, breaking the lock. Entering the room, she saw the body of her husband hanging from the rafter by a rope that was so long that it allowed the body to sink almost to the floor, so that Jim's legs were crossed tailor fashion. His head was thrown forward as if he had deliberately held it there till he was strangled. She claimed that she climbed up and loosened the rope from the rafter and then laid out the body."

The rest of the story is what transpired after she had told her neighbors of the death. The body was taken to the mission, where it was prepared for burial.

Friends of the dead man, including the chief of his tribe, were present. The shirt and blanket of the dead man were removed and his shoulders and chest washed. When the friends attempted to remove the rest of his clothing to wash the lower portion of his body the woman objected and would not permit it. The remains were buried without further cleansing. Later investigation of the premises where the death occurred revealed the fact that the lock of the door was uninjured, although Mrs. Spokane Jim had said that she broke it kicking the door open. It was also found that there was no way, by which she could have climbed up high enough to release the rope from where she said it had been fastened. These circumstances and the peculiar conduct of the woman at the funeral and before have aroused suspicion and the remains will probably be exhumed this week for examination.

Document 85

County Taxes and Land Sales

August 18, 1898

Source: Ignace Paul to Commissioner of Indian Affairs, received August 18, 1898, letter received 37,724/1898, RG 75, National Archives, Washington, D.C.; "'All Same M'Kinley,'" *The Anaconda Standard*, August 24, 1898, page 10, col. 2.

Editors' note: In 1898 many tribal members were upset about federal efforts to purchase the northern part of the reservation, and the continuing efforts of Missoula County to collect taxes despite the decision of the Commissioner of Indian Affairs. The newspaper coverage reflected the bigotry and prejudices of the county officers who must have aggravated the situation.

Ronan, Flathead Reservation, Montana

To the Honorable the Commissioner of Indian affairs, Washington, D.C.

Sir:

There is at present on the Reservation Three men who claim to have been sent here by the Government to buy a part of the Reservation. We are not disposed to deal with them, because our Reservation is already small enough. The Spokanes, Kallispels, and West Kootanies have been sent here. So we have not too much land for the number of people there is here. The Government has not done with us as the Commissioners of the Treaty of 1855 agreed to do.

We were to Keep the land for 25 years at the end of that time, to make another treaty. During the 25 years Ignace Paul Chief of the Kootanies to get five hundred dollars per annum, Metchtla chief of Flat Heads, and Alexander, chief of the Ponderies. Were to get the same amount five hundred dollars each per year, during 25 years. We do not Know if the chiefs of Flat Heads, and Ponderies got any money, But Ignace Paul chief of Kootanies got $250 for eight years or 2000. in all.

After Micheal became chief We do not Know how much money he got. The Tribe of Ignace the Kootanies, were to get $5000 yearly the Ponderies and Flat Heads the same amount.

The above amount was to be paid to the Tribes in goods, Indian supplies, if not, to be paid in money. In 1893 the white people took a piece of our land.

The year before in 1892 Major [Peter] Ronan came to Dayton, the Kootanie camp, and told Ignace Paul that his people must take land and improve it, and that he would furnish them everything necessary to farm. There was 12 of his people who took farms and improved them. The Major took the names of Indians that had taken the land. Those were the farms taken by citizins. The Agent Ronan came, I asked him why after taking land according to his orders, that it was taken away from us. The Agent said he would write to Washington, and the Citizens would be sent away. One of the men on our land said that if orders came from Washington for them to leave that they would go. It is now five years, and I have not yet got an answer, Major Ronan died and that was the end of the matter. I told Agent Carter about this affair, but he told me to wait. The Commissioners who are here at present want the best part of our land. At the last meeting we had with the Commissioners all the people were there, also the Agent, the agent did not say anything either to the commissioners or to the people. We ask first of all for the Government to do as they agreed in the former treaty, to pay us the money due us and also our Supplies as promised.

The Commissioners told us that in one month sometime in September we would have another meeting. The Agent is away at present. There is here at the present time two County officers collecting taxes. They have already collected some money from Half Breeds and from citizens married to members of the tribes. We told them to go away that we did not want taxes collected here.

Of the chiefs who made the treaty of 1855 (the writer) Ignace Paul is the only one living. The Mill we have here at Ronan was to be free, now they charge us for sawing our lumber and grinding our grain.

I ask of the Commissioner of Indian Affairs to Write to me at once so that the People and myself may Know how the matter stands.

Please address Ignace Paul Ronan, P.O. Montana. In care of Basil Finly Missoula Co.

* * * * * * * *

"All Same M'Kinley"
Chief Aeneas' Conception of His Power and Authority.
He Warns Mr. Hess Off
Mr. Hess, on the Other Hand, Warns the Big Chief to Pull in His Horns or He will Send the Sheriff After Him.

Missoula, Aug. 23. — Deputy County Treasurer Hess, who is collecting the disputed personal property taxes on the reservation, came down from Ronan last night and returned this morning after a brief conference with County Treasurer Cave and County Attorney Murray. He is making good progress with the collection of taxes and has had no trouble with any of those who were assessed since the visit of Under Sheriff Curran last week, which resulted in the prompt payment at that time of all the taxes that had been in dispute up to that date. The added penalties for the costs of the sheriff and the collector are rather heavy and those who find that they are compelled to pay, do not care to make the expense any heavier than necessary.

Mr. Hess says that the reservation is very dry this summer and that thunder storms are frequent in the hills. Several fires have been started by the lightning this month in the timber and they are spreading rapidly. One house was struck by lightning and one man has been slightly injured. A stock of grain was set on fire in another place by the lightning, and it is a common occurrence during the evening to see a bolt of lightning strike in the timber and a blaze start immediately afterward. Mr. Hess is of the opinion that the fires at the head of Jocko have been started in this manner.

Messrs. Hess and Woodworth had a call the other day from Chief Aeneas Paul, who came to Ronan with about 30 bucks and demanded an interview. At first Mr. Hess refused to talk with the chief at all, as he was satisfied that the purpose of the visit was to drive him from the reserve. The Indians were so persistent, however, that the interview was finally granted, Bill Irvine acting as interpreter. Chief Aeneas Paul would not talk till Will Woodworth, Mr. Hess' assistant, was sent for. When Will came the chief proposed to lay down the law to the intruders. He told them that all that valley belonged to him; that the government had given it to him; that he was the chief, "all same McKinley"; that all these braves were his children, and that the intruders must not round up the cattle of his children or collect taxes from them. As he referred to McKinley, he pointed to an old campaign button, bearing the likeness of the president, which he wore pinned to his coat.

During all this talk the bucks were drawn up in a circle, in the center of which sat the chief and the two intruders. When the chief had concluded his long discourse about his possessions, his people, his domain and his authority. Mr. Hess said to the interpreter: "What I want to tell that old Indian is that he may go to h——. You needn't use that language, but tell him something that means the same thing. Tell him that in town all of the little children wear those McKinley buttons, unless they are silver advocates, and that he needn't point to it so proudly. Tell him that this is not his country, but that it belongs to the government at Washington. Tell him that there is an agent on the reservation to whom he may apply for aid and who will deal with me. You tell him that the sheriff will be here in the morning and that if he makes any trouble he will be arrested."

That night Under Sheriff Curran came in to attend to the Sloane and Clairmont cases, and when Chief Aeneas saw him he thought that it was all off with him. From that day he did not say a word. The collection is going on quietly and the work will soon be finished. Considerable revenue will be added to the county's income by this collection, and it is not likely that there will ever be another year in which the tax is resisted.

Document 86

Chief Charlo Rejects Land Sales

September 27, 1898

Source: "An Eloquent Old Man," *The Anaconda Standard*, September 27, 1898, page 10, col. 2.

Editor's note: The commission that met with Charlo and the other tribal leaders in 1898 was called the Crow, Flathead, Etc., Commission. Despite the refusal of the tribal leaders to consider the sale of reservation land, the commission kept up their efforts to obtain Flathead Reservation land by persuasion or coercion through the early years of the twentieth century. See also article about earlier negotiations in March 25, 1897, above.

An Eloquent Old Man
Chief Charlot Tells Commissioners His Opinion of Them.
A Big Pow Wow Was held
Conference Between the Head Men of the Confederated Tribes
and the Treaty Commissioners on the Reservation.

Missoula, Sept. 26. — The meager reports that have been received here concerning the conference between the head men of the Confederated Tribes and the treaty commissioners on the Flathead reservation have not given much idea of the details of that important meeting. It was known, as reported in the Standard at the time, that the proposition of the treaty commissioners for the opening of the reservation for settlement had been rejected by the Indians, but further than that not much was known. It is now learned, however, that the meeting was one of the most interesting ever held on the reservation. Its chief feature of importance was the address delivered by Chief Charlot of the Bitter Root Indians in reply to the commissioners. The old man was very eloquent, and those who heard his address, even with the loss of effect that always follows translation, say it was a remarkable effort. It produced a marked effect upon the Indians and it must have afforded the old chief considerable satisfaction to be able to tell the commissioners what he thought of them and to relieve his feelings of the wrath that has been accumulating for these many years.

The proposition of the commissioners, as it is understood here, was that the Indians cede to the federal government a strip of their land 25 miles wide, running east and west along the northern border of the reservation. This would include that part of the Flathead valley that lies within the reserve, the Flathead lake and the Mission valley as far down as Crow creek — about 640,000 acres in all. For this the commissioners agreed to pay the Indians 60 cents an acre. Of this sum the red men were to receive 5 cents per acre in cash and the remaining 55 cents was to be expended for them by the government in improvements and stock. All of the Indians know, of course, that the sum the government has paid to the Nez Perces, the Crows and other tribes who have ceded to their government their reservations. They know that the average sum that has been thus paid has been about $3.75 per acre, and when they were offered the insignificant sum named above they were justly indignant.

Charlot made the principal reply to the commissioners. He said, in the first place, that he and his people had no confidence in the commissioners. He did not believe that the commissioners ever came from Washington. He did not think that they had any authority any way. He and his people had treated with commissioners too often, and they were through with that business until some of the promises that had been made by the previous commissions had been fulfilled. When he had any treaty to make he wanted to go to Washington and make it with somebody that would speak with authority and would keep his promise. He referred eloquently to the sufferings of his people as a result of the broken promises made by commissioners, and said that he would deal no more with them. He said: "You think this land is good. So do I. You want it. I propose to keep it for my people, their children and their children's children. You want to give us a cow apiece for our land. I am afraid that the cow would hook me."

The old chief became very ironical as the address progressed and he paid his respects to Professor Barge of the commission in strong language. He told how the professor and his commission had brought all of the Indians together at the mission and then had not come to meet them at all. To Professor Barge he said: "I thought that I had cut your tongue out, but I see that another is growing." He refused to treat with the professor at all.

It looks now as if the whole matter was as far from any practical settlement as ever. It is of much importance to the people of this section, and it is to be hoped that a commission will some day be named that will be more successful in treating with the Indians. It may be that the department is at fault for not giving the commissioners sufficient authority. Anyway, there is something wrong somewhere. If the matter could be properly handled, there is no doubt that some satisfactory arrangement could be made with the chiefs and their people. They certainly have not been properly treated.

Document 87

Blind Mose Remembers Old Time Powwows

Late 1890s and later

Source: Don Matt, "Blind Mose Remembers," *Char-Koosta* (Dixon, Montana), vol. 6, no. 5 (July 1, 1976), pages 6-7.

Editors' note: The Salish, Pend d'Oreille, and Kootenai Indians had always held celebrations, but the early pow-wows did not begin until the late 1890s. In the 1970s, Blind Mose, a tribal elder, remembered the pow-wows as a time of joy and camaraderie. Before the 1890s, the government tried to suppress traditional dances and celebrations, but they continued and in the twenty-first century are still an important part of tribal life.

Blind Mose Remembers
Memories of past Pow Wows light his darkness.
an in-depth interview, by Don Matt

Everyone has seen him, this blind Indian with grey hair in braids and wide-brimmed uncreased hat. "Blind Mose" seems almost a permanent part of the old Mission town, St. Ignatius, with his carved cane and his large, aging dog. It almost seems like he comes from a different time. When he was born, there were no jets or cars here. It would be over a month and a half before Chief Charlo would abandon his stand in the Bitterroot Valley to join the others on the reservation.

Mose Chouteau, born September 6, 1891, was not always blind. He was born to Louie and Nancy Chouteau, in St. Ignatius, by the Father's Pond, next to the flour mill. His father was a farmer and wood cutter who helped built the Mission Church. His mother worked in the school laundry during the winter. Mose helped cut and deliver wood to the townspeople. He helped plow and harvest his father's grain with the old hand scythe. Two of his sisters, Annie and Lucy died at ages three and five. They were buried by the school. The other sisters, Katherine, Jolene and Mary Lucy faired better, as did his brother Louis Pierre. He also has a half-brother Charlie Lewis, at Colville, Washington. Mose had learned catechisms from the Fathers, but he never attended school. He learned to recognize a few words in English, but he never spoke it. He remembers the old people taught the young ones religion and culture, whether they were related or not. He remembers the three times he got to go hunting over in Swan Valley with his family. They would go just about this time of year to get fish and game in preparation for the pow wows. They also got scent glands from beavers for perfume.

Other Indians at Camas Prairie used to hunt in the mountains to the West. All that seemed like play to Mose, as did picking huckleberries, service berries, chokecherries, elderberries and wild raspberries. He claims he liked eating peeled sunflowers stems in the spring. He also enjoyed digging bitterroot. Some of his favorite memories include the dancing and singing, which was learned at private get togethers in people's homes. Whenever his family heard of a dance, they would hitch up the horses and go, without ever thinking about how cold it was. Sometimes they would dance all night.

Naturally, some of the best fun the family had came from participating in the big annual pow-wows. Some of those pow-wows lasted up to 15 days, and Mose danced in them from as far back as he can remember.

Life was not without its troubles though. Mose was about 11, when a boy threw ashes and he turned around just in time to catch it in the eyes. He lost the sight of his right eye. The boy who threw the ashes was later killed with others in an incident with the game warden in Swan Valley. The sight in Mose's left eye was very gradually fading. By the time mose [sic] was 18, the camp crier who was appointed to pass out drums only to the best singers, selected Mose as a drummer. By the time he reached 25, he was almost completely blind. This did not stop him from being head drummer for the pow-wows for 36 years.

Today, as Mose tried to explain the old songs and dances, he often sings examples and weaves in his chair as he relives the dances. Sometimes his fingernails tap out the rhythm of the drum.

Mose misses the old pow-wows. He says they used to be different. The wagons used to be set up in a circle around the pow-wow and drinkers would be tied to a wagon wheel and not turned loose until the next day, with strict orders not to drink again. He says there would usually be one or two women and about three or four of the men in that embarassing position. Out of the whole camp, not more than a dozen got in trouble this way. Another thing that was different was gambling. Horse races were a major part of the celebration, taking up three or four days. Betting was allowed on the races. People would bet horses, blankets and hides. But the stick games and card games were forbidden. This was suppose to prevent hardships on those who would lose everything. People still tried gambling and some got caught. Mose says he witnessed public whippings for gambling on four different occassions. This was supposed to be followed by a month in jail. A group of men who didn't like this met with the Chiefs and priest all day, and into the evening to try to change things. That was in equity hall before it burned down. Mose says that when the proposals were rejected, the group of men secretly wrote Washington D.C. and praised stick games as a harmless pasttime of tribal custom, and got it legalized.

The pow-wow and its activities were such a big event that people started drifting in as much as a week beforehand. Mose says the Chief would tell people not to allow their kids to play until after the war memorial items and clothing were put away. People would put on clothes from some relative or friend who had been killed in battle, and go to a special area to mourn, at the start of the pow-wow. This lasted until noon, and helped to prepare them for the war dancing. After the ceremony the kids would be turned loose.

They would war dance until after supper, when they would dance in file back to their teepees to change to more regular clothes. Sometimes, they would do the Camas dance all night. In the morning came the wake up song. Anyone reluctant to arise was in danger of having his covers pulled off, and find himself covered with water instead. They would say, "We are here to celebrate, not to sleep!"

People who came from far away to attend the Pow-wow were not unrewarded. At the give-away dance people would grab a partner and then at the end of the dance, give him something in appreciation of his attendance.

One of the things those attending enjoyed was a re-enactment of the highlights of past battles, with six or seven warriors leaving the camp to return in the role or raiders. The scout would ride his horse back and forth giving war whoops when he spotted the intruders. People would then throw a stick which hit him in the back, and he would tell of raiders after the horses. With cries and war whoops, warriors from the camp began a horseback pursuit, resulting in a battle about a quarter mile away. Shots were fired, although not directly at anyone, and the scalps taken were actually wigs. They would return singing the victory song and there would be a scalp dance the next day. After telling this, Mose said, "I sure miss the old time pow-wows. They were really good."

If he remembers correctly, the first pow-wow in Arlee was in 1896, and then in Mission in 1898. The pow-wow sites moved around several years before they finally went back to Arlee.

He also recalls that when people returned from the east from a visit to the Crees, they brought back a couple of Owl dance songs, or round dances. These dances proved popular immediately.

When pow-wows were not going, the difficulties of earning a living returned. Even though Mose was blind, he still cut wood and sold it to people on into his fifties. He lived with his folks until they died. Then he moved in with Pete and Mary Barnaby. They are gone now, but Mary made a provision

Blind Mose
Source: Salish–Pend d'Oreille Culture Committee, St. Ignatius, Montana.

in her will that Mose could stay there until he dies. Mose says he has sufficient income from things like property to keep him going.

He used to walk to town daily until he was struck by a car about three years ago. He still fixes his meals, sews, washes clothes and takes care of himself. He even chops wood once in a while in emergencies. Bill Durgeloh says he'll ask people to take him somewhere and then insist on footing the bill. Mose said that some of the old women say his blindness is a blessing. Maybe otherwise he would been mean and violent and raping women. He contends that even today he could do those things if he wished, but he doesn't.

Sometimes now life is lonely for Mose, with most of his friends gone. Pete Woodcock seems to be the only one who takes much time for Mose. Mose will tell stories for hours to those willing to listen. Bill Durgeloh said he should tape all the coyote tales.

In spite of the loneliness, most of the time Mose enjoys the independence of living alone. He keeps a pistol for intruders.

When loneliness and boredom close in, Mose does not always have a way to get out and go. He does not get to many pow-wows anymore. He will only go when someone that the knows he can trust to stay with him and help him. He still enjoys sweat lodges and the annual medicine sweat rituals that may last from four to eight days.

Once in a while the darkness closes in, and Mose doesn't know why, but he gets scared of the end of the road. He says a few prayers and gradually he forgets. He gets lonesome for his parents and his brothers and sisters who are gone. Once in a while he cries, out of loneliness. Sometimes he puts on his coat and hat and walks around until he feels a little better. Sometimes when things bother him he takes his little drum down off the wall and signs [sings] until he feels better. Sometimes his little drum brings back the memory of all those who are gone, and he has to quit.

Document 88

Missoula County Attempts to Collect Taxes on Reservation
April 3, 1899

Source: W. H. Smead to Commissioner of Indian Affairs, April 3, 1899, letter received 16,086/1899, RG 75, National Archives, Washington, D.C.

Editors' note: Agent Smead reported on the friction resulting from continuing efforts of Missoula County to collect taxes from mixed blood tribal members. Apparently in this case, the county was claiming that mixed bloods on the reservation whose Indian blood came from the Blackfeet or other tribes than the Salish and Kootenai were not wards and were subject to taxation. The conflict continued into the early years of the twentieth century. Some typographical errors have been corrected.

Department of the Interior,
United States Indian Service
Jocko, Flathead Agency, Mont., Apr. 3rd. 1899.

Commissioner Indian Affairs,
Washington, D.C.
Sir: —

The persistent efforts of the officials of Missoula County in trying to assess and collect taxes from mixed blood residents of this reservation is causing much excitement and uneasiness among all classes of people here, Indians as well as mixed bloods.

Mixed bloods who have been on this reservation nearly all their lives, and whose legal rights here have never before been questioned, are being assessed, and last year taxes were collected from several, under protest, who I am satisfied have rights here.

A deputy assessor of Missoula County who was last year ejected from the reservation, was recently arrested at my request and taken before a U.S. Commissioner. This man was trying to assess persons who in my judgement are wards of the Government, he however did not confine himself to this work, but apparently desired to create a disturbance with these people, offering to bet that this was not a reservation as well as making untrue statements of various kinds.

When given a hearing before the Commissioner, he was discharged on the ground that he was an officer of Missoula county and was on the reservation in the discharge of his duties.

The cases of several person who are supposed to have been illegally compelled to pay last year are now in the hands of the U.S. Attorney for Montana and he will he informs me soon bring suit against Missoula County for the sum so collected. The people here are very impatient and are unwilling to await the decision of the courts and some of the mixed bloods here are desirous of coming to Washington at once to confer with you in relation to their rights on this reservation:

There are great numbers of mixed bloods on this reservation and if the officials of Missoula county continue in their determination to tax them all, it must necessarily result in almost endless litigation as very few of these mixed bloods rights, could be settled by any *one* court decision, their claim to rights here being very different in nearly every case.

I shall be pleased to receive any further instructions you may deem necessary.

Very respectfully,
W. H. Smead.
U.S. Indian Agent.

Document 89

Good Friday Services at St. Ignatius Mission

May 1899

Source: Katie Ronan, "Good Friday at St. Ignatius Mission," *The Kaimin* (University of Montana, Missoula), vol. 2, no. 4 (May 1899), pages 4-5.

Editors' note: The daughter of Agent Peter Ronan wrote this description of the Good Friday service at St. Ignatius Mission in the 1890s for the University of Montana student newspaper.

Good Friday at St. Ignatius Mission.

The most solemn ceremony we witnessed during the Holy Week we spent at the St. Ignatius was on Good Friday evening. We went early to the church in order to procure a good seat, for we had been told that the crowd would be even greater than on the preceding days. However, on reaching the church, which had just been completed and is the largest in Montana, we found it well filled and had to content ourselves with a back seat.

The church was almost dark, save for the mellow light shed by the many candles on the altar and the soft red light of the sanctuary lamp. In the dimness the real Christ seemed to hang in agony on the crucifix suspended above the altar and one could easily imagine that the shadowy forms of the kneeling Indians were the Jews who believed in the Savior. Indeed, these children of the forest presented a very novel picture. All of the men were on one side of the church and the women occupied the other. As the Indians prefer to set on the floor, the benches which extended a half way down the church, were occupied by the school children, their tutors, the whites, and the mixed bloods. Scattered among the men were a few Indians decked out in all the glory of policemen's uniform. And woe to the maiden, old or young, weary with kneeling during the long prayers dared to set down, for the man with the brass buttons, the envy of all his friends, was very soon at her side ordering her to "kneel up." If she persisted in keeping her position, she was forced to her knees; and if that girl, being of a stubborn disposition, refused to comply with his stern commands, the door was shown her. We say many other incidents that greatly amused us, but what surprised us was the great devotion of these simple Indians.

Our attention was soon drawn to the altar by the appearance of many acolytes coming from the sacristy, each carrying in his hand a lighted candle, followed by a white haired priest. From where we sat, the priest looked more like one of those apostles of Christ we read about, than a man living in our day. His face expressed saintliness, heroism and humility. After a brief sermon, the procession to the graveyard was formed. First went a little boy holding aloft a cross, next all the men some of whom carried banners, followed by the women with sleepy babies in their arms or strapped to their backs; then came the Mission band composed of Indian boys attending the Fathers school. Six little girls in white, with veils covering their heads and carrying nails representing those used on Calvary, the acolytes two or whom swung sensors before the priest, and a large statue of Christ borne in nearly the same manner in which he was to the tomb, brought up the rear.

It was a most weird scene. The driveway from the church around the cemetery was lighted by bon fires, and the men and women, in gay costumes that contrasted strangely with their solemn faces, chanted hymns in stranger Latin, except at brief intervals when the band reminded us that were not out of civilization and wandering in some ghostly realm.

Having made the circuit of the grave yard, the procession slowly wended back to the church where prayers were said; and then the redmen stalked off to their lodges, anxious only for the next good Friday, for the Indian loves display of any kind. But his pale-face brethren walked homewards deeply impressed and awed by the piety of the savages.

Katie Ronan.

Document 90

Lolo Convicted of Murdering Ambrose

December 3, 1899

Source: "They Have Bad Records," *The Anaconda Standard*, December 3, 1899, page 14, col. 2.

Editors' note: Lolo was convicted of the murder of Ambrose near Missoula in November 1899. Duncan McDonald gave background information on the two men.

They Have Bad Records
Characters of the Principals in the Indian Murder.
First Class Drunkards
Ambrose Was a Tough Citizen and Played Gay Lothario With Great Ability — Interesting Bits of Indian History.

Missoula, Dec. 2. — County Attorney Denny has received from Duncan McDonald an interesting letter regarding the principals in the recent Indian murder for which Lolo was sent to the penitentiary last week. According to Mr. McDonald, both Ambrose, the murdered man, and Lolo, who did the killing, have bad records and the killing was not altogether unexpected by those who were familiar with the habits of each. Ambrose had a bad record as a roue and libertine among his people, and was an habitual drunkard and gambler. He was called Young Ambrose by many, but he was a man 50 years old, and his record of late years had been a bad one. In referring to Ambrose, or "Ambroise," as the name should be spelled, Mr. McDonald says:

"This dead Indian is now, I presume, a good Indian where he is."

He was a son of Chief Ambrose of the Flathead tribe, and his father was a man of exceptional ability and recognized integrity. His son, however, had for years been a bad man and the only wonder seems to be that he was not killed long ago. He was a reckless fellow, whose boast was that he could win any wife away from her husband, and whose record showed that his boast was not altogether vain. At the time of his death he was living with another Indian's wife. He had a habit of dropping these unfortunate women as soon as his fancy led him to choose another, and he has caused much unhappiness and

suffering amongst his people. There has been, apparently, little mourning over
his violent death.

In connection with the death of Ambrose, Mr. McDonald recalls an incident
that is remembered by the older residents of Missoula. When the Northern
Pacific people were treating with the Indians for a right of way through the
reservation in 1882, A. B. Hammond, then a resident here, assisted in the
council of the Indians at the agency. While this council was in progress on
the treaty ground near the agency, Ambrose became angry and opposed the
advances that were being made by Assistant Attorney General McCammon
and Mr. Hammond. In the course of the discussion he attempted an assault
upon Mr. Hammond, but was prevented from carrying out his purpose. He
was a man of high temper and base motives. Mr. McDonald writes:

"Young Ambrose, as you call him, was about my age, 50 years. I remember
him in the spring of 1859, I think about March. My father and Chief Ambroise
were camped where the city of Helena now stands, and this young Ambrose
was a good sized lad. Lolo is a cousin of mine and Little Mary is his aunt.
The news that we get here is that Ambrose had gone to Lolo and told him
that he would take away his (Lolo's) wife before his eyes. That is probably the
provocation that Lolo had. Still it is good for Lolo to be where he is, in jail.
Both men, Ambrose and Lolo, were first-class drunkards and gamblers."

In speaking of the two men Mr. McDonald says, further: "These two
men Ambrose and Lolo, were both descendants of Mohawks and Iroquois
blood, from their mothers' side. Both women were Marys and their brothers
and cousins immigrated into Montana with the Hudson Bay company. They
intermarried with the Flatheads, Kootenais and Sill-cat-com-schints. The last
tribe named is what you call the Pend d'Oreilles. The French word was intended
for the Calispellums and not for the Sill-cat-com-schints, as it is now used. The
Calispellums live in the Calispellum valley, about 50 miles north of Spokane
Falls. The city of Kalispell should be Calispelum.

"The cause of the immigration of these Mohawk and Iroquois Indians was
the continuous wars that the Spanish, French and English waged with each
other for the possession of North America. The white nations introduced a
bounty upon the scalps or heads of their enemies and whenever the savages
killed any of these whites they presented them for the bounty, bringing in the
scalp for evidence. This was the reason that the Indians used the scalping-knife.
The knife was not originally used by the Indians, but was given to them by
the whites, who are forever damned for it. In this muddle the Mohawks and
Iroquois had a hand in turning over scalps to the nation that paid the highest
bounty. Their part in the warfare caused them to skip out for Montana for
safety. It was from these same Iroquois that the Flatheads learned of the Black

Robes and their religion, and it was this news that led the Flatheads to send runners to St. Louis for Black Robes. Rev. Fr. [Pierre] DeSmet was, I believe, the first to respond to the call."

Document 91

Indian Complained About Flathead Agent and Traders
December 28, 1899

Source: Roman Nose to "Secatory Indian Afairs," December 28, 1899, letter received 547/1900, RG 75, National Archives, Washington, D.C.

Editors' note: Most of these complaints involve traders on the reservation. The Office of Indian Affairs did not reply to this letter. Some periods have been added.

Flathead Reservation
Dec 28/1899

Secatory Indian Afairs
Wash D.C.
Sir:

We respectfully call your Attention to the way We are Robed and Treated here on the Flathead Indian Reservation. By our Indian Agent. in the first Place he is useing our County to Run his Big Band of Cattle on. We made a Kick about it to him, and he say the Goverment gave him a right to have all the Cattle he Wants to on the Reservation. And now he has Fenced in a Big Pasture and Says it [is] for the Goverment. But we see it for his Own use. him and the Post Trader at Arlee used it All Summer. to Keep Horses in. Witch they killed to Feed to there Hogs, and he has the Boss Farmer to go on the Cattle round up to Brand his cattle. The he trades our Wagons of For Grain and Stock. he Traded one Wagon to Joe Howl and one to John Morrigeau and one to Frank Ducharme and one to Pete Irvine. These men are Rich and can Buy Wagons and are men Dont Belong here. We have now only one good Store here Now and the most of us have to go along Ways to trade Since He closed the Best Store we had at Ravalli. the Store at St Ignatius and Arlee are no good to us. neather Of them has 5 Hundred Dollars Worth of Goods. and We Demanded for him to Put a Store at Ravalli again. the Trader at Arllee. We Want Put of. he was Put Of once By our old Agent And the new Agent Put him Back Again. We think the Agent and Trader are in Partners. is the Reasons the Store at Ravalli Was Closed up to make us go and Trade At Arlee or St Ignatius. Since the Store at Ravalli is gone We have to go Along Was to trade. We respectfully ask you to have a Indian Inspector to Investigate this matter as Wee can get No Satisfaction from the Indian Agent. Let the Inspector call on the New or old Indian Judges.

Respt yours
Roman Nose.

Document 92

Snapshots of Life on the Reservation

1899 plus

Source: Excerpts from Morton J. Elrod, "Indian Quirks: Stories Sent to McClure Newspaper Syndicate," box 14, folder 13, Morton J. Elrod Papers, MS UM4, Toole Archives, Mansfield Library, University of Montana, Missoula.

Editors' note: Elrod spent a number of summers doing scientific field work on the Flathead Reservation, starting about 1899 and continuing through the early years of the twentieth century. He also took a number of photographs of the people and scenic sights on the reservation. These vignettes of everyday life at the turn of the twentieth century gave insight into daily life on the reservation. Seven of the 28 articles submitted by Elrod have been reproduced here. Some typographical errors have been corrected.

Indians Make Tourists Pay.

The old mode of crossing the Pend d'Oreille or Flathead river at the outlet of Flathead lake, a distance of perhaps a half mile, was by an old flat-bottom ferry. It was rudely made and rowed by heavy pole oars made from red fir trees or saplings. The boat was always on the other side of the river, and much hallooing was necessary to arouse the indigent ferryman to the performance of duty. Never did he know whether or not he would be paid, so why hurry.

A half day was considered necessary for the passage, when now by bridge and auto the time is about two minutes. The return would be about the same, with the ferry always on the wrong side.

The team to be taken across drew a spring wagon and six passengers. Six dollars was the price, and a dollar then was as good as two now. Too much. Can't pay it. No sense in holding people up and robbing in this way. Be reasonable.

"Its only a dollar a head," he argues. It is like ferrying so many cattle to him. And the traveler knows he may [must] pay or stay on this side of the river. But he must argue a little on the way, for his pride and pocketbook are touched.

"How much do you charge Indians to cross?"

"Oh, we don't charge Injuns nothing. They go across free."

Ah, that's the idea. Make the tourist visitors keep up the ferry. The Indian is not the only one who play that little game. It is well nigh universal.

* * * * * * * *

Indians Like to Gamble

Indians, like all other primitive tribes, are great gamblers. Whether it is a horse race, a card game, a stick game, or anything else of a gambling nature, they will stake a pile with reckless abandon, and lose with a careless "So long, see you again." They seem like children at play. And yet they are seriously in earnest. Happy-go-lucky, better luck next time, always believing in what we are pleased to term a lucky star, they never hesitate to jump in if there is a place in the game. This does not, of course, apply to all individuals, but seems to be a racial instinct.

"Where's the Major?" said one, coming round the trader's store at Flathead lake, long before the white man built Polson. "Major" was the Indian agent, representing the father at Washington.

"He's just going over the hill. He'll be gone out of sight by the time you get out the deck."

The blanket is spread on the ground. The players squat or idly sit around. The spectators are grouped behind. Only a few expressions are heard, and they usually are of banter for the dealer or some slow thinker in the game.

"Hold on. Hold on. Wait a minute. I had two bits on the queen. Who got the money? It is mine, wait — "

But the game goes on, and he is sqelched by the laugh at his expense. It usually ended only when the dealer was "bloke," and ceased to turn them over. Perhaps after much banter some one else would grab the deck, with such expressions of approval as "goo boy; goo boy," until he, too, was reduced to penury.

* * * * * * * *

Indian Teaches White Manners

Indians have their ideas of honor and honesty, and are quite consistent in their views, from their standpoint. Their antipathy to those who would unsuspectingly take their photograph is well nigh universal. And yet it is as easy to get pictures of Indians as of whites. Suppose the case was reversed and an Indian visitor assumed such a privilege of whites?

A visitor at the Indian dances held near St. Ignatius on the Flathead reservation was treated to a bit of Indian argument which will illustrate the point. The Indian village circle of tents was on an open prairie, on the bank of a creek, with a most wonderful mountain background. The Mission mountains are among the most beautiful of the world. It was too tempting for the photographer. Three Indian tepees, no white man's impediments, a marvelous background, was too fine to miss. Just as the shutter was to be opened for the exposure an Indian emerged from the middle tepee and made a bee line for the camera, wrath in his countenance. In vain he is told, "Ketchum teepees and mountains. No ketchum peoples." He knows better. Why not go over yonder if you tell the truth. And he emphatically concludes the discussion by relieving his mind of a great burden. He must say it.

"You askum fellow take his pitcher, dass all right. You no ask him take his pitcher, dass all same stealum."

Having thus told the visitor his manners, he stolidly walked back to his tent.

* * * * * * * * *

Indians Appreciate Favors

Years before the present wonderful dam was constructed across the outlet of McDonald lake in the beautiful Mission Mountains of western Montana, on the very spot where now an end of the dam rests, we were camped a week, making a report on the lake for irrigation purposes. It was a beautiful Sunday afternoon, as we idled by the tent, that an Indian and his s...., a delicate looking little thing with a heckling cough, tied their ponies and sandered [sic] up the rocky shore to the inlet, fishing as they went. Later a lone Indian similarly secured his horse, and laboriously paddled the old flat bottomed scow up the lake, slowly disappearing.

A sudden storm came up, rain fell in torrents, thunder echoed and reverberated from the tremendous cliffs with crash and deafening roar. During the downpour of rain the lone Indian came down the lake in the leaky boat, soaked but erect, a piece of board his only paddle and steering gear. We met him at the shore and asked about his trouble. We could not understand his wants, until he picked up an axe. Ah, yes, we knew at once. No teepee, no fire, no food, no matches, "no nottin," as he stated it.

Matches in a bottle, dry kindling in protective covering, a can of corn and another of tomatoes, and he was told to hurry. An hour later a wisp of blue smoke with the magnificent mountain background told the tale of warmth, perhaps comfort, for the s....

In late evening, when the sudden storm had passed, when the crags were bathed in the soft rays of the fast disappearing sun, and the bow of promise had spanned the lake in brilliant colors and again faded, the three came for their tethered ponies, restless for hours. But before untying the horses each Indian came quietly to our camp, stopped politely and gave expression in their own way of appreciation for the courtesy we had shown. There was only one word, "Tank" (thank you), but it said very much for them.

* * * * * * * *

Indians Repay Kindness

Indian have a keen sense of honor. They are appreciative of favors, and will return them whenever occasion offers. They have doubtless been deceived so many times they have become somewhat skeptical, and naturally defend themselves whenever possible. Childlike in many ways, they are far above children in returning a good deed.

On one occasion years ago, it was necessary to travel from Polson to Camas Hot Springs, Flathead Reservation, Montana, some thirty miles. On the way was a very steep hill on either side of a long hogback. On one side it was a long, winding, steep incline, on the other a steep pitch for a quarter of a mile, a runaway for two or three miles further. Going over was to go down the steep incline, coming back was to climb the hill.

We went down with wheels roughlocked, a tree as large as four men could handle tied to axle for a drag, two men riding the drag. The horses held back all they could, but had to make it on a run. Coming back the team drawing the light spring wagon was stopped at the foot of the hill, and unloaded of people. A council was held to determine how to get up, when there strangely appeared a party on the top of the hill, all on horseback. Stranger still, one of the men led a horse fitted with heavy harness, a singletree hanging from the hames, all as though just prepared for our use.

The Indians was hailed, our name and destination stated, and request for help made. The response was instantaneous.

"You bet I will. You took a picture of me and my outfit at Ravalli two years ago, (I had forgotten), sent me some prints and I never paid you for them. Where shall I hitch on?"

With much wild yelling and wheel chucking the summit was reached, men and horses alike panting and breathless, but not a cent of pay would our Indian take.

* * * * * * * *

Indian Justice

In the early nineties, when the Flathead Lake region in Montana was unsettled, an Indian reservation, the tribal laws of the Salish Indians governed most of their actions. Since they were, and still are, considered wards of the

Federal government, they were given much freedom of action, quite as during the years prior to the entrance of the whites.

A very singular case, illustrating their ideas of justice, and involving murder and the unwritten law, came under observation. An Indian buck, jealous of his s...., objected to the little attentions shown by a young man, and upbraided her for her acts. She was accused of infidelity, which she vehemently denied. Unlike her white sisters, she took matters in her own hands. no divorce courts existing with her tribe.

The s.... was a little thing, of about a hundred pounds, slender and rather delicate. But she had true Indian spirit. The Indian in question was asleep in a teepee, even at midday. To prove to her lord and master that she cared not for the one whose charms were claimed to be so potent, she picked up an axe from the wood pile, walked into his tent, and clove his skull with the sharp edge. He was not killed but died some two years later, an imbecile.

Thus did she prove her innocence. She was immediately arrested by Indian police, and was escorted, on horseback, by two powerful Indians to the agency. The trial by Indian method resulted in acquital and freedom. The proof of innocence and the action of the Indian judges was speedy.

* * * * * * * *

Indian Beliefs

The various tribes of North American Indians have largely passed into history. The few remaining Indians have been so influenced by contact with the white race and their customs that their native habits have almost disappeared. Yet they unconsciously retain many superstitions, obey tribal laws, and have religious beliefs, uninfluenced by civilized man.

The Salish Indians of Montana, residing on the Flathead Reservation, among other religious rites, have shrines in various places, upon which in passing they deposit an offering to the memory of the departed, as we would place flowers upon a grave.

Duncan McDonald, whose father was a Scotchman in the employ of the Hudson Bay Company, and whose mother was a full blooded Indian, tells a story of his Indian wife who forgot to place an offering on a shrine along the trail. After camp was made about sundown she called attention to her forgetfulness, and expressed a desire to return to the shrine, some five or six miles, to perform this sacred duty. Without a murmur he saddled the horses and accompanied her. The return was long after dark in the long days, but conscience was satisfied.

If all mankind showed the same spirit of devotion and sympathy as this untutored Indian woman the world would be better and happier.

Morton J. Elrod
Source: Toole Archives, Mansfield Library, University of Montana,
Missoula, Montana, photo 84-0184.

Index